Dear Bob and Pat,

 I can't imagine those better endowed to appreciate to fullest measure what I have tried to create in this book than you two, who have experienced you share of emotional triumph and tragedy.

 Succinctly, to explain why I have composed *Quest*, I can do no better than Don Quixote's answer when Aldonza asked why he did the things he did: "I hoped only to add some measure of grace to the world." Fondly,

  John Filsinger

The cover flap and Preface reveal the origin and nature of this book. Vital information about the cover, dedication, and introductory pages is found in the Notes Section, beginning on page 322. Because of the large number of pictures included to make vivid this life in song, and to keep the facing pages uncluttered and aesthetically pleasing, I chose to put all background and clarifying material, including picture identifications, in that section, page by page. With this arrangement, identifications are not necessarily limited to succinct captions.

       -- The author

In Quest of
Truth and Beauty
A Life In
Song and Image

John Filsinger

The A. G. Halldin Publishing Company, Inc.
Indiana, Pennsylvania

"A thing of beauty is a joy forever;
It's loveliness increases; it will never
Pass into nothingness; but still will keep
A bower quiet for us, and a sleep
Full of sweet dreams, and health, and quiet breathing.
Therefore, on every morrow, are we wreathing
A flowery band to bind us to the earth,
Spite of despondence, of the inhuman dearth
Of noble natures, of the gloomy days,
Of all the unhealthy and o'er darkened ways
Made for our searching; yes, in spite of all,
Some shape of beauty moves away the pall
From our dark spirits."
                              --John Keats, Endymion

Copyright © 1993 by Mr. John Filsinger
ISBN: 0-935648-44-5

To my gracious helpmates, Marjorie and Elaine,
who shared meaningfully with me
the music of the first and last of life--
understandingly, steadfastly, passionately...
envisioning, laboring, and learning
in our ongoing quest for truth and beauty.

Preface

This book started to come into being long ago, gradually, piece by piece, although I was unaware of it then. Something inherent prompted me, even as a boy, to try to articulate in written form significant emotional experiences. These were not necessarily major ecstasies or tragedies, but largely private discoveries of intriguing beauty, or harsh reality. I watched with wondering eyes the miracles of Nature unfolding, as Pennsylvania's varied seasons turned in annual cycles. I loved to kneel and press my face close to the fragrant, delicately tinted blossoms of trailing arbutus, half hidden in reviving grass of early spring, or to lie on my back on a warm summer lawn, charmed by the night music of country insects. Sometimes, on a clear night, I'd climb a tall hickory tree to marvel at the starry sky, or, on a bright day, I'd mount the lookout of an old oil derrick to be thrilled by distant scenes of cultivated fields and hardwood hills. In winter I relished the shivery sensation of snowflakes falling against my upturned face...and the sparkle of sunlight or moonlight on snow-covered slopes. Perhaps the most poignant sense of natural beauty came with the stunning colors of autumn. It was sad to see the tints fade and the drying leaves fall, but sheer delight to ramble shin-deep through their accumulations....

Inevitably, I learned that Nature, and human involvement in its processes, was not all wondrous beauty, but at times destructive, even cruel. Shame and remorse overwhelmed me when I stood over the struggling body of a squirrel I had wounded for no good reason. It could not be justified, as could the unfortunate but natural necessity of one animal killing another for food in order to survive. My candid idealism was harshly pierced by the incredible extent to which human cruelty could go, when a sadistic neighbor poisoned my yearling German shepherd. The wrenching pain and disillusionment I suffered were almost more than I could comprehend or bear.

However inadequate my vocabulary in those youthful years, I found happiness or solace in attempting to compose poems about these emotional experiences...or sunsets...God in Nature...infatuations.... It was a necessary learning process. Gradually the imagery improved, and occasionally there seemed to be a great leap forward, as with the early poem, "Serenade to Harbingers of Spring", which needed only a bit of polishing to include in Part I. College, marriage, self-education during three years of World War II military service, university study, work experience, adventurous travel--all added material and refinement to my private literary efforts. As the years rolled on, I wrote numerous articles and poems for mountaineering magazines and journals, but I made no effort to publish the accumulating pieces which comprise a large portion of this book. I must have sensed that many momentous experiences were yet to occur and be described before I could consider the work a meaningful whole.

The idea of an autobiography entirely in poetic form occurred to me sometime during the middle years, but I was too fully occupied with maintenance obligations to give such a project much concentration. Academic years were brimmed with preparing for and teaching five or six Spanish language and literature classes daily, correcting countless themes and tests, coaching golf, preparing for and participating in musical activities, as well as teaching my own children string music and other skills. In summer I guided at mountaineering encampments in western ranges, and on climbing expeditions to South America, Europe, and Asia. Some of these demanded extensive planning and preparation throughout the preceding year. Not only did I write about these adventures, but I was obliged to give countless illustrated lectures on them in school, community, and sometimes farther afield. Considerable time and energy went into remodeling a country home, and maintaining it and a large parcel of land in an aesthetically pleasing condition. Occasionally, notable diversions, such as exploring the West Branch of the Susquehanna River by canoe, or creating my "Family in Sculpture", were sandwiched in. From time to time, deeply moved by some new revelation of Truth or Beauty, I'd add another poem to the pile.

The concept of a lyrical life story became a firm conviction as a consequence of the profound emotions experienced during my first wife's long struggle with cancer and eventual death. Instinctively, I knew that AN ELEGY TO LOVE, a long series of poems composed in the aftermath, would become the centerpiece of my book. But, even as I slowly lifted myself out of grief, I realized that there might still be significant episodes of life with lyrical overtones yet to be lived, recorded, and added to the repository, before final sorting and arrangement.

At last, retired from teaching, stirred by the recent deaths of long-time friends, I set myself to the task, feeling keenly the personal relevance of Andrew Marvell's poignant seventeenth century petition to his coy mistress:
"But at my back I always hear Time's wingéd chariot hurrying near;
And yonder all before us lie Deserts of vast eternity."

As I proceeded, I chose to divide my story into two volumes. Since my mountaineering experiences have constituted such a distinctive and extensive part of my life, I have gathered them into a separate volume of prose and poetry entitled A Lifelong Love Affair with Mountains, which, in and of itself, may appeal to mountaineers and lovers of wilderness. In Quest of Truth and Beauty, which deals with other emotional, intellectual, and physical highlights of my life, I've opted to keep entirely in lyrical form, except for this introduction and necessary explanatory notes.

To give my "Life in Song" a meaningful pattern, I've frequently used musical terms in section titles and titles of many of the poems. In these, and throughout the body of the poems, I've not hesitated to use uncommon words. My "Quest for Truth and Beauty" has included a relentless search for words with just the right connotations, which may enable the reader to sense the subtle nuances of each episode. My creative process has also been heavily weighted by the sounds of words and phrasings, for these can immeasurably enhance the emotion being shared. I've always loved to read aloud the splendid, finely textured language of such classical poets as Shakespeare, Jonson, Wordsworth, Keats, Cullen Bryant, Longfellow, Hardy, Yeats, and Teasdale. They have been fountains of inspiration. It is my fervent hope that the reader will read my poems aloud, and endeavor to hear their distinctive music, to feel their inherent cadences, to savor their internal and climactic rhymes. Perhaps my personal account has evolved in this form because long ago I sensed the wisdom of Wordsworth's premise, in his preface to Lyrical Ballads, that poetry originates in the overflow of powerful emotion recollected in tranquility--that it is "the breath and finer spirit of all knowledge."

Since this is an autobiography, though an unusual one, much of it has chronological order, but not all of it. The poems were not necessarily written in the order of appearance. For example, "A Medley of Childhood Tunes" and "Remembering Anna," in SOME MELODIES OF LONG AGO, have the perspective of an elderly man recalling scenes and salient influences of childhood and youth, whereas the other poems in that part actually originated in the early years, most of them after graduation from high school, while I worked to save money for college. Those comprising LOVE MUSIC MIDST THE DISSONANCE OF WAR were composed during my first semester at Thiel College and three years of service in World War II, culminating with my return home at my father's death. CHANGING THEMES AND TEMPOS derives from my return to college, graduation, a year of graduate study at Syracuse University, and first settling in to a teaching career in Clearfield, Pennsylvania. It was a time of expanding perspectives, soul searching, and increasing awareness of contradictory human concepts. LEITMOTIFS FOR FAMILY PLAYERS principally portrays our somewhat isolated lifestyle, parenting, and uniquely bountiful sharing with our children. DISCORDANCIES philosophizes about incongruities and injustices experienced and observed during many stages of life. REFINING THE ARPEGGIOS OF LIFE embraces a wide spectrum of creative fulfillments over many years, up to my first wife's death in 1977. RHYTHMS AND MOODS FROM CHOSEN LANDS and MONUMENTAL ODYSSEYS highlight impressive experiences over forty years of foreign living, travel, and exploration, supplementing the mountain-related cultural and historical material covered in A LIFELONG LOVE AFFAIR WITH MOUNTAINS. Some of these poems were written long ago, and others composed recently from memoirs and recollections.

The first half of AN ELEGY TO LOVE, through the poem entitled "Midway through Adagio of Grief," was completed during the summer following my first wife's death in May, 1977. The rest followed during the subsequent autumn, winter, and spring. It was a year when not only piercingly intense present emotions but also myriad past ones were put through the refiner's fire. In fact, many of the most significant aspects of the previous three decades of our life together are revealed in this section. It's a detailed, very intimate portrayal of sublimating grief by starkly confronting, and giving aesthetic if painful expression to, the lost but lasting beauty of a deep, long-time love relationship. Sara Teasdale expressed better than anyone else how I felt during that bittersweet year:

> "My heart cried like a beaten child, ceaselessly the whole night long;
> I had to take my own cries and thread them into a song...
> One was a cry at black midnight, and one when the first cock crew--
> My heart was like a beaten child, but no one ever knew.
> Life, you have put me in your debt, and I must serve you long--
> But oh, the debt is terrible that must be paid in song."

The final section, OUT OF DEATH AND TIME CONCORDANCE WITH NEW MELODIES, is a tapestry of ongoing life up to the present--sharing fresh joys with my second wife--sorrows at more frequent deaths of other loved ones, and at man's pollution of the natural environment--new experiments, discoveries, disappointments, fulfillments--a never-ending quest for Truth and Beauty.

--John Filsinger

"Where there is an open mind
there will always be a frontier."

Searching

for

Shangri-La

I mark a far-off mountain's crested face,
Which movingly impels my searching sense
To go and know the essence of that space
Where earth and sky define pre-eminence.

What insights might that venture stir in me,
Scanning the nighttime's shoreless, starry sea
For truth? Beneath a midday's undiluted sun,
Above the circling landscape's complex entity,
Might I behold the hidden sources run?
Or would I scale that massive paragon
To have a mere diversion when it's done?

It may well be that I shall only see
Vast slopes that stretch to nebulosity
Around that skybound tower; but possibly,
If I go forth that prospect to assay,
Open to fresh perspectives of a way,
I'll find the thing my soul is questing for--
A final force of beauty at the core--
A wiser synthesis than known before.

Table of Contents
In Quest of Truth and Beauty--A Life In Song and Image

Dedication III

Preface IV

Theme Poem: Searching for Shangri-La VII

Part I: Some Melodies of Long Ago XII
    A Medley of Childhood Tunes 1
    Serenade to Harbingers of Spring 5
    Fantasia from Youth 6
    Pastorale--Vibrations from the Past 8
    Remembering Anna, Maestra Virtuosa 9
    From Many Themes I Now Must Choose 10

Part II: Love Music midst the Dissonance of War 14
    I've Found My First Sweet Fancied Love 15
    Too Soon Aufwiedersehen 16
    March Militaire in 13/13 Time 18
    Our Yesterday Might Never Have Become Today 21
    Unexpected Signatures and Counterpoints 22
    Nostalgic Refrains from Mexico 24
    Honeymoon Song 26
    In Midst of War's Loud Clangor, Muted Descants Rise 28
    A Windfall of West Indies Essences (Jamaica) 30
    Green Laurel Keeps a Vibrant Presence Sure 36

Part III: Changing Themes and Tempos 37
    An Illusive Harmony 38
    Valedictory 39
    Resurrection 40
    A Mentor's Heritage 42
    Prelude to Perennial Concert 46
    A Doomed Apple Tree's Recitative 48
    Processional? Recessional? 49
    Arrowhead Soliloquy 50

Part IV: Leitmotifs for Family Players 52
    Cradle Song 54
    Sonatinas Impromptus 55
    For Every Child a Never Never land: Allegro con Spírito 56
    A Tone Poem of Autumn Dancing 57
    Chansonette Celeste 58
    The Force of Destiny 59
    Childhood Duets 60
    Variations for Tuned Quartettes 62
    Roundelay with a Wren 64
    A Tribute to the Most Persistent Flower 65
    Swiss Hat Novelette 65
    An Art Too Evanescent 68
    Ballets of the German Shepherds:
        Allegro Grazioso (Rusty) 70
        Andante Maestoso (Thor) 71
    Parting Song for Rusty 72
    Like Milton Writing "Paradise" 73
    To Shape in Solid Segments Out of Time 74

Part V: Discordancies 76

    Lament for the Wounded Alleghenies 77

    A Century of Glory Here in Ashes Lies 78

    Interrupted Concert 81

    The Broken Terrarium 82

    Like a Finely Written Manuscript Destroyed 83

    Requiem for One Too Young 84

    Obscenities 85

    A Forest That Became a Gravestone Hill 86

    A Fury of Percussion 88

    Perhaps It Was Sylvania's Oldest Tree 89

    The Dilemma 90

    A Cadenza of Cacophonies 92

Part VI: Refining the Arpeggios of Life 93

    Intuitively My Spirit Sings 94

    The Theater Where I Sing Was Wont to Grow 95

    Appalachian Etudes:

        A Time to Go 96

        A Time to Stay 97

    My Friend the Cello Waits 98

    To Restore a View 100

    Each Bell I Ring Becomes a Living Thing 102

    I Love the Full Crescendo of the Surging Surf 105

    A Cavatina for Old Christmas Trees 106

    A Recurring Essence of June 107

    A Means for Years to Far-off Spheres Now Disappears 108

    A Collage of the Best of Teaching 109

    A Symphonic Ode to the Susquehanna 112

    An A-door-able Shed Takes Shape 117

    A Quartette of Unordinary Weddings 118

    Uplifting Golf to Lifelong Art 122

Part VII: Rhythms and Moods from Chosen Lands 125

    Climbing Pyramids (Mexico) 126

        From the Moon to the Sun and Beyond (Teotihuacán) 126

        Ascending to the Temple of the Serpent (Chichén-Itzá) 128

        A Mountaintop of Antique Artistry (Uxmal) 130

    A Kaleidoscope of Time and Place (Mexico) 132

        Like Ghosts of Prayers Whispered Long Ago (Acolman) 133

        A Place for Honeymooners (Xochimilco) 134

        Birthplace of a Nation's Liberty (Dolores-Hidalgo) 135

        Where Some Long Dead Still Render Testament (Guanajuato) 136

        A Solitary Trumpeter's Unpeered Antiphonies (Yucatán) 136

        A Monument of History Day (Taxco) 137

        A Crystal Moment Graved in Memory (Acapulco) 137

    Tenochtitlán at Christmastime (Mexico City) 138

    Glaciers and Gardens (Canada) 141

    Like Going Home (Austria) 142

    Musicians, Glockenspiels, and Dancing in the Park (Germany) 144

    Music Box Songs (Switzerland) 146

    A Glimpse of Immortality (Switzerland) 147

    Improvisations by the Sea (Costa Rica) 148

    Burros I Have Loved (Mexico, Spain, and Peru) 151

    A Tale of Two Pearls (Japan) 153

    Where Buddha Is Reclining, Solid Gold, and Emerald (Thailand) 154

    The Long, Long Path of Prayer (Nepal) 156

    Where Aged Pilgrims Come to Bathe and Die (India) 158

    The Taj Mahal--So Lovely, but So Costly (India) 160

    A Gauge of Great Ideas Here Was Formed (Greece) 164

    The Faces of the Children (Nepal, Japan, Mexico, Spain, Peru) 168

    Sevilla--City of Reflections (Spain) 172

    Interlude on the Isle of Birds (Spain) 178

Part VIII: Monumental Odysseys (Japan) (Peru) (Spain) **179**
  Roaming the Islands of the Rising Sun (Japan) 180
    Drenching Flesh and Mind unto Satiety (Tokyo, Hitoyoshi) 180
    Uncommon Sounds in Unaccustomed Places (Kuma River Rapids) 182
    Concerto Grosso of an Empire's Past (Kyoto) 183
    A Hymn of Murmuring Solitude (The Silver Shrine) 184
    Stone Lanterns of Antiquity (Nara) 186
    An Album of Oriental Novelties (Noto, Osaka, Beppu, Kamakura, Nikko, Matsushima) 187
  Along the Ancient Highways of the Setting Sun (Peru) 190
    Bass Notes and Overtones (Lima) 190
    A Place of Towering Mysteries (Sillustani) 192
    Life among the Reeds of Titicaca (Puno) 193
    Unfathomed Incan Walls Held Us Enthralled (Tambomachay, Kenko, Ollantaytambo) 194
    A Panoramic Pageant of the Sun (Sacsayhuaman) 196
    An Elevated Scale of Human Craftsmanship (Cuzco) 197
    Savoring the Sacred Valley of the Incas (Pisac, Urubamba) 198
    A Vital Harmony of Sun and Snow (Machu-Picchu) 200
  A Consummating Journey through Iberia (Spain) 202
    A Real-life Sense of What We'd Taught 202
    The Glory Wheel of Spain Was Axeled Here (Madrid) 203
    A Salient Centerpiece of Legacy (Toledo) 208
    The Trumpets of Glory Then Called Us to Ride (LaMancha) 210
    Bread and Wine for Soul and Flesh (Alcázar de San Juan, Valdepeñas) 212
    A Poet's Dream of Paradise (Córdoba) 214
    Our Quest for Truth and Beauty Lingered Here (Granada) 216
    A Song of Loss Is a Sad Song (La Rábita) 220
    Out of History into Legend (Sagunto) 222
    Cathedral Spires and Citadels of Earth (Picos de Europa, Cuevas de Altamira) 224
    A Shadow of Man's Yearned-for Immortality (Salamanca) 225
    A Firm Grasp of the Distant Past (Avila) 226
    A Palace for a Vengeful God (El Escorial) 227
    The Valley of the Fallen 228
    A Perfect Place to End an Odyssey (Segovia) 230

Part IX: An Elegy to Love **234**
  O Aching Fragrance of Spring 234
  Madrigal of a Last Bright Day 236
  Then Came a Surge of Anguished Consciousness 238
  Immortal Overtones of Elements 238
  Accolade at Home 239
  Still Echo Here the Drumbeats of Our Fate 240
  Carillions in the Towers of the Mind 240
  The Sounds of Hymns Triumphant 241
  Modulation to a Darker Key 242
  Midway through Adagio of Grief 242
  A Few Sweet Notes that Fade at Summer's End 244
  A Tribute to the Best of Friends 244
  I Went Today to Play at Treasure Lake 246
  Still Burn the Fires Perennial 246
  A Monument in Sound 247
  Out of the Fabric of Past Christmases 248
  A Tapestry of Continuity 248
  O Come, My Love, Come Lead Me to the Fire 250
  The Reddening Maple Blush Is on the Trees of Winter Silver 251
  And Gently Comes a Calming May at Last 252

Part X: Out of Death and Time, Concordance with New Melodies 254
Nocturne by the Sea 256
Grandfather's Reverie 257
Intermezzo at Farnam Creek 257
A Twenty Minute Emperor 258
The Chimes of Love Ring Clear Again 259
We Framed Our Wedding in a Highland Park 260
Our Tender Love Fulfills the Seasoned Years 261
Steep Snow Arabesques 262
A Rash of Unrecorded Rainbows 267
On Playing Don Quijote 268
A Song for All Winters 272
In the Realms of Titans 276
Revisiting the Needle Mountain Wilderness 277
Harmonics Still Echoing 280
In Praise of a Worthy Life 282
Fifty Springs Too Soon 284
Cycling Country Roads 285
In Retrospect of Colorado Friends 288
Fare-thee-wells for Troubadours: 290
     Zion, Hyner View, Cathedral of Learning, Everglades, Sinnemahoning, Niagara, Yosemite,
     A White Sand Beach, Torremolinos, Bryce, Ticonderoga, Jefferson's Monticello, Bok's Singing Tower
Good-bye, My Great Good Friend 304
Return to Bilger's Rocks 307
I Feel Such Boundless Pride in You 308
WQED-FM, We Love You 310
Watching Grandchildren Playing 312
A Canticle of Sunsets 'round the World 314
A Toast to the Wonder of It All 316
Looking Up, Still Singing 316

Coda: Remembered Beauty Kindly Tints the Graying Mind 319

Notes and Identifications 322

Since the pictures are located in close proximity to the text they are illustrating, their identity is usually clear. If they merit further elucidation, it may be found by page and location in this section at the back of the book. Where origin is other than the author, it is indicated there parenthetically.

Acknowledgements

My boundless gratitude to the following persons who demonstrated inspirational interest in contributing to the beauty and quality of this work: my wife, Elaine, for constant literary counsel and painstaking proof-reading of the text; Dorothy Loddo, of D and J Photos, Clearfield, for creating excellent black and white pictures from color transparencies; Dr. Bob Freeman and Bonnie Riggle, of Hi-Tech Color, Indiana, for carefully producing high quality color separations, often from old and worn transparencies.

"How to the singer comes the song?
At times a joy, alone;
A wordless tone
Caught from the crystal gleam of ice-bound trees;
Or from the violet-perfumed breeze;
Or the sharp smell of the seas
In sunlight glittering many an emerald mile."

Thus to the singer comes the song:
Gazing at crimson skies
Where burns and dies
On day's wide hearth the calm celestial fire,
The poet with a wild desire
Strikes the impassioned lyre,
Takes into tuned sound the flaming sight
And ushers with new song the ancient night."
--Richard Watson Gilder

Some Melodies of Long Ago

A Medley of Childhood Tunes

O callow lad of long ago,
How difficult to really know
From this far-off review,
Your hurts, defeats, triumphant schemes,
Your candid ways, what you esteemed--
The dreams that bloomed in you.

There must have been a normal score
Of growing pains, things boys abhor,
Of mischief, perhaps fights;
Somehow I don't remember these
As dominant, but clearly see
What gave you most delight.

I certainly can well recall
Enthusiasm through it all,
Innate desire to see
And feel kaleidoscopic life
Reveal its harmony or strife,
Its mobile entity.

The novel home your father made
Is gone, as is the summer shade
Where giant locust boughs
Arched high above that valley view,
Where dairy farmer's avenue
Framed cherry orchard rows.

You often glanced at that fair scene
While playing in your child's demesne
Of apple trees and lawn;
You sometimes climbed a hickory
To wonder at the mystery
Of what must lie beyond.

You pruned that orchard frequently,
Knew every branch of every tree,
Expressed proclivity
For climbing through those leafy routes,
Where yearly blooms became sweet fruits;
You sensed affinity.

How vividly I see the place
Where first you went to school--a trace
Of perfume lingering
From orchards seen from every room—
Tall plums, pink peaches bright in bloom,
In those idyllic springs.

And during recess in the fall
Your friends and you while playing ball
Hit homeruns to those groves,
For license then to hasten there
To find the ball, and seckel pears,
Their succulence to prove.

On way from school your friends and you
Would scale the cliffs where trains sped through,
Rejecting highway bridge;
Adventure there was taking shape
Which later led to mountain scapes
Of precipice and ridge.

You'd play at marbles for a time
With friends, but soon your questing mind
Felt urge to ramble on.
Absorbed, you leafed your aunt's old books,
Made friends with cows by stoney brooks,
Heard Nature's antiphon.

The quiet woods, orange orioles
Stirred kinship in your budding soul
For Nature's fresh milieu;
You climbed old oil wells' derrick towers,
And many tall trees' swaying bowers,
For love of distant views.

The haying farmer let you ride
His mammoth draft horse; there astride
Its fragrant sweating back
You savored strength's accomplishment,
Learned Nature's sure replenishment
Of fertile country tracts.

You learned to golf on caddies' day,
Then made your lawn a links, and played
Full tournaments with names
Of those renowned; there in your own
Yard's privacy, in time were sown
The seeds of tempting fame.

Sometimes by winding valley creeks
Where cattle kept rich pastures sleek,
You'd lure a friend or two,
To shape secluded golfing fields
And make a lazy summer yield
Constructive revenues.

On perfect moonlit nights you'd take
Some friends along to North Park Lake
For swimming in the nude;
Then, walking back, you often crossed
A field where golf balls might be lost,
Your stockpile to renew.

With childhood awe and German phrase
You shared your Grandpa's closing days--
His bearded, godlike face....
For unknown reasons you alone
Enjoyed the strained victrola tones
His old recordings traced:

Caruso, Scotti, Shuman-Heinck,
You sang their thrilling melodies,
Strange language mimicking;
Then Grandma bought a violin;
More music trembled deep within,
Art's instinct nourishing.

Your German shepherds taught you love's
Fidelity, as prize above
All venerated traits;
They showed you perfect symetry,
And, through one's death, first tragedy,
Stark grief to sublimate:

That shepherd was entirely white,
A constant presence, strong and bright--
Your foremost early friend;
How someone with impunity
Could feed him lye so callously
I still can't comprehend.

Your mother, brimmed with energy,
Would sample with alacrity
From all life's offerings;
You seemed to catch those eager ways--
To see, to taste, stretch every day
To fullest reckoning.

But most you were your father's friend,
Companion in a quiet blend
Of artful work and play;
He taught you careful carpentry,
How wine was made, shared willingly
With you his Saturdays....

He showed you early morn's appeal,
Its effervescency to feel,
Its hushed expectancy.
He led your thoughts to starry skies,
And what's beyond the reach of eyes
In that infinity....

"How to the singer comes the song?
How doth the night bring stars?
How yields darkness to happy dawn?
How to the summer fields come flowers?"
--Richard Watson Gilder

A Serenade to Harbingers of Spring

Hale Forsythia!
Steadfast harbinger of spring!
Uplifting out of melting snow,
What special message do you bring?

Sudden brilliancy!
Lutescent pageantry of spring!
Close galaxy of daytime stars!
Would that your voiceless choirs could sing!

Offspring of the sun!
At last I trace your mute design:
To ring with radiance in my eyes
And my heart's spring--event divine.

Fantasia of Youth

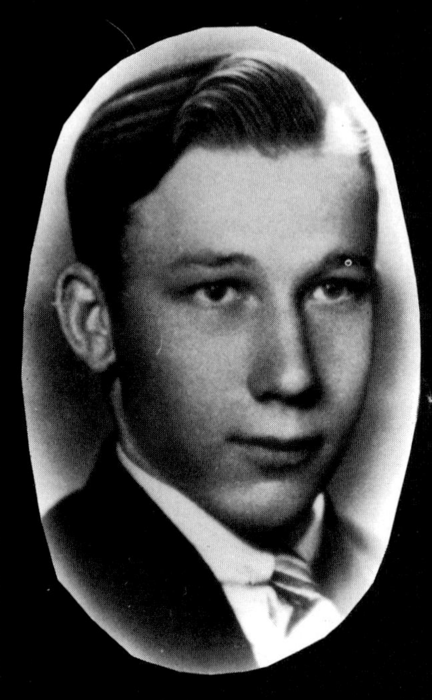

There is a Shangri-la beyond
Some far horizon line,
Where I shall find fulfillment of
My life's ideal design.

I do not know precisely how
Or when my quest will end,
But, ranging where my heart direct
My hopeful steps extend.

Perhaps through clamorous cities
Or complex forestries?
Up snow-hung fortress mountains?
Past vast forbidding seas?

Out somewhere in that theater
Of unknown future scenes,
I'll shape with subtle shadings
The substance of my dreams.

I fancy placid valleys, far
Away from troubling blast,
Wherein perchance I'll realize
True beauty that will last.

I envision well-spaced cottages
By brooks with ample views
To tranquil scenes of textured hills
In seasonal tatoos.

Classic music of the masters
Will complement clean air;
Polished eloquence of poetry
Will be exalted there.

And I shall know romantic love
Beside a spring cascade,
Or on a slope of sylvan flowers
Near patterned palisades.

Unfolding art will recompense
The care that I invest;
Productive days will not be tense,
Still nights will nurture rest.

With hope I venture out of youth
To seek that goodly place,
Where valued is maturing love
Of Beauty, Truth, and Grace.

Pastorale
(Vibrations from the Pas

I love to leave the dusty road behind,
And walk between long rows of aging pines,
Which settlers placed with purpose long ago
As seedlings, unaware, perhaps, they'd grow
Someday to shape of green cathedral halls
More lovely than the temples normally
Raised up by men to worship deities....

Respectfully, insatiably I breathe
The sylvan incense of their needled fronds,
Which join aloft from either side to arch
My private saunter through domains where Pan
Shares custody with self-sustaining man.

On contoured slopes I wander thoughtfully,
Past warped, abandoned farms where briared sward
Holds sway--where huckleberries dry unpicked--
Where old unbarbered apple orchards hint
Of May-time blossomings...of harvest tints....

Not wholly lonely seem these altered sites,
Where once squint eyes of farmers looked with pride
On what they'd done with Nature, tirelessly
Through decades laboring, unto the time
Of rest on mossy height with river view,
Where now I sit, instructed by the past,
Inspired by phantom friends I never knew.

Remembering Anna, Maestra Virtuosa

When I was but a growing, pliant soul, in awkward stage
Somewhere between a boy and man--between a simple heaven
And complex world, both undefined to point of verity,
She taught me voice, piano, and, through music's subtle signs
And rhythmed harmonies, a way to think and point my life
On proper course, replete with cultural discoveries.

With great anticipation every week, I'd climb the stairs
To her small home, ears primed to hear her voice call out
My name with bell-like clarity, before I'd reach the door;
Then, entering, I'd blush a bit ingenuously to see
Her snow-white ringlets, and her classic face, glowing with blend
Of virtuoso poise, warm mother love, and teacher pride,
Which I could not then aptly phrase as now, although I tried.

As soon as practice etudes and solfeggios ran their course,
Anna would rise, go to another room, and bring to me
A brand-new piece, then say, in her inimitable way:
"My dear, let's try this song. I think that it will suit your voice."
When afterwards we'd go into the kitchen, to partake
Of apple pie or gingerbread she'd made "because it was
My lesson day", she'd say the music was for me to keep,
The only pay required a promise to forever stir
My voice to song, and in the singing to remember her.

When I was far away in war, I learned that she had died,
And sorely grieved she could not ever play again for me
To sing, nor could I hear the clear pure beauty of her voice
Speak truth to me.... But I could still keep rendezvous in song
She long ago conceived. My old piano bench and heart
Are filled with gifts she freely gave, and when I sing, I see
Those snow-white ringlets shining through the notes persistently--
I hear her courteous words--I feel her matchless quality.

From Many Themes I Now Must Choose

I love to make things with my hands, to see
Results take final form from careful plans,
To give things individuality;
I relish spicy fragrance of cured wood,
Well-driven nails, joints fitted skillfully--
Constructive work that stands for all to see.
This seems the quickest route to mastery
From where I stand. Should I choose carpentry?

In first chair of our grade school orchestra
I keenly felt responsibility
To strive for more secure dexterity;
Unlike so many of my schooltime friends,
I've loved my violin, sensed beauty throb
That my instructor's faith was gratified.
But would my skills eventually compare
With fine musicians that compete out there?

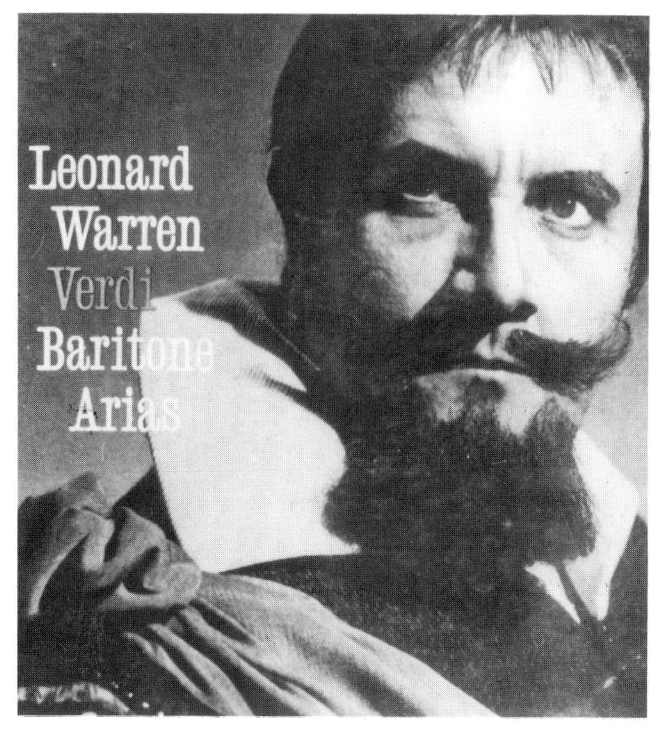

From Grandpa's quaint old classic opera discs
I learned the drama of majestic sound;
On afternoons of autumn Saturdays,
I seldom miss the broadcasts from the Met,
While other boys my age cheer football teams;
I study voice with one whose cultured grace
Leaves deepest mark on my emerging face....
Would I be good enough to make her proud
Among great bassos singing clear and loud?

Among the pastimes of my growing years,
I've greatly fancied golf--the fresh-cut scenes
Of satin greens, ambrosial fields that roll
In clever manicured designs to goals
Set artfully by copse of trees, or hill,
Where shapely hazards challenge hard-won skill....
I've had success in this aesthetic game,
Becoming champion of the county's youth;
In high school I rose up to premier player
On expert team that triumphed over most....
Should I become professional, and try
For fame and fortune some have prophesied?

James Ramsey Ullman's book on Everest,
And Hilton's <u>Lost Horizon</u> touch the core
Of all my imaging. Are there perchance
Great explorations still to do, far off,
Beyond high reaches of some glaciered range,
Or deep within some unknown wilderness?....
Dare I imagine that it might be I
Who might discover some uncharted world
On earth, or in the cosmic night unfurled?....
But how should I prepare for such a thing?
Make practical such wild imagining?
What studies should I make? What school attend,
To turn my life toward such adventurous end?

"O world, thou choosest not the better part;
It is not wisdom to be only wise,
And on the inward vision close the eyes,
But it is widsom to believe the heart.
Columbus found a world, and had no chart
Save one that faith deciphered in the skies;
To trust the soul's invincible surmise
Was all his science and his only art.
Our knowledge is a torch of smoky pine
That lights the pathway but one step ahead
Across a void of mystery and dread.
Bid, then, the tender light of faith to shine
By which alone the mortal heart is led
Unto the thinking of the thought divine."
                              --George Santayana

St. John's historic chapel on the hill
Is filled with seasoned beauty and repose.
What peace in stained glass windows' muted shades!
What jubilee in organ serenades!
The eloquence of King James' Bible phrase
Stirs deep poetic instincts in my soul,
Instilling some security or whole,
It would be so felicitous to work
In such a quiet splendrous atmosphere....
Could I succeed in church's ministry?
Help folks through life, assuage death's agony?

The three hard years I worked to save for school
Were education in the rough, profane
Academy of Groups of Men--their harsh
Abrasive words and ways disheartening
For one whose frequent dreams were imaging
Some lovely, gentle race which could evolve
In some idyllic place....I then resolved
To enter college primed with high ideals,
Inclined to study for the ministry,
Intent on steady scholarship for ways
To aid a floundering humanity.

Love Music
Midst the Dissonance
of War

I've Found My First Sweet Fancied Love

I've found you in reality at last,
Just as I've always somehow known I would
Since in my early fantasy you stood
On pedestal of cloud high in the sky,
Calling to me to come with fleet reply.
I sorely yearned in that discovering hour
To answer you with passion-carried flower--
Ascend to you on sparkling, terraced beams.

But then it could not be more than a dream
Because, through learning years, I had to strive,
Anticipate, prepare a golden bowl
Of essences to prime my flesh and soul--
Gain wisdom for a more sufficient goal.

With wistful resignation as my prize
To bear away, I focused on your eyes
So distant gleaming, my heart redeeming,
And as your fading figure turned to mist,
I swore I'd someday touch and warm your hands
Which only far, insentient winds then kissed.

Too Soon Aufwiedersehen

I loved the ivied bricks, the antique rooms,
Old burnished books arranged enticingly,
My teachers' individualities,
The cultured atmosphere, the chapel choir,
Where every morning you and I would meet
To sing, and feel the comfort of our love.

I found you first among the walls of books,
With recognition in your tender eyes
That years before had bridged the frigid skies
To fill my own with hope. Instinctively
I sensed your unadulterated warmth--
Your quick intelligence in helping me
To source my studies sought....I soon forgot
My tasks, so captive were my eyes to watch
Your grace unfold; and then my lips were bold
Enough to sing to you "The Evening Star"
On amphitheater stage, where first we kissed
And cleared away all past forbidding mist.

Our lives at last entwined in warming clasp,
We danced together toward a promised land,
Exultantly, securely, hand in hand.
But suddenly we heard the clam'rous call
To war! Our trails, so recently combined
In choric pace, must separate, and I
Must quickly journey to some unknown clime
For undetermined length of precious time.

How hard to take as ordered destiny
Such rude intrusion on our new found joy!
But well we knew that we must cast our weight
Against the evil carriers of hate
Who moved with cruel, accelerating gait.

And so we parted with committed hearts
To nurture love while acting out our parts.

Marche Militaire

in 13/13 Time

With <u>thirteen</u> letters in my name, perhaps my eyes were prone
To find that emblem of supposed misfortune everywhere
I turned…. Thus was it I took note it was the <u>thirteenth</u> of
The month when we were called away from pleasant college days
To serve our country in the throes of escalating war.

Perhaps the friendly faculty and student body who
Paraded with us from the campus to the railroad stop,
To send us off in proper style with fanfare and applause,
Were unaware that we were <u>thirteen</u> souls who disappeared
Along that track that led to unknown ends, but I was not.
Two times, in changing trains, we passed through gates <u>thirteen</u>, an
And then when I received my air force serial dog-tag numbering,
I must have wryly smiled, for it began with <u>two-thirteens</u>!

In spite of all this seeming prophesy that ill might fall,
The fates sent me for basic training to the lovely parks
Of old St. Petersburg's Venoy Hotel, on Tampa Bay;

We rose for reveille with tints of dawn reflecting there,
Then marched beneath tall royal palms, past bougainvillaea blooms
And flowering jacaranda trees, which dampened some degree
The strident orders of the crusty sergeant drilling us;
Not even that tough, surly man could dint our firm belief
That we were lucky to be there, instead of barracked at
Some dismal fort, or marching in some frozen habitat.

But as so frequently in life when some good fortune comes
To settle unexpectedly around us, it endures
For such a precious little while; with cruel abruptness
I was stricken with a nearly fatal malady--
A deep infection after surgical emergency.

There followed several sick and suffering weeks at Pas-a-Grille,
My buttocks penicillinned to a sorry hurtful state;
Bed-bound, made sad with brooding on the omen-numbering,
I watched bright sunsets flood the Gulf of Mexico, wondering
If all along, behind those pleasant scenes, it had been functioning,
And shaping chains to bind me in some dire catastrophe....

Auspiciously, that scary sojourn, on the rim of Death's
Grim Valley, was not warranted to be my final scene;
Regaining strength, I traveled north more than a thousand miles,
Assigned to cryptographic school near New York's Quaker Hill,
Where, unbelievably, among the countless rooms of its
Hotel-sized dorm, I found that I was quartered in Thirteen.

Still facing such incessancy of bodeful overtones,
I somehow graduated from that most forbidding course,
Knowing those who didn't likely would be sent to infantry;
And then I traveled on, inexorably, to many chance
Assignments, with the fateful number reappearing time
And time again; but always there was some redemption in
Each new experience that rescued me from fearful end....

Although I felt a constant need for what I'd left at home,
The long-range tenor of my military years was such
That, oddly, I might even have been led to speculate
That Thirteen was for me an emblem of good luck, not bad....
Till full maturity of thought brought me long since to see
That superstitious figments, of whatever source they be,
Have little place at all in shaping human destiny.

Our Yesterday
Might Never
Have Become Today

Today I have to pinch myself to realize that I
And my companion, Billy Hannibal, are still alive.
But for the merest chance of time and space, our yesterday
Might suddenly have slipped away to everlasting night.

This air base close to Smyrna, Tennessee, where bombing crews
Are trained, was just to be a brief delay en route for us
Who graduated recently from Air Corps training in
Cryptography. Awaiting further orders as to where
We'll be assigned, we've been seizing opportunities
To go up with the bombing crews on training runs, to gain
Experience in flight, and knowledge of the latest planes.

Thus yesterday my friend and I went out to where the line
Of bombers was preparing to take off. We headed first
For number Sixty-three, whose crew seemed set to go on board,
But they informed us that there was no room. Then we approached
Plane Forty-nine, which fortunately did have space for two. .
For several hours we circled over pleasant countryside,
Apparelled with new April greens, beneath a cobalt sky....

Both past and present happenings combined to make us feel
Abnormally contented as we flew: We'd recently survived,
Where many failed, some really challenging instruction in
Cryptography. With fascination we observed the crew
Go through what they will have to do to guarantee success,
When fate calls them to deal with real ferocity of war.
And bearing "bird's-eye-witness" to revitalizing spring,
Performing its appointed work on seeded fields and trees,
Inspired us with a quickening sense that our own fresh vitality,
And new-made skill, will play a needful role in what must come to be.

While such instinctive optimism governed thus our minds,
Although we still knew not where we were bound, our olive plane
Made contact with the ground, and taxied to its parking place.
We thanked the pilot, disembarked, and walked across the field;
Then, like a sudden bolt through yesterday's blue heaven,
Our hearts were pierced with tragic, wrenching news: Plane Sixty-three
Had crashed!! The crew beneath the wing who told us they were filled--
The riders who were just ahead of us--all had been killed!!!
How fragile is the thread of human destiny. To think that we,
Arriving moments sooner, would have been the ones who ceased to be.

Unexpected
Signatures and Counterpoints

Surprisingly, I'm now in old Tampico, Mexico,
Encoding cryptic messages that deal with Air Force flights--
Pursuit planes bound for Africa, and cargoes coming back
With wounded soldiers from those odious desert battlefields.
By virtue of my language skill and lucky circumstance,
I find myself attired in full civilian masquerade,
Instead of military garb; and, quite improbably,
I'm billeted within a private residence, the property
Of agéd Spanish immigrants from old Navarre, near Spain's
Cantabrian Sea.
        Señor Mendive long has been retired
From building mansion homes for wealthy foreign families,
Lodged here to exploit Mexico's petroleum industry.
As stolid as the handsome Husky dog who stoically
Attends nearby, the master of the house seems uninclined
To speak more than "hello", and plays an endless game
Of solitaire on porches of his self-made residency,
Renowned as Pine Street, Number One, in High View Colony.

But the petite sēnora of the house, who's asked me to
Address her in endearing terms as "Abuelita", plays
Quite fitting counterpart to mister's quiet reticence;
With silver hair piled high atop her less than five-foot height,
She's pert as any energetic girl one-eighth her age;
When her attendant frees that bun of hair to brush it out,
Incredibly, it nearly reaches down to touch the floor.
Vivacious and informative each time we're face to face,
She's come to be my trusted confidante-companion in
Extensive coloquies through which I'm honing fluency
In oral Spanish use.
                    Although she tries to "mother" me,
She does so with a winsome edge of gentle irony,
Assuming as her daily liability to see
That I am dressed and ready to depart for work on time;
But what engraves her image even more in my esteem
Is that she does respect my privacy on my days off,
If I go out to use her palm-tree-shaded balcony,
To read, or write long letters home, or study Greek.
I feel a certainty that even when I'm old and gray,
As Abuelita is today, when recollections fade,
I'll not forget her undiminished spry agility,
Nor her petite endearing look of tasteful amity.

Nostalgic Refrains from Mexico

To muse the cemetery's marbled art
And lawn-sealed griefs, then cross the antique bridge,
That spans Shenango's calm or rushing flow,

To balance on the endless railroad tracks,
And search for pleasant brook-bank bivouacs....
One Sunday we were caught in gentle showers:
The golden rod had browned, as had the flowers.
Our slow-paced day spun out--we read aloud
From Keats and Wordsworth till a massive cloud
Arrived to spray the thirsting grass and us,
Eliciting an earthly fragrance while

We sought the trees for shelter, hugging then
More earnestly as vistas of the fields
Around were drowned from view.

We knew its thrust,
For soon the lists would come to separate
Our paths and blur the landscape of our fate.

From Miramar I scan the Gulf's wide waves
With tempered thoughts to Allegheny's bend,
Among the moderate hills where you attend
A teaching schedule with long-range resolve,
Preserving, planning, as the war evolves....

Past mounds of time I walk beside the sea,
Embracing hope undeviatingly
In gray acceptance of my separate way,
Rehearsing visions of our future day.

"I sent thee late a rosy wreath,
   Not so much honouring thee
As giving it a hope that there
   It could not wither'd be;
But thou thereon didst only breathe
   And sent'st it back to me;
Since when it grows, and smells, I swear,
   Not of itself but thee!"
                    --Ben Jonson

Honeymoon Song

All this seems like a dream--too good to be
Reality--since I received my leave
From Mexico so suddenly, then came
Across slow, long-anticipated miles
To walk into your classroom as surprise,
And see your incredulity that I was there
Within your firm enveloping embrace.

With dancing thoughts and hearts in perfect rhyme,
We quickly settled that we would be wed,
And reap the fullness of our deepened love
Within that granted span of rushing time,
Uncertain of what fate might lie ahead.

Our parents, friends, your students, all the town
Excitedly shared our festivity--
A brief surcease from war's adversity;
And Nature, too, bestowed its alchemy
With apple blossoms blessing every tree.

These images will go with me to war
When I must say goodbye to you again:
The quaint white church on orchard-scented hill--
Gold candlelight to match your eyes' soft look
Of caring warmth--our vernal ecstasy
In privacy of mountain forest camp--
Our carefree swim in cold lake's clarity--
All we compressed into brief woodland walks,
Ephemerally, but with serenity,
Will bear us both beyond the unknown strains
Of harsh war music, back to old refrains
Of love and peace, made doubly meaningful,
For what has passed will preface what will last.

In Midst of War's Loud Clangor,
Muted Descants Rise

As through strange trees and foreign fields I range,
I secretly evoke familiar eyes
Whose soft look may assuage dejecting thoughts,
And fathom starlight in the bursting skies.

The grinding motors of this war-wrought art
Deafen the list'nings of my midnight hour
To all but urgent chimings in my heart,
Commanding forcefully your present power.

And in the midst of nameless, rushing throngs
In crowded cities where mixed speeds converge,
I sense your face, your voice, your laughter's song,
Obscurely somewhere as the masks emerge.

The treadmills of our waiting lives run on,
With merely imaged touch on warming flesh;
O when will yearning yield substantial trace
Of sunlight's morning splendor on your face?

A Windfall of West Indies Essences

I couldn't have imagined, when I went away to war,
I'd eventually be assigned to live and work a year
On the Island of Jamaica, in the blue Caribbean Sea.
The United States and England made a trade of battleships
For airfields, after which Jamaica's Vernam Field became
A training base for our B-29's, ostensibly
Because those isles were like the ones that dot Pacific seas.

"Quite overwhelming" was my first impression of that
Tropic flourishing, when our drab olive-painted air force plane
Descended from a perfect sky to runways bordered by
Broad fields of sugar cane at harvesting, with fragrances
So densely laden with intoxicating sweetness
That I could taste and savor them with every sensuous breath...
Thus did I step onto that isle of lush fertility,
With all my senses swelling to aroused facility.

But even as I deeply drew those heady opening breaths,
Sensing that the fates had maybe sent me to a privileged place,
I hardly could conceive the wealth of new experience
That year would bring. The very day that I was billeted
At Vernam Base, I could not keep my eyes from straying, time
And time again, beyond the fields and foothills to the east,
Where mountains, blue as any flower could be, were calling me
By name....Before that year had run its course, I managed to
Persuade two groups of friends to ford fast streams, and climb exotic
Mountainsides, so we could gather orchids in the wild,
Consume fresh berries resting on Blue Mountain's highest peak,
And scan the island's eastern half, from north to southern seas.

"...The sounding cataract
Haunted me like a passion; the tall rock,
The mountain, and the deep and gloomy wood,
Their colors and their forms, were then to me
An appetite.... And I have felt
A presence that disturbs me with the joy
Of elevated thoughts; a sense sublime,
Of something far more deeply interfused,
Whose dwelling is the light of setting suns,
And the round ocean and the living air,
And the blue sky, and in the mind of man...."
                                    --William Wordsworth

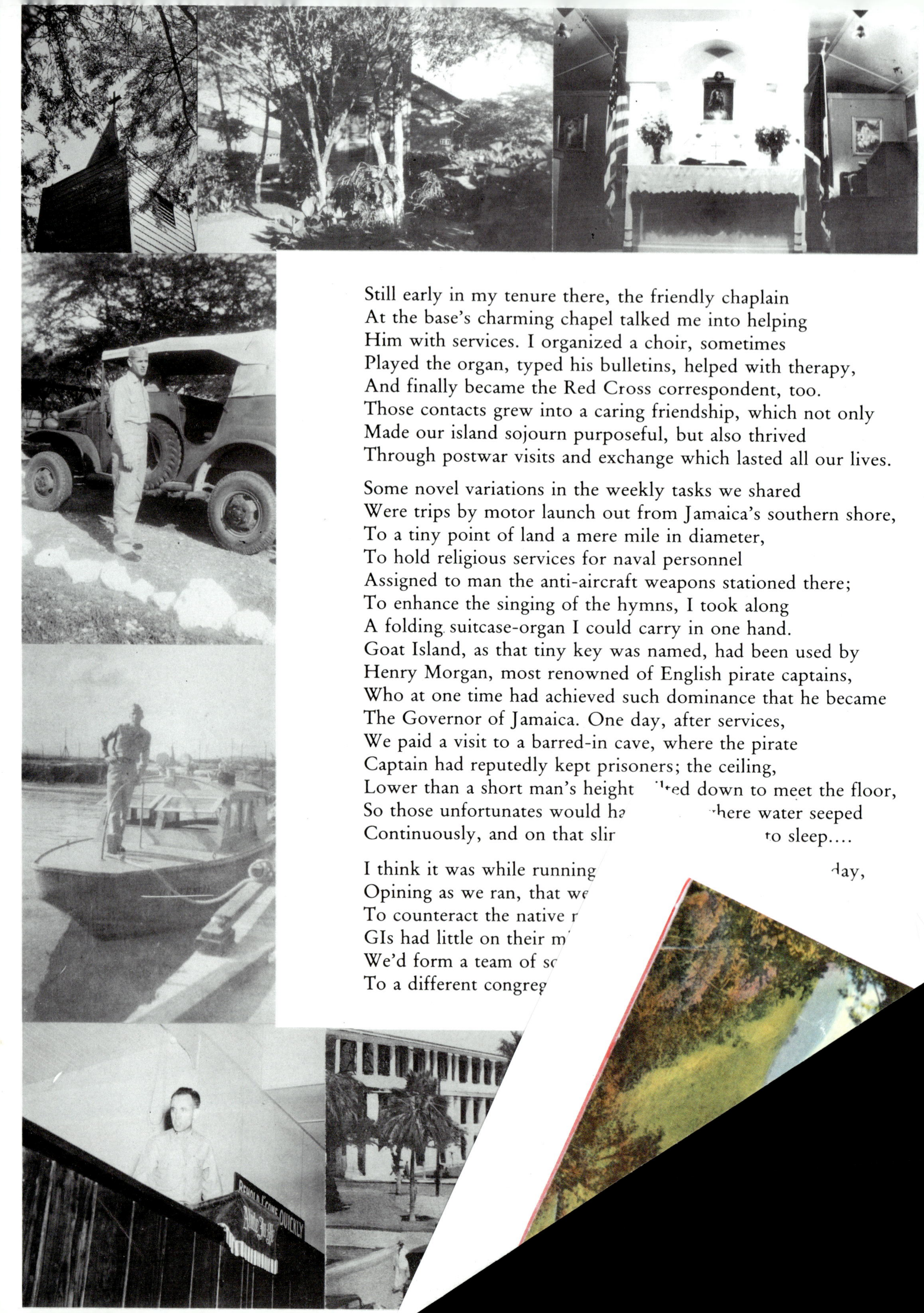

Still early in my tenure there, the friendly chaplain
At the base's charming chapel talked me into helping
Him with services. I organized a choir, sometimes
Played the organ, typed his bulletins, helped with therapy,
And finally became the Red Cross correspondent, too.
Those contacts grew into a caring friendship, which not only
Made our island sojourn purposeful, but also thrived
Through postwar visits and exchange which lasted all our lives.

Some novel variations in the weekly tasks we shared
Were trips by motor launch out from Jamaica's southern shore,
To a tiny point of land a mere mile in diameter,
To hold religious services for naval personnel
Assigned to man the anti-aircraft weapons stationed there;
To enhance the singing of the hymns, I took along
A folding suitcase-organ I could carry in one hand.
Goat Island, as that tiny key was named, had been used by
Henry Morgan, most renowned of English pirate captains,
Who at one time had achieved such dominance that he became
The Governor of Jamaica. One day, after services,
We paid a visit to a barred-in cave, where the pirate
Captain had reputedly kept prisoners; the ceiling,
Lower than a short man's height ⸍ted down to meet the floor,
So those unfortunates would ha   ⸍here water seeped
Continuously, and on that slir   ⸍o sleep....

I think it was while running   day,
Opining as we ran, that we
To counteract the native r
GIs had little on their m
We'd form a team of sc
To a different congreg

Appealing songs and hymns; a couple of the men would give
Their personal accounts, explaining what our mission was;
And then the chaplain, in his winsome, finely tempered way,
Would share some well-phrased wisdom as the climax to the day.

Our project ranged from Kingston's major churches, through average
Towns, to little hilltop chapels at the end of winding roads,
Where people walked all day just to hear the services;
Everywhere we went, we were acclaimed enthusiastically;
Frequently, in rural settings, windows would be opened wide
So that overflow attendants would not have to be denied.
We learned a great deal of the life of the Jamaicans and
Their history, as well as much geography, as we
Traveled here and there those fragrant Sunday afternoons;
And we experienced so many stirring high points, that
It's difficult to choose which ones to tell. For me there is
One image highly personal that I've reviewed so many times
It's past forgetting: We'd gone to hold a service in perhaps
The grandest church in all of Kingston; the chaplain had
Enthralled a large assembly with his thoughtful eloquence;
A pin could have been heard to drop in that great hall, as I
Stood up in organ loft to face that full observant mass,
And raised my voice to sing the prayer that Jesus gave, set to
The ageless music of "Finlandia." It was as though
My voice became some other voice, more beautiful than mine;
As I went on, the tones poured out so rich and deep, they seemed
To have no bounds; the words were crisply clear; I seemed to hear
Them as if I had stepped outside myself; and at the end,
It was as though I were a statue standing there, reluctant
To relinquish its immortal pose; it might have been for me
The closest I shall ever come to art's sublimity.

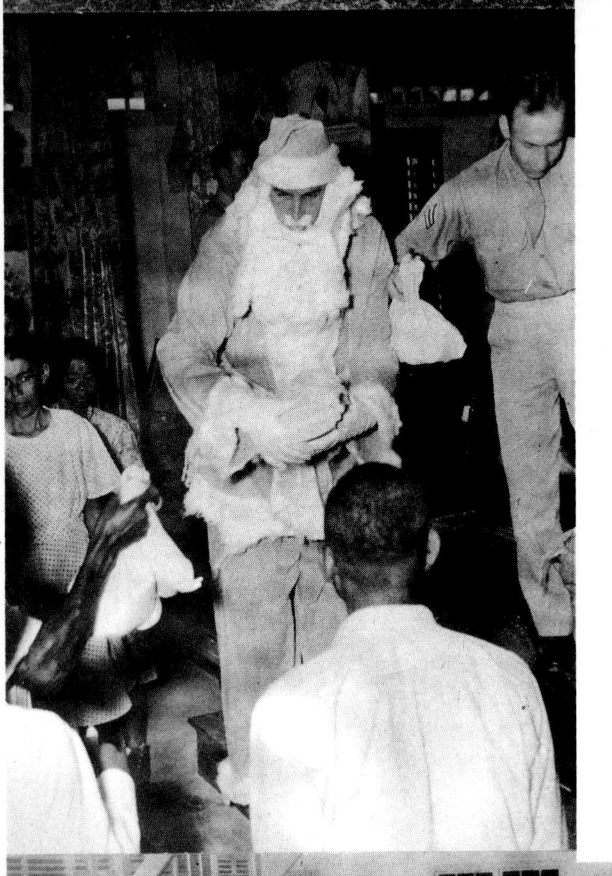

Of vastly greater merit, in the human chain of being,
Was the Christmas celebration that we planned and carried out
In behalf of lepers, living in a colony in
Spanish Town, Jamaica's two-time capital. Unselfish
Catholic nuns gave wondrous care to those poor suffering folks
The dreaded malady had overtaken. The sisters thought
Those shut-ins would enjoy one of our Sunday services,
But, as we planned it out, we felt that we could do much more—
Perhaps enlarge our visit to include a Christmas party,
With a special treat and gift for each and every patient....
Even though it all transpired nearly fifty years ago,
I can vividly evoke those sad disease-distorted faces,
Trying to lift up their voices, as I stood in front of
Them to end the service with the lovely words of "Silent Night"
Aware how hard it was for them to feel "all calm, all bright".
A band of soldier instrumentalists then played, while one
Of our team members, dressed as Santa Claus, gave out the gifts
And, insofar as possible, in view of their distress,
We shared with them at least a bit of human happiness.

Close on the heels of that heart-rending try at charity,
I got the shocking notice of my father's sudden death,
And left that sugar-scented isle, never to return again

To see the candid, sun-drenched, white-toothed faces in the churches...
To meander through Hope Gardens' orchid paradise...
To sit for hours reading Thoreau's <u>Walden</u>, where I could see
The matchless mountain blue, and breathe the peerless fragrancy.

Green Laurel Keeps a Vibrant Presence Sure

I've traced your likely steps near gurgling brook,
Then up steep pasture hill to overlook
At edge of maple, ash, and oak domain,
Where you had slowly come to cope with pain,
Perhaps to rest beneath these birdless boughs
Of winter trees, which nonetheless somehow
With wildwood wisdom speak to human ear,
And shelter sense and thought at Death's frontier.

Sparse clinging foliage, braving the cold spear,
With melancholy language quavers here--
A private windsong of a fatal hour
When, nestled by a fallen oak, you lay
From sleep to death that solitary day.

In tender grief I contemplate your bed
Where years of fallen leaves are lying dead,
All once bright thriving green, then flame or gold,
Soon crackling dry, then dank and merged to mold,
Their form and pith long lost but manifest
In tiny curling roots, whose darkling quest
Strives ever upward through unfrozen sod
To sunlit growth which man ascribes to God.

It may be your quintessence now will stay
Within these leaves; or have you gone away
To ride the breeze through peaceful valley mist,
To seek the gold of sunfire's alchemist?

I cannot know, but most I feel you here
Within my prizing heart, as through the years
Green laurel keeps symbolic presence sure
Where every autumn, life, downthrown, endures.

"High upon the mountainside,
Under scourging thong
Of wind and sleet, the oaken tree
Toughened and grew strong.
Close beside, the slender birch--
Delicate of form--
Writhed in ashen agony,
Bending to the storm.
Why the gale brought down the oak
At the summer's end--
While the birch stands straight and tall--
Who may comprehend?"

--Jessie Wilmore Murton

Changing Themes and Tempos

"Like a flower now we grow,
Like the sea we ebb and flow,
Still uncertain is our change;
Like the wind so do we range."
--John Attey

"I sent my soul through the invisible,
Some letter of that after-life to spell:
    And by and by my soul returned to me
And answered, 'I myself am heav'n and hell'."
--Rubáiyát of Omar Khayyám (Trans. by Fitzgerald)

"When truth stands in your way,
you're headed in the wrong direction."

An Illusive Harmony

When wheeled away from school to serve in World War Two,
I carried forth resolve to garner gain from what
The fates of place and circumstance might cast my way--
Not lose, but nutrify, incipient tendency
To ponder new ideas, to stretch my growing mind
To highest reach, to sift and spell the undefined.

I walked and talked with natives in their rooted place,
And used my skill in foreign tongue to taste firsthand
Their brew of truth--to comprehend their different ways.
I read as well great books of classic master worth:
Thoreau seduced me with his <u>Walden</u> rhapsodies,
The scope of Tolstoy's <u>War and Peace</u> enlarged my frame,
While Shakespeare's sonnets brimmed with wise experience
And lured my soul to thrill of well-phrased eloquence.

I shared long letters with my love to bridge the miles
And years, and in this rich detailed exchange we learned
In many ways more deeply of each other's thoughts,
Refined with more dexterity the loving art,
Than if the fated war had not cast us apart.

Throughout it all a subtle change was taking shape
Within the mental corridors that led me on.
Returning to my college with a clearer view
Of life's complexities, and more aware of man's
Propensity to shape his universe and creeds
To suit his needs, I found myself now more inclined
To study languages and English literature--
To crystalize some broad, discreet philosophy
Wherein my intellect and heart might harmonize
To deal with basic doubts and life's inequities,
Perhaps therein enlarge my capabilities
To think, to write, to teach at universities.

Valedictory

The vast gymnasium is filled with students' relatives
And friends, assembled here with pride to recognize long years
Of study, trial, discovery, evaluation, choice—
Pursuit of dreams with unspoiled hope they may be realized.
While stirring tones of Pomp and Circumstance teach solemn poise
To slowly moving gowns and faces crowned with tasseled boards,
The college president and dean, and chosen candidates
For high degrees, take elevated seats...How can it be
That only I among my fellow students join them there?

Inside my chest, all tremulous, I feel an awesome weight
That I must summarize in graceful, compact terms what we
Have learned--what values we've refined--the meaning of it all
For us as we now say farewell and go our sep'rate ways.
Will my voice fail? Shall I let down all those with faith in me?
Will my oration measure short of some expected eloquence?

I hear the president pronounce my name; I rise to face
A broad complexity of peopled seats, and at my feet
The tensely full expectancy of faculty and peers.
Is that my voice I hear acknowledging distinguished guests,
My fellow graduates, an audience unknown? And with
No hint of tremoring? My words pour forth just as I've planned;
A calming confidence pervades and bears me smoothly through
To climax with the sapient words of Carl Schurz: "Ideals
Are like the stars. Although we may not ever touch them with
Our hands, we may, like seamen on the vastness of the sea,
Chart out our courses by them and thus reach our destinies."

Applause ensues; the smiling faces in the frontal rows
Give ample benediction to my part; then suddenly
That crystal moment of my life leaps into history.

Resurrection

When I attended graduate school in Syracuse, New York,
My wife and I found pleasant lodging in a hamlet twenty miles
Southeast, where summer tourist cabins had been winterized;
One Sunday morning, friendly neighbors asked if we would like
To go with them to church in the hilltop town of Pompey,
Half a dozen miles along a highway going west;
Somewhat uneasy as to whether we would find the kind
Of tempered atmosphere where intellect and spiritual
Conceptions could be reconciled, we felt we hardly could
Refuse their cordial, well-intentioned overture. Quite soon,
However, it became apparent in that little church
That there were persons with uncommon capabilities.
The owners of the Snow White Inn, with cabins shaped in guise
Of Seven Dwarfs, were cultured and imaginative folks,
With beautiful soprano and high tenor choral singing skills;
The Minister was quite intelligent, experienced,
And tolerant, as was his winsome wife--a music teacher
And a master organist; she led a small but gifted
Chancel choir, and, finding that my wife and I had music
Backgrounds, too, she felt quite sure that we would like to sing
The kind of classic anthems they were weekly rendering.

All that was merely background for the quite extraordinary
Happening that we would help to realize that fruitful year.
In Syracuse, a large cathedral's congregation was
Remodeling, and planned to have a brand new organ built
As vital part of their extensive renovation scheme.

We didn't even have an organ in our church, so our
Inventive pastor promptly went and asked what plans they had
As to the old pipe instrument that they'd be taking out;
They told him we could have it free of charge, if he would take
Responsibility to disassemble and remove
It from the premises within a designated time.
Using as a guide some books on organ building, which my
Wife located at the university, we labeled
And enumerated every single part and pipe as
We dismantled it; and then we laid them out in careful
Order, using half our little church's pews and walls to
Store them temporarily…till we could resurrect its
Earthly shape, and hear its muted voice vibrate anew.
It took a long, long while, but finally it stood complete,
In place of several pews back in a corner of the nave;
Then anxious hearts leapt up when first our master player
Deftly stirred the keys to music worthy of angelic prayer.

To dedicate such rare accomplishment, our choir planned
For Holy Week a gala gathering for which we would
Prepare a polished rendering of Stainer's "Crucifixion";
So many people came that there was need to open all
The windows and the doors, and gather chairs to put outside
So those who could not fit within at very least could hear.
Although I'd sung the solo bass before in my home church,
One of the greatest honors of my Life in Song was being
Asked to sing the words of Jesus in "The Agony", and share
The moving male duet, "So Liftest Thy Divine Petition",
With the "Snow White" man who had the lyric tenor voice;
Our organist and choral leader managed to inspire
Our compact choir to lift itself up to the artistry
Which that unique event deserved; and the salvaged organ,
Which we ourselves had boldly toiled to resurrect, aesthetically
Enlarged its celebration with celestial harmonies.

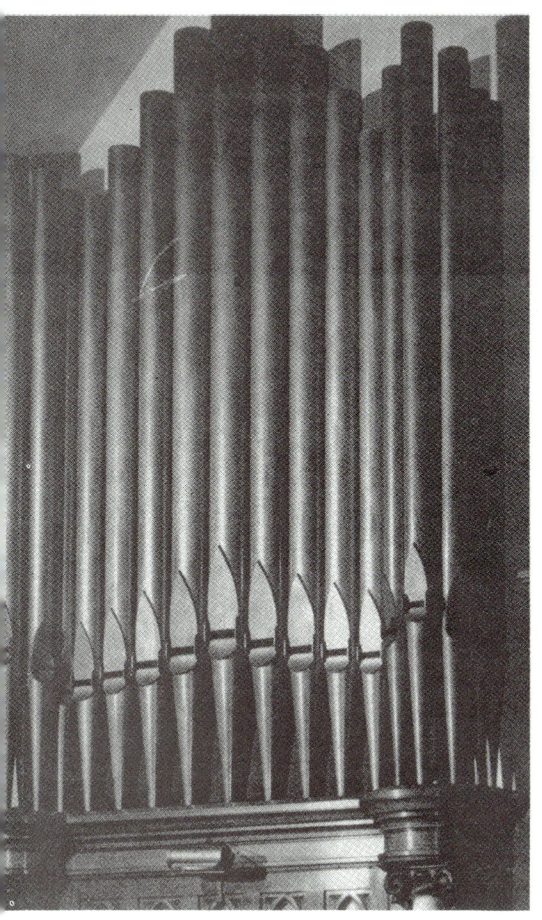

A Mentor's Heritage

Somewhere ascending education's long-term rise,
The poetry of William Cullen Bryant touched my
Soul, and moved and shaped me with its cadenced throng
Of thoughtful images that ranged through Nature's realms
With tender reverence for all her various forms,
And counseled me to court her beauty with a song.

In June-time when the graduate year was rounded out,
Our striving minds stretched taut and tired from long-time
For salient facts and adequate philosophies,   quest
On verge of moving to new work's uncertainties,
My mate and I went forth to look for restful scenes,
Unpressed by institutional necessities.

We wandered through New England's literary shrines:
Communed with Thoreau's ghost at birch-lined Walden Pond,
Mused Alcott's novel school, saw Hawthorne's tales unfurl,
Evoked a living pulse from cemetery stones;

We pondered Whittier's site of "snowbound privacy"
And surging Plymouth tides of Pilgrim history;

We strolled through Harvard...loved Longfellow's stately home;
And French's apt memorial to his characters;

We mused by Emerson's "rude bridge that arched the flood"
With Minute Men who "fired the shot heard 'round the world",
And sat upon the chair where he would strive to tune
Considered words to "the vast soul that o'er him planned;

We sensed with Lowell the rareness of "a day in June";
But most of all we prized the shades of Berkshire scenes
Where Bryant made his youthful strides and ponderings:
His early country home en route from which he rode
To Barrington, alone, his future to assay,
And marked the solitary moving "waterfowl",
Across a crimson sky, fly surely on its way.

And then we climbed the "Mountain of the Monument"
(As Bryant had), and stood at beetling edge of precipice
From which, as legend says, a heartsick Indian maid
Snuffed out her torment leaping to the rocks below.
We keenly felt the darkling sorrow of that tale,
But as we stood aloft, enamored of the scope
Of Nature's forms, attuned to finalizing truth
Of all her processes, we felt peace subtly glow
Within, as when we first read Bryant's stirring words--
The peace of merging death in life's ongoing flow.

"When thoughts of the last bitter hour
Come like a blight over thy spirit...
Go forth under the open sky, and list
To Nature's teachings:--Yet a few days
And thee the all-beholding sun shall see
No more in all her course....
Earth, that nourished thee, shall claim
Thy growth, to be resolved to earth again;
And, lost each human trace, surrendering up
To mix forever with the elements...
So live that when thy summons comes to join
The innumerable caravan that moves
To that mysterious realm, where each shall take
His chamber in the silent halls of death,
Thou go not, like the quarry-slave at night,
Scourged to his dungeon, but, sustained and soothed
By an unfaltering trust, approach thy grave
Like one who wraps the drapery of his couch
About him, and lies down to pleasant dreams."
                              --William Cullen Bryant

Prelude to Perennial Concert

We chose the Alleghenies as our home,
Where arborescent slopes, southeast-northwest,
Store and outpour in seldom-ending flow
Fountains which sometimes rush and sometimes rest.

Quite early on, to exercise my limbs
And rest my mind, I went to hike beside
A nearby forest-chambered mountain stream,
Where Nature was companion to each stride.

Through pregnant odors in a fern-decked woods,
I scrambled onto boulders splashed with spray;
Beneath a dam's fast-sliding overflow,
I pondered sparkling images of day.

Through instruments of rock and fallen trees
Legato brooklets funneled fluently;
Staccato springlets fluted root-held leaves
With muted, peace-inducing harmonies.

Cloud-pictures moved across the mirrored-lake;
My daydreams rode the surface silently:
"What brought us to this region, to this town?
This forest dam? What is our destiny?"

I could not guess then if we'd linger here
To work and play--what joy, what grief we'd know.
We've traveled 'round the world, but never left;
Some forty years have crossed that overflow.

A Doomed Apple Tree's Recitative

Near gate with rail ajar I stand,
Where pasture yields to oats or wheat;
Deep-rooted in this antique land,
I cannot opt to seek retreat.

Through rustic fence my orchard peers
Reflect the seasonal advance;
How was it I was rooted here,
Away from that more fit expanse?

With sad presage I contemplate
The dust, the roar, the pungent fumes,
Of riding men who cultivate
The annual stalks that raise their plumes.

Through many springs my blossomed dress
Fragranced the cattle's grazing pace,
And children's upturned faces pressed
Into my aromatic lace.

In those days I felt loved, but now
I crowd the growling tractor's turn,
And cramp the labor-saving plow,
By comrade gate which too must burn.

Anon a saw will cut my heart
To gain a grain-extended span,
Where countless years my fruitful art
Has straightway blessed the mouth of man.

Processional? Recessional?

On scooped-out shelf of old-time hillside farm
(Choice balcony for odd persipients
Of serpentine creeks that thread sequestered vales)
Are strewn the bones of old abandoned wells:
Warped, bleached boards with rusted bolts; old lead pipes
Cradling a twisted mass of cable loops;
A broken wrench receding into soil;
And over all the odor of old oil.

Residuals of earth's charcoal blood spilled here
Repel persistent growth of weedy turf
No more, and tranquil cows laze and graze nearby,
Untroubled by large strident disks and rods
Sucking out fuel to foster mobile man's
Acceleration through his standard span.

Eventually, it seems, Nature will
Effectuate a total erasure
Of the vestiges of power which throbbed here;
These blackened blocks of greased wood and plied wheels
Will, as strong men who made them, decompose
And intermix with basic elements
In leisurely but certain vanishing--
The normal long-time destiny of things....

But now, man holds a torch of deadly sparks
Whose power can, in awful paradox,
Infect with speed traditional decay;
Perhaps this massive base of concrete slab,
Then crumbling at its ends, will fascinate

Some future-century tramper through the wilds,
Or make a seat for some eccentric seer
Of labyrinthine Pennsylvania streams,
Evoking possibly some antique theme.

Or maybe powers malignant will explode,
Even here, which will burst this solid block,
And fine inventive minds, and ticking clocks,
To fast oblivion, as a lump of sand
Crushed by a playing child's unthinking hand.

Arrowhead Soliloquy

Below high palisades that overlook a horseshoe curve
Of Clearfield Creek, on wooded slope half way from top to b
A great primeval prow of rock projects out through the trees
And holds upon its beetling edge a mammoth chestnut oak.
I used to go and sit in that improbable, secluded nest,
My back against the bark of that surviving masterpiece
Of long-time Indian woods, my boots at verge of air and rock
My eyes upon the rippling water curving slowly through
An intervening, loose-knit, mottled veil of leafy fronds.

I'd meditate awhile upon the fates and destinies
Before I'd put my climbing rope around that hermit tree,
And then around my body for an old-time free rappel,
With awkward start to get my hands beneath the narrow edge
Of that sharp overhanging cliff; but as the rope embraced
My leg and chest with friction's grasp, I'd savor scenic turns
In air, descending through high private chambers of gray squirrels,
Until my feet would sink to dank and shaded forest mesh.

Unbound from doubled rope which touched the ground full twenty feet
Out from the base of that protruding, gnarled precipice,
I'd search for routes by which I might regain my outlook seat.
One day while straining up a route just barely possible,
I chanced to find a perfect arrowhead of weathered quartz
Upon a ledge where no one else had ever stepped before--
Where only eyes of birds or squirrels could see its marble shine.
I took it to the top with me, sat down against a tree,
And tried to fathom how? how long ago? it came to lodge
In that remote, unlikely storage shelf of history.

Perhaps two hundred years ago, I thought, some native brave,
While hunting game, had spied an owl fly to this rocky place;
His speeding arrow must have missed the mark and settled there
For centuries, for he could not climb up to get it back.
Or maybe where I sat and mused a peerless stag once stood
To watch a group of Indian canoes drift down the stream;
Perhaps an optimistic brave arched here his flint-tipped shaft,
Without awareness that it then would lie unnumbered years
Untouched, until a mountaineer in practicing his strange
Unheard of craft, would find its unadulterated glow,
Unyoked of mortal shaft which flew it there long time ago.

Whence Comes This Rush of Wings ?
(Carol of the Birds)
(Story on page 18)

BAS-QUERCY

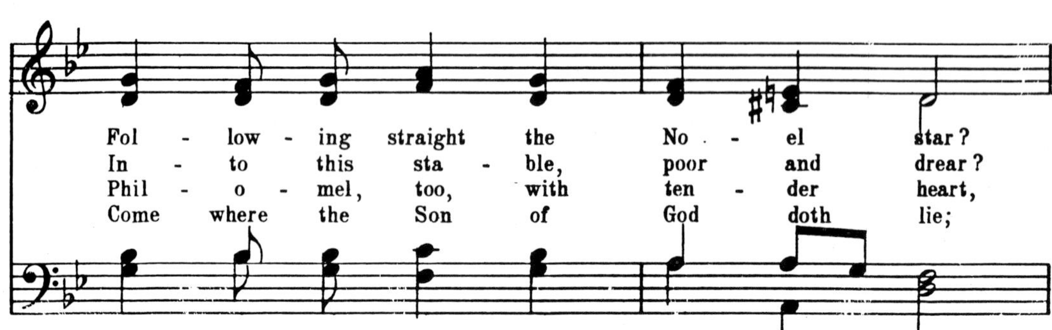

"Whate'er the theme, the maiden sa
As if her song could have no ending
I listened, motionless and still;
And, as I mounted up the hill,
The music in my heart I bore
Long after it was heard no more."
--William Wordswor

Leitmotifs
for
Family Players

Aura Lee

GEORGE R. POULT
Arr. by M.G. Groen

Cradle Song

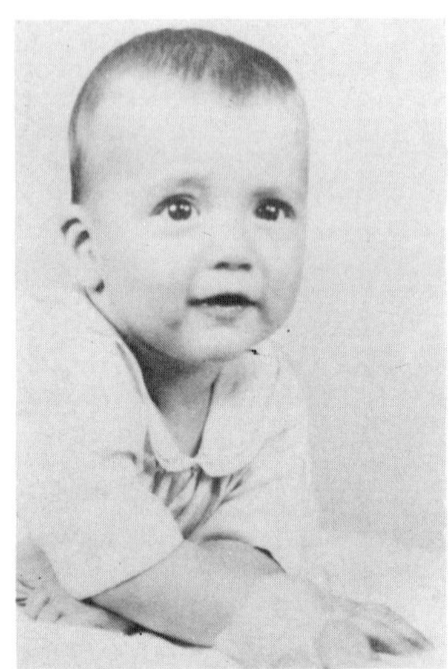

In course of normal April blossoming
You come as fragrant hyacinth appears,
Expected, but astonishing, when spring
Transforms the barren season of the year.

We look upon your tiny, puzzled face,
Adjusting to the light of outside sphere,
Fulfilling in your first vague answering gaze
Deep-seated longings of two hearts' career.

Your simple presence stirs parental pride;
We brim with new responsibility
To filter human values, fathom how
Love's beauty flows through life's complexities.

We cannot know precisely what we've wrought
In tuning mingled instincts of our love,
But sense some hint of immortality
In your fresh life, not some veiled realm above.

Sonatinas Impromptus

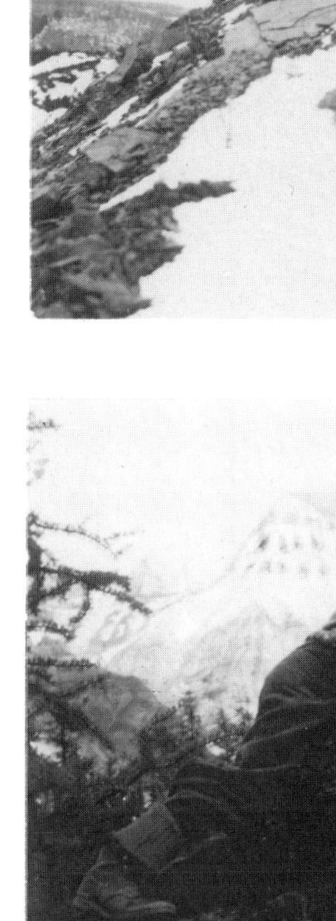

You sit for hours at your little desk,
Pouring over books intensively,
Playing school, perhaps, or making plans
For ventures yet to be.

While I paint murals on the cellar wall,
Depicting mountain realms where I have climbed,
You play and dream of scaling greater heights
In Fairyland's far clime.

On fireplace I made from river stones,
You fancy cliffs as stage for pantomimes
Up which your tiny soldiers, linked by strings,
Contrive new routes to climb.

The gentle hillside just outside our door
You picture as a grand olympic scene,
Where on your little skis you race and jump
To fancied fame, quite credibly.

Our yard becomes a course for golf's great names;
All by yourself you play full championships--
Strike every player's ball from tee to green,
Keep track of every chip....

Intense excitement shines in your pure eyes,
As leaders strive to win the closing holes;
Your final putt for victory is real,
Though it be figment's goal.

For Every Child
a Never Never Land:

Allegro con Spírito

As Tinker Bell with twinkling elfin gleam
Performs her nimble scintillating dance,
Somewhere between reality and dream
In Never Never Land,

You turn our yard into a magic place--
Like spectral humming birds among fresh flowers,
Or ambient butterflies, with transient grace
You flit and dance for hours.

I love to watch you deftly emulate
A prancing pony with blond mane awry,
Cantering through an early summer glow
Of buttercups, beneath a bright blue sky
Which duplicates your eyes.

Indoors, when I'm inclined to recreate
The lilting old-world strains of Johann Strauss,
I sweep you up into my Austrian arms,
And waltz about the house.

Quite frequently you mount my dining chair,
With sprightly innate knack and health-bright face,
To ride upon my shoulders clingingly
To some enchanted place.

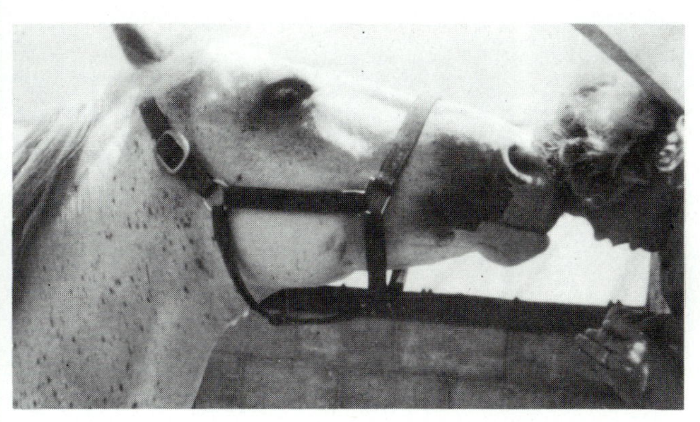

A Tone Poem of Autumn Dancing

Kristan is a golden leaf
Carried on a winsome wind;
Kristan's cheeks are sumac red,
Shining like her violin.

Kristan's hair is gossamer,
Where our hilltop's maple bright;
Undulating saffron frames
Capture her in vibrant light.

Moss and leaves enthrall small feet,
Delving whither fancies may;
Where the blushing dogwoods meet,
Kristan complements the day.

Chansonette Celeste

Two stars, and the moon--
A celestial spoon.
Come, my son, share this delight;
Partake all you may
Of that cosmic display,
Spilling the nectar of night.

I recall how you stood,
In your late babyhood,
Through the showing of Peter Pan,
With your eyes glistening wide
To see Tinker Bell fly,
Spreading star sparkle with her hand.

Look for stars as you go…
Though your faculties grow,
Keep your wide-eyed envisioning;
In that far-reaching sky,
You may find, if you try,
An elixir that sweetens being.

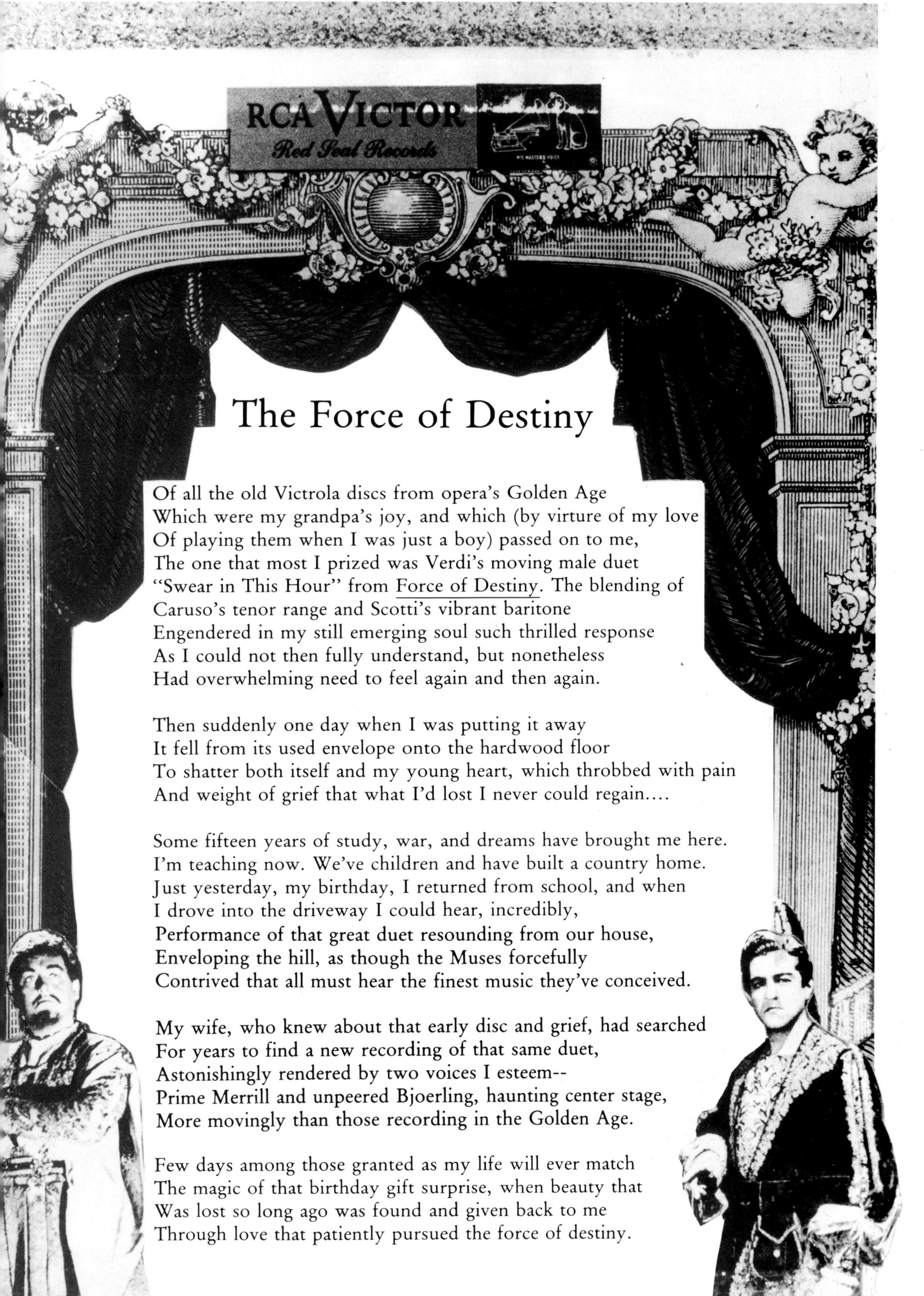

The Force of Destiny

Of all the old Victrola discs from opera's Golden Age
Which were my grandpa's joy, and which (by virture of my love
Of playing them when I was just a boy) passed on to me,
The one that most I prized was Verdi's moving male duet
"Swear in This Hour" from Force of Destiny. The blending of
Caruso's tenor range and Scotti's vibrant baritone
Engendered in my still emerging soul such thrilled response
As I could not then fully understand, but nonetheless
Had overwhelming need to feel again and then again.

Then suddenly one day when I was putting it away
It fell from its used envelope onto the hardwood floor
To shatter both itself and my young heart, which throbbed with pain
And weight of grief that what I'd lost I never could regain....

Some fifteen years of study, war, and dreams have brought me here.
I'm teaching now. We've children and have built a country home.
Just yesterday, my birthday, I returned from school, and when
I drove into the driveway I could hear, incredibly,
Performance of that great duet resounding from our house,
Enveloping the hill, as though the Muses forcefully
Contrived that all must hear the finest music they've conceived.

My wife, who knew about that early disc and grief, had searched
For years to find a new recording of that same duet,
Astonishingly rendered by two voices I esteem--
Prime Merrill and unpeered Bjoerling, haunting center stage,
More movingly than those recording in the Golden Age.

Few days among those granted as my life will ever match
The magic of that birthday gift surprise, when beauty that
Was lost so long ago was found and given back to me
Through love that patiently pursued the force of destiny.

"We are all of us dreamers of dreams,
On visions our childhood is fed;
And the heart of the child is unhaunted, it seems,
By the ghosts of dreams that are dead."
--William Henry Carruth

Childhood Duets

's certain that our isolated country living style
redestined you to formulate your childhood play alone
'ith one another, rather than with other playmates, as
ou doubtless would have done had we preferred to live in town,
'ith constant traffic of the neighbors' children all around.

s supplement to each one's solo trips to Fairyland,
ou frequently would join your fertile minds productively
o activate adventures, mixing real with make-believe.
he characters you played were sometimes painted Indians,
ho spoke with graceful signs, just like the Laubins whom we saw
spire a Teton campfire group with their refined display;
r maybe you were Roy and Dale, appropriately dressed,
rsuing evil cattle thieves who were invisible,
ut nonetheless, through long-extended horseback rides across
he sagebrush plains, through deadly shootouts at unsung corrals,
hey were alive for you, at least till each received just due.

nd you were crusty pirates, who perhaps kidnapped Bo-peep;
r matadors who braved precarious moves to win esteem
f royal Spanish ladies; or gallant knights who might
ngage in jousts, astride white charging steeds laboriously
haped from snow, with climbers' axes serving as your weaponry.

e loved to watch you feel delight in all the episodes
our teeming minds conceived, and sometimes we were truly moved,
s when you beautifully staged a wedding to each other,
ear the urned-geranium in our front yard, incredibly
he very place where Kristan chose to take real wedding vows
wo decades hence--a sign that early play sometimes may be
he seed of what in later life becomes reality.

Just as our living somewhat off from settlements inspired
Our little ones to hatch their games alone, so we were moved
To undertake more enterprises as a family--
To take the time and care to teach and share what we had learned--
Than is the mode of those who dwell in close communities.

When our wee siblings scarcely were of age to go to school,
We made a golf course on our property, with sawdust greens
Which could be rolled to efficacious smoothness, so that we
Could putt on them with some degree of accuracy; by chance,
I happened to possess old hick'ry shafted clubs, which could
Be shortened with a saw to fit the children's actual size.
Thus many a pleasant afternoon our kindred foursome moved
About the yard, through private nooks and bowers, and fragrant scenes
Of fresh-cut grass and sun-bright flowers, enjoying, without strain,
The subtle recreative boons of that refined, slow-paced,
Athletic, lifelong, most aesthetic human game.

Until our youngsters were in junior high, we did not have
A television set to steal away their time, as seemed
The normal way in households where young children were entrapped
And drugged, as often were their parents, too, by its strong lure.
Each evening after supper we would dedicate an hour
To instrumental music; my wife would teach piano
To one child, while in another room I'd give instruction
To the other on the cello or the violin. We
Seldom would permit another thing to alter that
Artistic hour, and presently they played their instruments
With such sufficient skill that frequently our family
Was asked to play in church or programmed social gatherings.

Variations

for

Tuned

Quartettes

In spring, or fall, before or after we were apt to head
Out west, to share with them the elevated beauty which we'd found
In rocky mountain tundrascapes, all four of us would go
To Bilgers' Rocks to search for primal essences, to breathe
Moist cavern fragrances; and on those cryptic, moss-draped cliffs,
We'd teach our boy and girl to safely climb and to descend;
Even in winter, after storms, our tuned quartette would go
To play among those natural chambers chocked with ice and snow.

But mostly when the cold months came, our family would ski
"Cross-country" over rolling fields, or through deep-shaded woods,
When cumulating powder had a velvet, cushioned feel--
Or "down-hill" on our private slope, among familiar trees,
Where friendly birds of winter were our only company;
We'd sidestep slowly up the hill, to pack the crusting snow,
So we could christy smoothly downward, freely to and fro.

Years hence, we could not help but yield to parent-teacher pride,
When witnessing that their achievements in these varied fields,
In which we had invested so much of our time and zeal,
Had sometimes reached a stage that could be titled "notable";
But well we know those momentary high points only were
The signposts of the daily unsung harmony we shared.

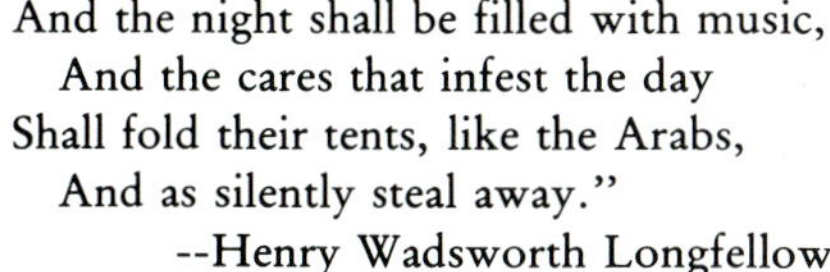

And the night shall be filled with music,
And the cares that infest the day
Shall fold their tents, like the Arabs,
And as silently steal away."
--Henry Wadsworth Longfellow

Roundelay with a Wren

Brave little bird, I must succumb
To such persistency--
You built your nest beneath my eave
A dozen times times three:

You strewed my porch with grass and moss
With hourly frequency;
I swept it off, you strewed again
With quick tenacity.

I moved your nest to other sites,
But unrelentingly
You flew again beneath the eave
And scattered more debris.

Completely undeterred by loss
Of time and energy,
You flew more swiftly back with strands
For mossy masonry.

The battle now more fully joined,
My broom moved endlessly
To sweep away each ardent start
With swift authority.

Day after day this game of wills
Continued senselessly,
Until you seemed at last to grant
The incongruity.

I put my broom away and turned
To other industry;
I went and came a dozen times
With fair impunity.

But then one day I raised my eyes
With incredulity--
Your woven nest was there again
In its entirety.

Instinct had made a work of art--
Amazing symetry;
In spite of mammoth counterforce
You plied your destiny.

And I, in face of such resolve--
Such artful husbandry,
Must now accept the scattered moss
With awed civility.

A Tribute to the Most Persistent Flower

Never failing, finely fettled flower.
Your tiny, robust sprouts peek out in spring,
At base of last year's stable, woody stalks,
When scattered daffodils are flourishing.

Then with slow pace you grow through summer heat
To backdrop green for your companions' hues:
And patiently you hold in rising fronds
Your bright surprise, till Nature beckons you--

Till autumn's late kismetic arbiter
Decides the hour when other blooms shall fade,
And you, at last, will come to center stage
To face chill winds and snowflakes, unafraid.

A Swiss Hat Novelette

I found it in a little shop somewhere in Switzerland--
The dark green hat of perfect shape and fine-brushed felt I'd long
Been searching for. When first I put it on, it felt as though
The hatter who had fashioned it had used my head as mold,
So soothingly did it caress my brow with soft, smooth warmth--
So comfortably clingingly did it my mind enfold.

I wore it on the Matterhorn when taking up a friend,
Who afterwards, as gift, pinned on it pearly edelweiss,
And lovely pewter images of peaks that we had scaled.
Affection deepened with the constancy of wearing it;
It was as though it had become a vital body part
Whenever I would go outdoors; on rugged mountain walls,
In howling wind or thrashing rain, it served me flawlessly;
On dress parade through city streets, I wore it pridefully,
Triumphantly, as would a king display his jeweled crown.

At home, my other hats stayed on the closet shelf, unused,
And if they could, would certainly have felt just jealousy
At my extreme inequity. But with no thought that I
Might wear it out, or damage it with such unbridled use,
I went on single-mindedly provisioning my pride.

One Indian summer day, returning from a weekend spent with friends
Two hundred miles away, I had to take it off to cool
My sweating head, so placed it on the back seat of our van.
Somewhere along the way, I stopped to give my wife the wheel,
And in the course of that quick change we failed to notice that
My cherished hat had rolled into the ditch beside the road.
Some thirty miles along, I felt a need to put it on,
Reached back for it, and with dismay discovered it was gone.

Unhesitatingly we turned around, and in great haste
Retraced our route back all those miles to see if it might still
Be lying by the road where we had made our quick exchange.
Real grief was in my heart along those lengthened miles, as if
A friend had had an accident and might not smile again....
A futile search...a hurtful journey home...the nagging thought:
"How stupid not to be aware, at every turn or pause,
Of things we dearly prize, which cannot ever be replaced,
With all the jewels of sentiment surrounding them effaced.

I advertised in towns near the vicinity wherein
My foolish loss occurred, but months went by with no reply;
And so, with dwindling hope, I settled to acceptance I
Would likely nevermore behold my crown of peerless green,
Nor feel around my head the comfort of its velvet cling....
Apppendant months amassed; a multitude of needful thoughts
And tasks replaced the substance of that painful memory,
Which was consigned, resignedly, to shelves of sad forgetting.

Then came a day of deep, late-winter, snowbound privacy,
And grimly I was laboring to shovel out the drive,
When suddenly my wife's excited voice called out to me
The words that truly seemed impossibilities: "It's found!!
Your hat's been found!!!" Mere witness can't convey my heart's high leap
And wild, wild dance at such unlikelihood. Ecstatically
I rushed into the house to hear the seeming fantasy.

Someone residing near Shade Gap, on passing by had seen
That special green stand out within the brown grass of the ditch,
And stopped to check it out. She took it home, and in the months
That followed it became a conversation piece, which all
Who visited were pleased to wonder at--the edelweiss--
The pins of mountain shapes adorned with foreign language names
That beautified its velvet green for reasons unexplained....

Then one day some new visitor recalled that long ago
She'd seen an item in her hometown press about a hat;
She asked the local newsstaff to research old Lost and Founds,
And, unbelievably, they soon supplied my name and phone;
Magnanimously, she took the task of phoning right away,
And we arranged to go for it the coming Saturday.
Substantial lessons vibrate from this song of"lost" and "found":
"Take care with priceless things. Love honesty. In midst of all
The selfishness around, kind human beings still are found."

The string quartette, which Marjorie and I
Contrived to teach our children music's charm,
Had played the concert with appealing skill,
And all of us returning home were filled
With keen excitement of success, were thrilled
That all that practice striving to finesse--
To stretch young minds and fingers to their best--
Had yielded ample value in the test.

Returning then to hilltop hideaway
To put our well-tuned instruments away,
Reluctant still to end a peerless day,
We chanced to see that trees and fields that night
Were heaped with new-made snow in full moonlight,
With sparkles of a million jewels bright
That matched the glitter of our hearts' delight.

With blood fast coursing through inspired veins,
We could not yet lie down to pleasant dreams,
In need of some activity or scheme
To give our minds repose. Then logically
It came to me that we should take our skis
And go out to soft moonshine on the snow,
To track through piney specters on the glow,
Or throw a crowd of diamonds into spray
Of graceful turns--create ornate display
Of interlocking patterns on the face
Of lustrous hill--glide over shadowed lace,
Too beautifully changing, too sublime
For us to fully know what we had framed
In speeding time--an art too evanescent
To stop and contemplate--to fairly see
Those splendrous shapes, those fine designs,
Except perhaps in sequent reverie.

Ballets of the German Shepherds:

Allegro Grazioso (Rusty)

With blend of symetry and might
Our German shepherd dominates
The spacious yard; his eyes excite
Attentively, as poised he waits
My slightest prompting.

Keen tracking up pine-scented hill,
Long scrutiny 'neath ridge-top maze
Of blue-hazed tall spruce woods until
Some creature echo turns his gaze
To stock-still watching.

Abruptly down a wheated slope,
Beige robust breast on surging flesh,
Then slow self-seeing, pawsteps grope
To statue pause in reedy mesh,
Faint earthsounds sensing.

Stark sentinel ears that never err
Respond, adjust, retune again,
As wind-gust stirs bright gold-rust fur,
Sun-blazoned crop of canine grain
Vibrantly changing.

Through natural ascendancy,
With bare-tongued haste or casual grace,
Or pose of inbred majesty,
With power and sureness in his face,
He rules our highland country place
As emperor ranging.

Andante Maestoso

(Thor)

Through layered snow he deeply pries,
Thick fur bedecked with frosted shapes
Too subtly fine for human eye
To fully see or contemplate,
But still enthralling.

He fathoms something here or there
As signs of wild ones tease his sense,
Then shakes soft diamonds from his hair
And turns to watch by brook or fence
Sky blossoms falling.

Across duned drifts of winterscapes
He contemplates some urgent quest
Less stirring other times--some hint
Of lost familiar wilderness,
Distantly calling...

Perhaps rememb'ring when still young
He went with us to Canada,
And from a high moraine looked out
Upon the rocky snowbound peaks...
Deep-breathing in primeval scents
Of highland spruce, and fir, and pine
Trees ever greening...

Some vague awareness in his chest--
Some rhythm of his ancestry—
Makes bittersweet his dreamy rest,
His wistful, mild captivity,
Forgotten soon in love for me,
Presently calling.

Parting Song for Rusty

First child of graduate marriage time
Who chose us out of all our peers
While rambling free mysteriously,
Then shared our pioneering years,
Watching and loving.

Now no more throb of rapid paws
Pridefully heard on hilltop sward;
No longer swell of sovereign bark
Swiftly alert on nighttime guard,
Disquiet assuaging.

No longer rush through autumn leaves
Playfully pacing creatures wild;
No circuit patterns etched in snow
Hinting ventures privately styled,
Duty discharging.

Peace now in loam he loved to dig,
Long summers waiting our return
From western trips he wished to share,
Somewhere out there, but stayed to earn
His keep, guarding and loving.

Like Milton Writing "Paradise"

We weep, and then we gaze upon
The handsome son of Rusty's prime,
To find allayment for our grief
In knowledge that those classic lines
Yet grace our seeing.

Our golden Thor waits at the door,
With breast and paws of ermine white;
Most beautiful of shepherd friends,
How tragic that you've lost your sight,
Midst your young thriving!

But still you function wondrously,
All other senses finely tuned,
And deftly cruise among our trees,
Or barriers at random strewn
Across your treading.

You greet our children at the gate...
It seems that in your blinded state,
Like Milton, writing "Paradise",
You have a mission to create
A beauty you yourself can't see
But which enriches others' being.

To Shape in Solid Segments Out of Time

Somewhere along the track of years, inspired by Keats' keen words,
I felt a most compelling urge to try to capture all
The members of our close-knit family, as they then were,
In aspect and in actual size--to mold and fashion them
As solid segments out of moving time, so they could still
Be seen, when our mere mortal flesh would wear away and die.

A friendly expert in the arts gave me a sack of clay,
And instruments of quite ingenius shapes with which to play,
In order to gain ample skill to reach the end I sought;
But quite amazingly, with no apprenticeship at all,
I found that I could recreate my wife and progeny,
As though a miracle were born by wanting it to be.

This friend then showed me how to make the molds with which to cast
Those cherished faces into forms more permanent than clay,
And then he most artistically arranged them for display,
When many came to hear the Obernkirchen Children's Choir sing
In our community. Within a month I brought them home
To our museum-living room, where they have staunchly kept
Their round-the-clock career of silent watching. And I
Pass by in wonder every day, with aging face and eyes--
With bittersweet awareness that in time I'll cease to be,
But also with a hope that they will watch unendingly.

"Thou, silent form! dost tease us out of thought
As doth eternity: cold pastoral!
When old age shall this generation waste,
Thou shalt remain, in midst of other woe
Than ours, a friend to man, to whom thou say'st,
'Beauty is truth, truth beauty,'--that is all
Ye know on earth, and all ye need to know."
                    --John Keats

Discordancies

From where I stand I glare at gaping scars
Where strippers mined the coal from hills around,
Outraging Nature where her arteries
Had nourished well the bearing overground.

Grey piles of shale and lumped infertile clay,
Bared to the air, seem to anticipate,
As the grim heap beside the churchyard grave,
A coming corpse to hide beneath their weight.

Earth's beauty here was killed for dollar gain:
Dispersed the soil which carpeted her stance,
Vanished the pleasant features of her face—
The colorings of seasonal advance.

I climb with slipping steps to the slate peak
Of this unseemly refuse mountain chain;
On northern side the lesser entrail piles
Hedge a clear view of one unbruised domain.

There beyond reach of ruinous wounding claws
The unsold farmer holds his firm intent;
Responsive to old loves and basic laws,
His shining harvest lifts its rich extent.

He nourishes long kinship with his land,
And prunes with pride his orchard with a view
From gentle knoll above extensive fields,
Where summer labor yields fair revenue.

But almost all elsewhere repulsive sores
Infect my sight. These hills which never reeled
From smash of cannon fire or shrapnel burst
Are yet undone and seem a battlefield.

A Century of Glory

Here in Ashes Lies

Our cherished church was at its loveliest, embellished for
The joyous pageantry of celebrating Christmas Eve;
Observant worshippers, on entering, would contemplate
The altar, tastefully embraced by royal red poinsettias,
And then, perhaps, their eyes would focus on the chosen pine,
All brightly lighted, and bedecked in mode to contrast with
The more subdued but ever satisfying antique glow
Of organ brass, and choir loft's oaken paneling,
Where green-robed choristers would stand in candlelight to sing
A well-rehearsed cantata for the birthday of a king....

How could we have imagined that it would not come to be
As other Christmas Eves it had for generations past--
That rather than the soft serenity of candlelight,
We'd see the fearsome violence of a seven-story flame
Consume in minutes all the structured substance which had stirred
A glory in our souls--that in the place of choral songs,
Filling the temple and uplifting hearts with love reborn,
Grim sirens would be screaming stridently above a throng
That hastened there to try to save, or just to see it burn.

In truth, a nightmare reigned that night, with dire macabre scenes,
In spite of great heroic efforts to assuage the force
Of molten heat and devastating rage; the canopy's
High-arching roof and rafters burst in wild explosive fire,
As if they were but kindling sticks, and soon collapsed into
The seething hell of the caldera which had been the nave,
Where worshippers sat normally in pews to think on heaven.

The valued stained glass windows, which had garnered silent praise
From galaxies of reverent congregational eyes,
Were shattered by blast furnace heat, or even liquified,
And crashed down to be swallowed in the chaos of debris
That writhed in black smoke agony to anonymity.

The most bizarre and cruelest irony, of all this mad
And tortured unreality, was kept till near the end;
Just when the steepled belfry caught the wildly torching flames,
The lovely Deagan chimes, which had for countless years rung out
In vesper hours for all the town to hear their charming tones,
Were activated eerily to ring one final hymn,
"Good Christian men, rejoice, with heart and soul and voice", before
They faded in the din to die forevermore.

The massive, hurtful loss struck harshly in my private heart
When later I stood silently among the roofless walls,
Whose mammoth stones incredibly had stayed the savage rage.
Inhaling the dank, water-saturated ash remains,
I thought of many features of interior design
That could not be replaced with current cost and workmanship--
The master-crafted beauty of the seasoned paneling,
And much of unbelievably unique utility:

In that dark hole there once had been a high-domed Sunday School
Assembly room that might have been a classic theater, with
A ring of second story classrooms which, when opened, could
Become a balcony; an even higher sliding wall,
Between the church's sanctuary and that heightened hall,
Could be rolled aside to make an outsize auditorium,
Where special services and even town-wide gatherings,
Such as the senior high school graduation, could be held.
How vivid still is memory of that expanded hall
When Stanley Jones, the famous missioner to India,
Inspired a massive gathering with trenchant eloquence.

Beside this barren wall, beneath which convoluted tubes
Of our great Moeller organ lie entombed, my gifted wife
Would sometimes sit at console and awaken from its pipes
Aeolean music with such graceful touch, it would inspire
A mystic beauty even deeper than mere words could stir.

At base of the still standing frontal wall, with high-arched, sky-
Filled opening, which housed the treasured stained glass window of
"Christ Kneeling in Gethsemane", I searched and found among
The ashes many pieces of that priceless work of art,
Then wondered if perhaps those remnants were symbolic seeds,
Which from our temple's grave our will and ingenuity
Might cause to spring into a bright new sanctuary--
A laudable successor to our lost sublimity.

Interrupted Concert

Once-stately boughs with drapery of snow,
Ice-cased by freezing rain, are drooping low,
Their burdens finery for human eye
To see, but for the trees incongruous tragedy.

Each weed and twig first finely dressed in glass,
Transparent fabrics, perfect tailoring,
Accumulating garmenture of glaze
Which weighs destructively the while it molds.

Strong limbs succumb, crack downward to the base,
Impaling in a spattered frozen paste,
Or mixing in a pile of shattered lace,
As tip-top fronds are strewn in disarray,
Choir lofts for birds turned fuel this dismal day.

Ironic such compelling power brings such
Conflicting ends. The crystal of this storm
Will melt beneath the rays that lifted up
These splendid trees--this fragileness of form.

Unfathomable Nature moves along:
Through unlogged time these friendly trees grew strong,
Nigh imperceptibly above the strife
Of us inclined to swifter styles of life;
Then in a day a rudely broken clan,
Their graceful beauty wasted, bent, and sheered,
They face a patient span of mending years.

The Broken Terrarium

They worked together happy hours to encase
In giant jar a vibrancy of Nature's face
That normally would only be and thrive outside--
A tapestry of dainty pads of moss and plants,
And rocks inlaid artistically, so they might be
Observed from every side, whenever there might be
A need to look up from a book, while studying
Inside a college dormitory room, and dream
Of other fresh young beauty, miles and days away.

As centerpiece, a blooming plant was hung aloft,
Suspended from the lid most carefully, so that
It would not bump against the thin transparent walls
That circled it. The boy and girl then stood and looked
With brimming pride at what they had so well achieved--
A work of beauty long to be enjoyed and prized,
As their own new-found mutual regard, if this
First project should evolve to meaningful reprise.

The holiday was over. Time to say goodbye
And go their separate ways. The work of art was tied
Into the seat beside the boy painstakingly,
But in the parting he'd forgotten to remove
The hanging plant. Before he'd driven out the drive,
It swayed against the fragile side and shattered all
That hard-won beauty, down to such chaotic pile
Of broken glass and plants, it could not be restored....

A pathos lingers still whenever I recall
That poignant autumn day, because that girl and boy,
Who carried on divergent paths the wrenching thought
Of that quick loss, would never have another chance
To beautify a glass terrarium, or life,
With unified, creative, lasting enterprise.

Like a Finely Written Manuscript Destroyed

It was as deeply hurtful as the death of a dear friend
To go back to the place where I'd grown up, and see that there
Was not a single remnant left of what had been the scene
Where first I had become aware that Beauty nurtures being.
The country home, which was the finely tuned fulfillment of
My city-dwelling parents' youthful dreams, had been torn down,
And in its place a large commercial enterprise was found....

Aided only by my mother holding joists and studs in place,
My father had sawed every board and driven every nail--
Hand-crafted every window frame and every cupboard door--
Imbued it with such charming individuality
That it became a masterpiece of private creativity.
Through sequent years he turned his energies to fashioning
In our high-postured orchard yard, a lovely parklike scene
Of fishponds, grapevine arbors, hedges, roses deftly placed,
And redbrick walks and driveways patterned with intrinsic grace.

Although I had a strong desire to venture out to see
New things, a counterforce of primal love urged me to spend
Much time at home to play, or cut the lawn, or trim the trees--
To help preserve the beauty of our self-styled entity....
When, in due course, I left to make my separate life, I think
I must have fancied, unrealistically, that even when
My parents could no longer function there, somehow at least
A semblance of the special beauty of the place would be
Maintained, although its destiny remained in other hands.
Vain hope.... Though mem'ries thrive, I feel recurrent sorrow when
It comes to me: I'll never really see that precious home again.

Requiem

for One Too Young

Our first "Denali" (which in Indian tongue
Means "great one") — our vibrant shepherd guard,
Has vanished from our yard; we find it hard
To reconcile such loss; we've searched and called
Through maze of empty streets with echoing walls,
Made wooded valleys throb with futile shouts;
Our largest hope was dimmed, then flared again
At some report that he was seen last night,
Curled by strange doorways out across the town,
Or on a pasture hillside running down;
We go to validate--again too late.

Nostalgically we name his salient traits:
Responding look of pert intelligence,
Statuesque wait for master sign to come,
Wise stoic patience with the family strings,
Strong shining back of haired obsidian,
Marvelous muscles that had just matured
In brimming growth, ordained to roam our yard
In long career as overseer and guard--
Suddenly voided without sight or sound,
As sadly we proceed with daily round.

Obscenities

Perhaps ten miles from where I'd chosen to create my home,
There is a wondrous concentration of great cloven rocks
Where, through millennia, the steep and sometimes overhanging cliffs
Have well withstood the falling leaves and branches which have
Overlaid their tops with rock-erasing soil and vegetation;
At most the shaded ledges of those mammoth monoliths
Have been embossed with fragrant coverlets of slow-growth moss,
Creating aspects of seductive semi-nakedness.

Long time ago I used those tempting verticalities
To hone my mountain climbing skills, and later took my wife
And children there for family adventuring, and to
Expose them to the novel beauties of that pristine place.
The children grew and moved away, and life's exigencies
Exacted such great portions of my time and energies
That many years passed by without my ever visiting
Those old familiar scenes of Nature's complex fashioning.

When finally I did return, I was apalled at what
I there beheld: ignorant, idle youths, or drunken, brutish gangs
Had used those wondrous chambers as a gathering place, then smashed
Glass bottles and spray-painted vile obscenities on every
Surface of those masterworks of Nature's creativity
That they could reach, trashing in brief aimless hours rare art
Evolved through patient genius of a thousand centuries.

A Forest

That Became

In Colorado's Frontal Range, among the knolls and ridges
That roll north from James Peak, emerging from luxuriant fields
Of alpine flowers, we came upon an unexpected scene--
A seeming cemetery hill. As we drew near, we saw
That all the monuments were weathered stumps of trees, which we
Surmised might long ago have been cut down by rough-hewn men,
Who'd ventured up onto those lonely slopes, quite probably,
To search for minerals that could be mined successfully.

At any rate, whatever were their purposes, they changed
A forest, which had taken centuries to grow in that
High clime, into a curious graveyard hill. Each tree they killed
Eventually became its own memorial stone, as wind
And sun transfigured it with orange and silver garnishment,
Slow-hardened over time to nearly petrified extent.

Stepping slowly up among those silent, deviant graves,
I felt the kind of pathos that I feel each time I go
To Gettysburg, and contemplate the melancholy stones
That mark the anonymous graves of those incongruously
Destroyed in ways that never should have been their destinies.

a Gravestone Hill

But even as we have transformed the basal mayhem of
That place into a scene of solemn beauty and repose,
So Nature has converted the destruction of this hill
Of trees, through time, into a tranquil beauty of its own;
Each stump has been transformed into a tombstone work of art,
With novel sheen and shape, arranged attractively apart.

As we attained the highest ground, we found a stubborn tree
That had survived both murderous storms and man's extremities;
Its structure had been stretched grotesquely, horizontally,
By thousands of unwitnessed gales, and still it had not died.
We wondered why the tough intruders who had cut down all
The others had allowed it to be spared? Was its small size
Unworthy of their enterprise? Or was there deep inside
Those rugged men a lurking sense that something should
Survive? Did they respect that little specimen's brave heart?

Whatever was their thought, for me that foxtail signified
A pristine flag that Nature will not wholly be denied;
Just when we think that something isn't as it ought to be,
Some feature of redemption rises from complexity;
Framed by that sign, the Arapahoes posed higher majesty,
And we still had the instinct and the strength to go and see.

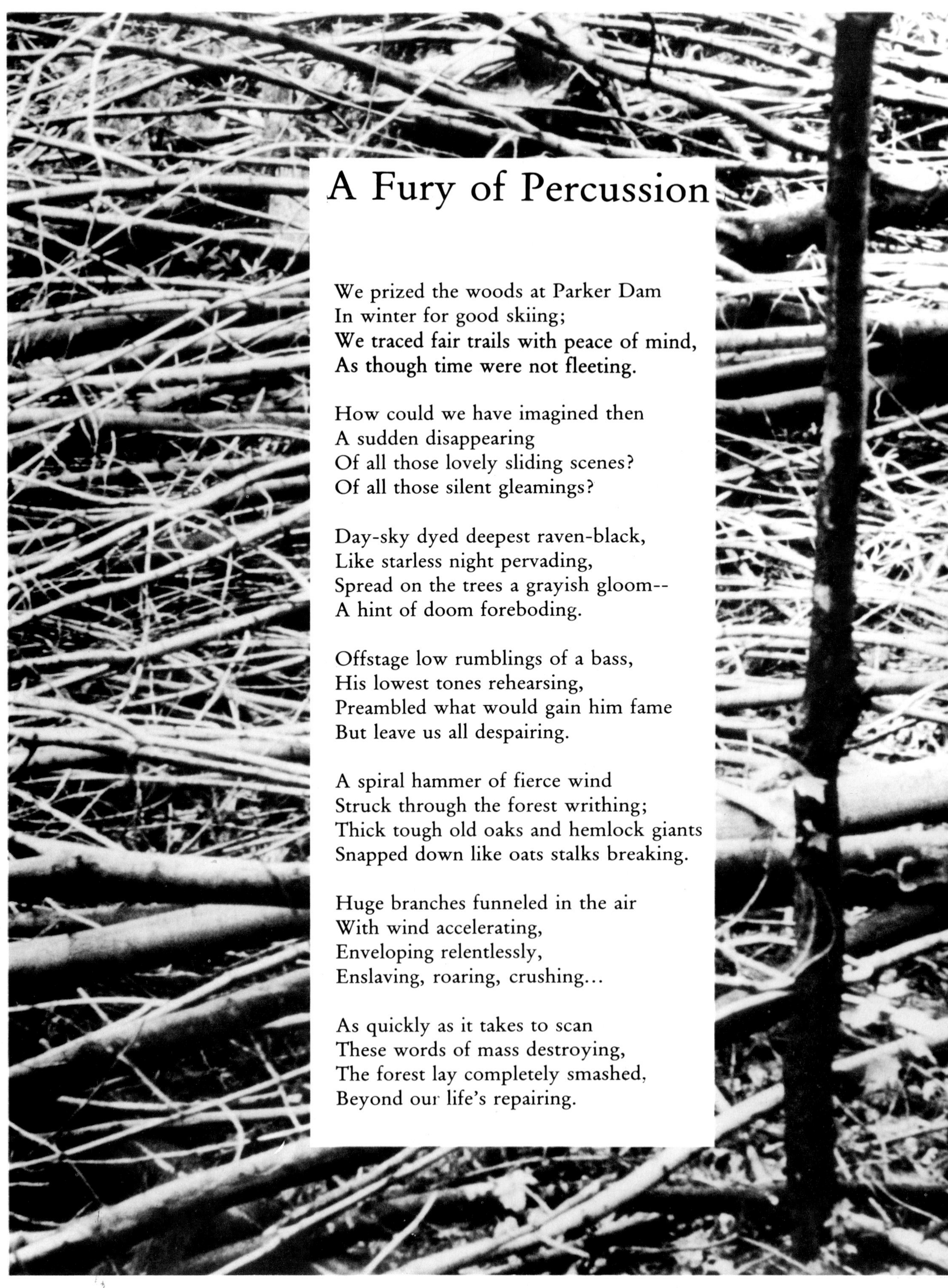

A Fury of Percussion

We prized the woods at Parker Dam
In winter for good skiing;
We traced fair trails with peace of mind,
As though time were not fleeting.

How could we have imagined then
A sudden disappearing
Of all those lovely sliding scenes?
Of all those silent gleamings?

Day-sky dyed deepest raven-black,
Like starless night pervading,
Spread on the trees a grayish gloom--
A hint of doom foreboding.

Offstage low rumblings of a bass,
His lowest tones rehearsing,
Preambled what would gain him fame
But leave us all despairing.

A spiral hammer of fierce wind
Struck through the forest writhing;
Thick tough old oaks and hemlock giants
Snapped down like oats stalks breaking.

Huge branches funneled in the air
With wind accelerating,
Enveloping relentlessly,
Enslaving, roaring, crushing...

As quickly as it takes to scan
These words of mass destroying,
The forest lay completely smashed,
Beyond our life's repairing.

Perhaps It Was Sylvania's Oldest Tree

Long time ago, a short while after building our new home
On one of Central Pennsylvania's wooded hills, we went
To ramble through the pathless trees, and came upon an oak
Of such extraordinary size it had the aspect of
A redwood giant; at shoulder height it measured three wide spans
Around; not any of the others standing near seemed half
As thick, and never through the years, on countless hikes that ranged
Much farther, did we ever come upon another
That superceded it in size, or shape, or majesty.

Quite frequently, when visitors would come into our home,
We'd mention that great oak, then take them out to search for it,
So other eyes and minds could verify our estimate
Of grandest scale. Sometimes we'd speculate about its age,
And wondered if, considering the slow, slow widening
Of hardwood growth, it could have been alive when Pilgrims came
To land on Plymouth Rock, before Penn's Woods yet had a name.

Each time we stood within its shade, we felt the aura of
Its sylvan link with history. Though branches quite as large
As full-sized oaks had died, or broken off in raging storms,
Its central heart continued its augmenting inner throb;
It kept its stately stance as woodsmen came to cut away
The neighbor trees, and float them down the Susquehanna floods
In spring; on, on it grew, as progeny of those lost friends
Began to rise beside their parents' graves; then farmers came
To clear and work large fields nearby, but spared the tract where stood
This great-grandparent-oak-survivor of Penn's virgin woods.

The saplings that had sprung nearby had grown tall and thick through
Slowly-moving decades of a hundred years or more,
Until they stood like palace guards, protecting royalty,
And insulating it from average eyes, except perhaps
Some hunter's chancing by more bent on game than size of trees....
Until we found and honored it with social frequency.

Alas, those visits now have come to sad finality;
The loggers, with their screaming power saws and heavyweight
Machinery, have been removing all the hardwood trees;
And close behind, a modern surface-mining company
Is gouging out colossal canyons to extract the coal,
Obliterating everything that's rooted in the soil....

When finally they've hauled it all away, their bulldozers,
By law, must push the upheaved rocks and earth back to a shape
That more or less restores the contours that were there before.
But it will never be the same. We've lost the mossy knoll
Where we would sit and have a picnic supper, looking out
Between white birches to a distant blue-ridge view; the lane
That passed beneath the snow-draped pines where we were wont to ski
Is gone, as is the whisp'ring eloquence of hillside springs
That faithfully, all year, were trickle-trickle-trickle-ing....

Of course, those private haunts, which were our own just in the sense
That Walden was Thoreau's, were only meaningful to us,
And have no weight compared to jobs and the economy;
But when I make comparison of that prodigious tree
And the empty slope that used to be its place in history,
I feel the weight that everything must die eventually.

The Dilemma

In recent years as May has grown to June, when fragrant tints
Of irises and peonies and roses grace our grounds,
When shrubs and trees profusely surge to healthy greens,
Vast hordes of tiny hairy worms have come to strip the leaves
Off everything; not even utmost branch of senior oak
Escapes the ruinous reach of their collective appetites,
As fuzzy shapes grow long and fat, chewing, chewing through the
nights...

Mid-summer they'll be spinning loose cocoons around themselves,
From which in weeks they'll resurrect as gypsy moths; the males
Will flutter but a frantic hour to find a mate, and these
Will seek a niche in which to paste a colony of eggs,
Which in another May will stir again to crawl as myriad worms;
On, on it goes, this plague of death and life, this selfless strife
To somehow guarantee a species' immortality....

In this mixed maze of Nature's ever mystifying prodigies,
We, too, seem destined to participate for our own boon;
Although inclined to reverence for earth's ongoing life,
We, nonetheless, must choose to kill one form in order that
Another may survive; to save the beauty of the trees
And flowers, we spray, we drown, we crush repeatedly, although
We feel an underlying sadness that it must be so.

This spring, as I was trying to control the furry worms,
I spied, upon a maple branch, a shape I had not seen
For many years; and soon I heard that strong unequalled sound--
That all-pervasive, whistling, whirring, multi-choral wail
Which is the ardent trademark of unbound cicada males.

Full seventeen bright Junes have come and gone since last I heard
The sob'ring music of that so-called "locust" plague--since last
Those transient mothers bored in twig or branch to lay their eggs--
Since last the quick-born wingless nymphs instinctively dropped down
To tunnel underground, and start their lightless earth-womb growth
Of seventeen slow years to gain maturity. The clock
Of their unerring instinct has kept silent track of more
Than thirty million ticks and tocks, and now they rise to fly
Into long-dreamed-of June-time light--the males to sing their long-
Awaited song of love--the females to accept a mate,
Deposit eggs, and thus another slow-paced cycle animate....

In face of such remarkable, intrinsic functioning,
I do, indeed, feel reverence for Nature's long-range schemes,
And I have empathy for these poor creatures who were bound
In subterranean darkness for near twenty years, and now
Have but a week or two to sport, and copulate, and fly
On missions of discovery among my cherished trees.

But then I fancy that my own intelligence must play
A vital role in Nature's still unfathomed reckonings;
I hold a vivid image how our favorite maple tree
Was gouged and gravely wounded when these insects last passed through;
Instead of thriving to magnificence, as might have been
It's destiny, it barely still survives. The double scourge
This year, of caterpillars and cicadas, probably
Will deal a mortal blow; and so, repeatedly I go
About the yard with conscious double force, to spray, to crush,
And trust my instinct and my acts in this unwelcome strife,
Will complement the underlying schemes of death and life.

A Cadenza of Cacophonies

Why thrives cruel prejudice of race?
Dumb bigotry and clash of creeds?
Why don't fine, humane traits prevail?
Essayed enlightenment succeed?

Why do the ruthless often win?
The merely mediocre rise
To presidential power? And why
Are those most qualified denied?

Why do St. Vitus freaks get wealth
For gross unbridled noise and jerks,
While skillful artists find small gain
For their well-tempered, seasoned work?

Why do great oaks get deadly plagues?
Why do those of moderate tastes
And genial ways have pain and grief,
While uncaught vandals widen waste?

Why did my sweet dog die so young?
Why are callous criminals freed
To steal, to rape, to kill again,
While "justice" takes the victim's fee?

I saw a fair Peruvian town
Completely buried under mass
Of avalanching rocks and mud.
Did Cosmic choice bring this to pass?

A fishing town in southern Spain,
With goodly friends I'd come to love,
Was swept away by sudden flood.
Was that ordained by Mind above?

At life's last breath, does living cease?
Why do the lovely gracious die
Before the evil ones are gone?
Is it mere chance, or planned on high?

How can we grasp the galaxies
That float upon an endless night?
Why don't all plants live after snow?
How can we know what's true or right?

No one can really justify
Incongruousness of human plight,
And so we strive in restless quest
To find some better lamp for light.

Refining the Arpeggios of Life

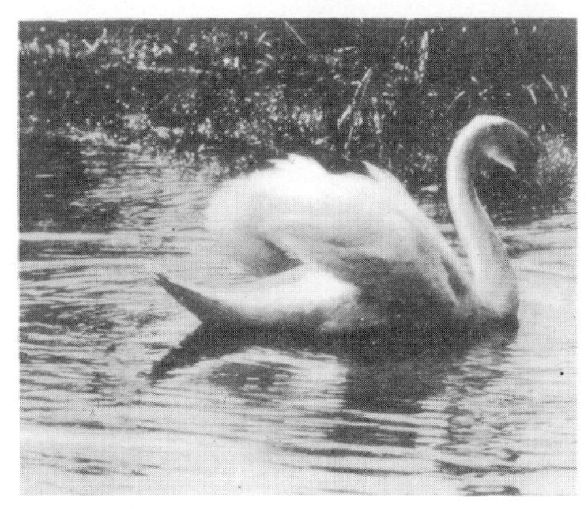

"It is not growing like a tree
In bulk, doth make man better be;
Or standing long an oak, three hundred year,
To fall a log at last, dry, bald, and sere:
A lily of a day
Is fairer far in May,
Altho it fall and die that night--
It was the plant and flower of light.
In small proportions we just beauties see;
And in short measure life may perfect be."
--Ben Jonson

(The Swan) C. SAINT-SAENS

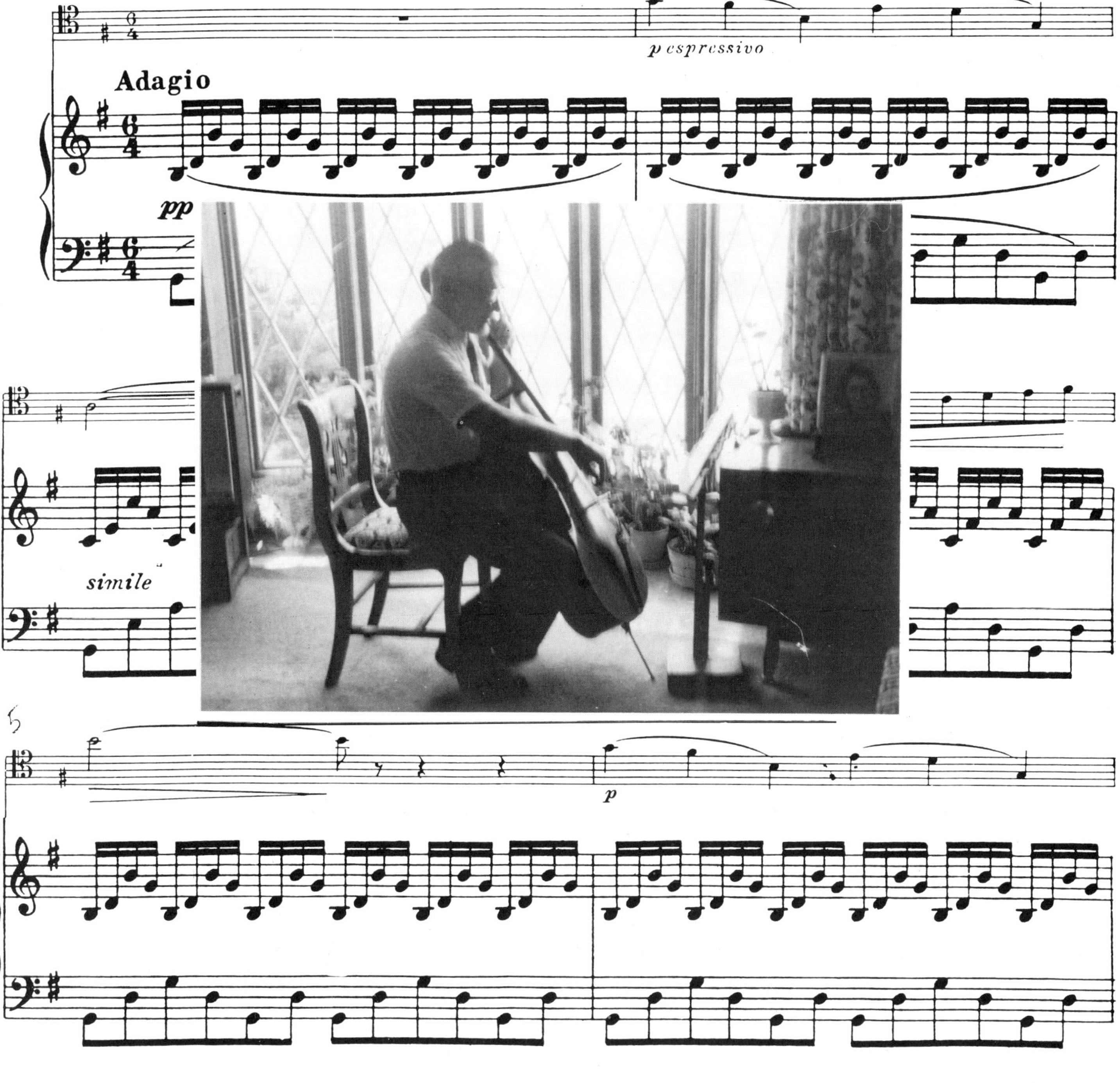

Intuitively My Spirit Sings

Through western window's curtained frame
An evening's painted image glides,
Absolves my mind from laboring,
Then lures me to the fresh outside.

The hills and clouds are torched with flame,
But grim alarms are not released;
No house or barn is sore imperiled,
No fire police--just crimson peace.

A melody of heart awakes;
Intuitively my ear partakes,
Enraptured as Aeolian harps
Hum subtly pleasing counterparts.

Cremona strings vibrate and sing,
And spectered pipers pioneer;
The chariots of the mind ride out
To trace the music of the spheres.

The Theater

Where I Sing

Was Wont to Grow

It grew out of necessity; our children reached the age
When each should have a separate room's respected privacy--
A refuge whereto each might go whenever there was need
To think, or post the signs of individuality.
Unsuitably, our cottage had been built with just a pair
Of bedrooms, and with little headroom under attic beams;
To add another room, we'd either have to spread the base,
Or raise the roof to make a garret-bedroom in that space.

One summer day, I climbed up on the roof and sawed by hand
The sheathing from the ridgepole down, just where the walls would be;
The neighbors came and helped us lift it to the proper height;
Within a single day we set the studs and closed the sides;
The outer wall we windowed from the ceiling to the floor,
And knotty-pined the inner walls, as well as cupboard doors....

That's how it came to be--the garret-room retreat where we
Have lived so much of life--where we have worked, and slept, and loved,
And dreamed, by day as well as night, for through the years the chair
Beside the windowed wall became a special place for me,
When I had need to plan or meditate--to think things through--
To deal with crises in my life--to grieve, or sometimes to
Remember ecstasy--to write long letters to my friends,
Or articles for magazines--and, periodically,
To try to give expression to my farthest-ranging thoughts,
My deepest sentiments, most meaningful experience,
Most consequential memories, in the only way that seemed
To satisfy my most instinctive needs--in poetry.

Somehow, while sitting in that chair, as on a balcony
Above the yard, gazing through that ample wall of light,
Past nearby maple branches, leafless, green, or red, or white,
Out over valley mist to blue-ridge peace, I seem to see
More clearly than most anywhere, and feel tranquility.

Appalachian Etudes

A Time to Go

While drifting down the widened tide
One Susquehanna spring,
We witnessed an exceptional
Display of venturing.

A Lilliputian chipmunk
Had launched into the stream
To try to swim that massive flood
As though to chase a dream--

To know firsthand what might be there
Across that far expanse
That he had not experienced
In former circumstance.

He seemed so insignificant
In face of that great sea,
But strove, unflinching, straight ahead
With strict persistency.

What prompted such capriciousness
To leave familiar place,
And set his sights so far away
At such frenetic pace?

Our craft succumbed to downward wash,
With him still struggling,
And we shall never know for sure
If he survived that spring.

But we shall not forget that gleam
Quite settled in his eyes
That focused on that distal shore
With will to go and try.

A Time to Stay

On that same trip we saw wild ducks--
The kind that yearly fly
Great distances in spring and fall,
Their cycled life to ply.

We saw the male first skimming close
To water's rippling crest,
And then he landed near the bank--
Perchance a transient rest?

But soon we noticed there were two
Within that reedy place;
A female with a broken wing
Could not depart her base.

Would then the male abandon her
And rise into the sky?
He chose to settle there with her--
Can you imagine why?

We felt great satisfaction
While gliding on our way;
We'd learned substantial lessons
From sylvan friends that day.

My Friend

the Cello

Waits

O vibrant friend of graceful, sensuous shape
And luring mellow voice, how I rejoice
To feel your curving firmness at my heart—
Your unrestrained response to fond caress
Of moving finger touch. Your feelings stir,
First tenderly at gently teasing strokes,
Then surge impassionedly at urgent grasp
For soaring climax in a higher range,
Before your throbbing pulses slow and tend
To calming resolution at the end.

How frequently as I pass slowly through
The dining room I fondly glance at you,

Aware of satin sheen on antique spruce,
Orange-ambered long ago by master hands,
Perhaps in candle glow. I cannot know
For sure but rather guess that you were groomed
When luminescent morning filled a room,
And nestled in your marbled maple curls
To wait in breathless brilliancy for me
To catch your warmth, your silent beauty see,
And bring to life our mutual harmony.

Confronting many tasks, it truly grieves
Me deeply that I cannot take more leave
To join with you. I seem to hear you say:
"How long must I in silent corner wait
For your delayed embrace? Take me in hand
That I may sing as I was born to do."
Then comes at last a Christmastime request
To play in church. With apprehensive joy
I strive to gain enough dexterity
To wake the splendors of your artistry.

Too soon comes Christmas Eve, and then in mid
Of bright poinsettias' festive scarlet glow
At front of church where faces overflow,
We share our private partnership in sound,
Endeavoring to render movingly
Franz Schubert's song of Christmas legacy,
Or Gounod's great exalting melody.
So is it that you do not die, but rather stand
And wait for special moments to arise,
Forever pendent on my enterprise.

AVE MARIA

FRANZ SCHUBERT
Transcribed by Gaston Borch

Andante

Ave Maria
(Meditation on Bach, Prelude in C)

BACH-GOUNOD

Andante semplice

To Restore

a View

When first we built our home up on this saddle, we could see
A long, long way, both to the west and to the north-northeast;
Quite frequently in evening hours we loved to sit outdoors
And face the northwest view, where forest-mountains rose above
A row of true-blue spruce that grew across a middle hill;
In summertime, especially, we loved to view the sun
Go down behind that higher rise of misty blue, flushing
The sky's complexion through a range of unfixed tones and shades,
As brilliancies receded into mellow pastelets,
And blue spruce branches blurred and merged to charcoal silhouettes.

At first we didn't notice, but eventually it seemed
The mountain was diminishing in size; in fact, it was
The evergreens that imperceptibly but constantly
Uplifted year by year, obscuring thus the lower slopes
Of that far mountain mass we'd grown accustomed to. There came
A time when we could scarcely see a hint of blue peeking through
The highest boughs. "What can we do to bring it back in view?"
I mused. "It's been a part of our estate right from the start."
And then a wild surmise flashed in my brain: "If I could climb
Just one of those gigantic trees, and maybe saw away
Its top, but not so much but that it likely would survive,
We'd bring the scenic mountain back into our daily lives."

The necessary art would be to plan the project so
That it could be accomplished without serious injury.
Convinced I could, with saw and forty meter climbing rope
Suspended from my shoulders, I carefully ascended to the
Topmost branches of the chosen spruce; I tied one rope end
To the tree, then hurled the coiled bulk out far enough so
That it cleared the lower branches as it fell to where my
Son was waiting to retrieve it. I then climbed down about
A dozen meters, at which point I interlaced my legs

Securely on the branches, just below the place where I
Intended to cut through the trunk. When I had sawed it half-
Way through, my son put tension on the rope from just as far
Off from the base as he could stretch, so he'd be safe and sound,
When finally that massive top would plummet to the ground.

I sawed and sawed diagonally away from where I clung....
Until I sensed the fateful moment was at hand. Shouting
To my son to pull as hard as possible, then quickly run
The moment it began to fall, I braced to move the saw
Again. Almost at once an ominous groaning-splitting sound
Surrounded me, accelerating to a strident pitch,
As that great top, itself the size of many trees, began
To tilt away from me, cracked violently and fell away,
With seeming slowness momentarily, then with a rush
And deaf'ning crush it struck the ground. Aloft, I found myself
As on a flagpole top, swinging back and forth, clingingly....
When movement ceased, I sat awhile in that unlikely place,
Which properly would be a perch for eagles, not for men,
Facing the far blue rise, which daily we'd now see again.

Each Bell I Ring Becomes a Living Thing

Among mementos brought back home from foreign odysseys,
I treasure most my store of bells; throughout the house they rest
In silent shapeliness on focal window sill or ledge,
Or china closet shelves among esteemed cut glass, where we
Are apt to pause at times to closely gauge their artistry.

Enticingly they hang from doorless archways joining rooms,
Inviting passing hands to activate their charming sounds,
Or swing from rods in front of sunlit window panes, to catch
Unique patina tones of antique bronze or weathered iron,
Or gleam of polished brass, or dainty porcelain veneer,
Or subtle damascene of plated silver souvenir.

In wintertime a phantom stir of circulating air,
Or gentle summer zephyrs passing through an open door,
Will motivate our pendent family of thin bronze owls,
Or clustered mobile of clay autumn leaves, to softly sway
And mingle evanescently in chiming roundelay.

Outside, on gateway span, or porch, or tree, they slyly wait
For touch of visitor, or surging wind, to animate
The vibrant music hidden in their cold metallic shapes,
And waken us from sleep or rest with urgent clangoring,
Or tease our passive evening thoughts with gentle tinkle-ing.

Occasionally I feel caught up in sentimental spell
To slowly go about the house and clearly ring each bell--
To relish meditatively each feature of design
That molds its personality, each radiating tone,
Creating novel shadings that pulsate from it alone.

I love each one, each long-time-tested friendly face and voice:
Uniquely tinted damascene from old Toledo, Spain,
Gold-covered, but distinctively endowed with silver ring;
Flare-bottomed bronze from ancient Cuzco's Andean marketplace,
With deftly-crafted llama body sculpture as its grip,
One similar, but brass, and more petite, with cormorant
High-poised, brought home from visit to North Maine's Acadia;
A bulbous, bass-toned cow bell found in rural Switzerland,
And many cute rectangulars from Alpine villages;
A trio of hexagonals bequeathed at parent death;
Exquisite portrait porcelains of varied foreign styles,
And many tiny, fine-brushed specimens with prayer flags
Attached, collected near Japan's intriguing, timeless shrines;
A giant masterwork of San Miguel Allende, Mexico,
Brought home two thousand highway miles to hang beside our gate;
A clan of clanging camel bells from Agra, India,
The city of the Taj Mahal; a gem from Thailand,
Tulip-shaped, with burnished Buddhist symbols set in bold relief,
Acquired from a naked swimming lad while floating down
The Chao Phraya River, near the Temple of the Dawn.

Although I cherish all of those, I'm bound to dwell, sometimes,
On favorites, envisioning the circumstance or place
Where these became a vital part of my own breathing space:

How Tenzing Norgay, near Mt. Everest, presented me,
As farewell gift, a seasoned yak bell from his native place,
Which, notwithstanding humble use, emits celestial strains,
Remindful of a templed land I long to see again.

In Kathmandu, Nepal, I searched a dozen craftsmen's wares,
Until I came upon a rare, embossed, Tibetan-fashioned
Bronze, with round and deeply mellow timbre in its singing soul,
Which any Himalayan monk would hear as pure and whole.

In Guanajuato, Mexico, I chanced to bargain for
A wonder-working bell quartette of horn-like clays, in guise
Of solid cross, which, shaken back and forth by hand, resounds
In multisplendored peal, like to no other I have found.

But king of all those marvels, which I lovingly re-ring
To add transcendent quality to any needful day,
I cite a masterpiece from Varanasi, India,
The sacred Ganges city where old pilgrims go to die;
The impact of its first unearthly quavering, at my
Exploring touch, can never adequately be defined;
I quivered then within, and tremble still each time I grasp
And lift its goddess-emblemed shaft in hand, to chime its sweet
Up-spiraling edifice of overtones far echoing....
Indeed, each silent bell I ring becomes a living thing.

I Love the Full Crescendo

Bare soles protest, although I haste across the sunbleached beach,
Until they rest refreshed on rippled margin of wet sand,
Agleam where latest, farthest-reaching breakers spin their foam;
I pause to let its cooling, soothing softness wrap my feet,
As though a mentholizing balm were lovingly applied,
While rhythmic rise and spread of coming waves invade my eyes;
The crash of each crescendo vibrates on the patient sand,
And stirs my soul with flush of water music overtones
Seductively, ineffably, like mermaids whispering.

Those subtle phonic images soon yield to chilling splash
On tender shins; I quickly move into the brine and brace
Myself to cut the height'ning power of every breaking surge
(each colder than the last) with upraised knee, with sidewise thigh,
Till fatefully I cast all reservation to the flow,
And plunge beneath the moving, salty blanket of the sea.

of the Surging Surf

Positioned where the highest heaving crests are apt to break,
I wait and contemplate the mustering parade of swells,
Until I spy the likeliest of all the ocean's mass;
Is that the perfect wave, conceived far-off, deep-down, sent here
Especially for me just now to fondle my small flesh,
To grasp and merge me firmly in its landward-racing thrust?

Entranced, I dive beneath its writhing curl expectantly;
Yes, this is prime; then comes the feel of ultimate embrace;
My stretching arms pierce through the vanguard wall
Exultantly; in full surrender now I give myself
Unto the mighty churning ocean's landward forcefulness,
Which takes me, bears me, throws me, pounds me, uncontrolably
To thund'ring climax of the sea's full-throated ecstasy.

A Cavatina

for

Old

Christmas Trees

A Christmas tree, if anything,
Is emblem of delight,
Adorned with globes, and angel choirs,
And twinkling little lights.

Why then an edge of sadness, when
We'd go to cut a tree,
And bring it to our living room
To dress with finery?

'Twas something like a Toltec maid
Selected from the rest,
As worthiest in form and face
To meet the gods' behest;

Apparelled with the finest jewels,
And fested for a day,
She soon was stripped of everything,
And cruelly cast away--

A dumb unneeded sacrifice,
It clearly seems to me,
To placate phantom appetites
Of gods they couldn't see.

In future, I decided that
I wouldn't kill a tree
At Christmastime, but rather dig
A little one, that we

Could bring inside, adore awhile
Its fragrant greenery,
And, when the festive season ends,
Replant it joyously,

Instead of setting it aside,
In sad necessity,
To see it slowly waste away,
Dry death its destiny.

Now we can boast a growing choir
Of former Christmas trees,
That grace our yard with living green,
And happy memories,

Of their display in glory days,
Touched with angel light,
Singing vibrant songs, not doomed too soon
To death's amorphous night.

A Recurring Essence of June

It was a late spring glory of my childhood country home
That draped my father's crafted arbor, arching brick-laid walk
With far-pervading fragrancy. In mellow June's fresh warmth
I passed beneath its shadows more than there was really need
To do, and pushed my freckled face and novice lips and tongue
Into those velvet-textured, moist and perfumed petal folds,
To sip with waking fervency the nectar gathered there
From pregnant soft-earth source, the dewdrop pearls of starlit air.

The years with quickened pace rolled on; I left that garden place
But always when I paused to think of it, I'd still inhale
That Van Fleet rose's subtle scent with sensuous memory,
And visualize the grace of its recurrent canopy....

My father died; my mother had to sell and move away;
I dug it up and brought it to a far transplanted home,
Where decades now it's tinged each entry into summer's span;
When gentle touch of June re-stirs its sleeping brilliancy,
I often go, as did that budding boy long time ago,
To drench my seasoned eyes and soul with its sweet pastel glow,
And still it shares its aromatic soft caress with me.

<h1 style="text-align:right">A Means for Years</h1>

<h1 style="text-align:right">to Far-Off Spher</h1>

You served us as a home away from home for many years,
In always-changing spheres, so as I watch you exit from
Our drive this final time, I feel possessed with wistfulness
For when, with growing children still in tow, we'd jam-pack you
With all our camp and climbing gear, apparel, and supplies
To last for months, and then we'd squeeze aboard excitedly
To share with you a new excursion of discovery.

      Two times you carried us as far as southern Mexico,
Where your staunch little motor-heart propelled us half way up
Steep slopes of high snow-capped volcanic peaks; you waited in
The parking lots of quaint historic shrines, kept nervous vigils
Close to speeding traffic while we dined, and other times
Dozed dreamily in patios, with hanging plants your hosts,
Till we returned to you, in need of sleep or change of clothes.

            You bounced us up abandoned, steep-shelved, Colorado
Mining roads to most unlikely termini, with just a few
Complaints or moans. Undoubtedly, you much preferred to rest
In shade beneath Yosemite's great trees and fabled cliffs,
Or feel the spray of surf along the coast of Oregon,
Or overlook Bryce Canyon's fantasy of ocherous spires,
Or roll along the Banff to Jasper Highway leisurely,
Where hanging glaciers grace rock mountains to sublimity.

I could go on and on, for there weren't many of our land's
Attractions, natural, historical, or cultural,
To which you did not willingly transport us when we asked
You to...until at last your worn arthritic joints, and tired
Internal organs aged to where your pain outweighed your joy
In venturing. But still we could not let your friendly form
Depart, and kept you standing in the yard, as if you were
A faithful agéd carriage horse, retired to laze and graze
For all the days that might remain to it. What's more, you st
Could function as a rainproof storage shed....And so we saw
You every day, although we drove a younger member of
Your family...until a nice enthusiastic youth

Inquired if he could utilize your cabinets and bed
In fixing up a camper of his own. Your body was
Succumbing to the rust of age; it seemed a goodly thing
That part of you, at least, could still live on, and still could be
A boon to that fresh spirit's journeys of discovery.

Now Disappears

A Collage
of the Best of Teaching

"The work will wait while you
show the child the rainbow,
but the rainbow won't wait
while you do the work."
--Thoughts for Teachers

In my career of teaching languages, I've been thrice blessed
In that I've had the choicest of my students stay with me
For three successive years. And since my wife instructed them
In their initial year, and often shared with me details
Of the outstanding traits of those most likely to persist,
It seemed I was custodian of their progress four full years.

That length of time enabled our relationships to grow,
In many cases, to dimensions far outreaching normal
Student-teacher scope--to deep and caring personal
Involvement in each other's lives, which often persevered
Long after those reciprocally enriching schooltime years.

Their visitations in our home, and letters keeping us
Informed of where they were and what they were accomplishing
Have been among the greatest satisfactions that we've known.
On melancholy days I feel uplifted looking at
Their portraits, given me with grateful, loving messages,
Or pictures which I took of them at Christmastime,
When they would decorate the chalkboard with their fantasies,
Or graduation time, when we'd invite them to our home
For games, a Spanish meal, group singing 'round our baby grand
Then fond, sad-happy "fare thee wells" and clinging-parting han

I contemplate those well-remembered faces, that so long
Attended mine and listened to my words: intelligent--
Sensitive--some shy and quiet--others energetic--
All genuine--prepared to learn--eager to be challenged--
Prophetic of accomplishment...and I feel a kind of
Surrogate parent love, as well as ample teacher pride,
To see them go their separate ways well-versed, inspired to strive
Whatever be their field, toward purposeful, fulfilling lives.

A Symphonic Ode to the Susquehanna

When errands take us down to nearby Clearfield town,
We glance or fondly gaze from fronting streets or bridge
At your enduring, slowly-moving form, more calm
With deep reflections since our bicentennial's
Authentic reconstruction of a raftsmen's dam.
If leisure grants us time to pause and contemplate,
More aptly do we feel your quiet pulsing flow,
And sense the stilled vibrations of your long ago....

Reflections of your early history appear,
When Indians alone perceived your mysteries...
Conceived Chinklacamoose from passing dug-out logs--
When pioneers canoed upstream remarkably
To probe your upland arteries, and fashion farms
From trackless woods, and mills to grind sustaining grains.

Then came the hearty foresters who used your floods
In spring to move their timber rafts to Chesapeake,
Through labyrinthine rapids, hidden rocks, and mud;
You were the avenue for giant, virgin pines,
Floating to be the perfect masts of great tall ships,
To hold their sails unfurled in winds around the world.

Through changing times you rolled along two hundred miles
Of West Branch forest slopes, past smoke, and curse or smiles
Of men, observing alteration of your clay
And sand and rocks to rust-iron glare from draining mines,
Then mix with human waste and slime of industry
To cripple and then kill your pure, wild legacy.

But happily in recent years a counterforce
Of wiser men has recognized the sanity
Of cleaning up the air we breathe--the earth where you
Can live and flow again with some impunity,
And we can fish, and swim, and ride your fresh clear tide
To feel a pride in Nature's pristine custody.

We love in wintertime to make cross-country tracks
With skis in new-laid snow across a treeless ridge,
And mark below your raven route past pillowed banks
Where rocky ranks held summer sway; another day
More frigid winds blow free, insistently, to lace
And seal with frozen glaze your wrinkled, seasoned face.

Sometimes in early spring when we are seeking out
The cryptic, fleeting fragrance of Arbutus trailing blooms,
We hear your distant horns' or flutes' full-throated rush
From bellows of fast-melting snows on northward slopes,
Then hasten to a clear strategic resting place
To see the gushing power of your quickened pace.

When warming days have urged the ice to break and flow,
Your frozen parts fulfill their postponed destiny
To go downstream; at first they strive impatiently
To rush away, then gentle down more distantly,
Diminishing to merge into your liquid whole...
We're waiting now for perfect time to launch canoes,
And share resurgence of the budding hills with you.

The winds of March have calmed; the bear has left his den;
The daffodils have flowered; the wren has come again;
And now we feel an urgency that we must choose a day
To take an April ride with you along your winding way,
Through northern woods, where banks give hint of rising grass,
Where thick-packed rhododendron growth and laurel mass
Will burst in June to myriad blooms of pink and white.

The mottled slopes that rise above show subtle shades
And tones, as hardwoods resurrect from winter freeze
To frame tall pines and hemlocks' fine viridity,
While early silver maples' erubescency
Preens o'er the tilted hills and fills our springtime mood
With thrill of nature's saving liberality.

In fullest spring we feel your flow more pointedly:
The sun upon your rippled face is multiplied
Ten thousandfold--divided into quaking sparks
Of nearby clustered galaxies in speeding flight,
Caught for us briefly in your effervescency,
As though we ride through stellar realms in miniature,
Beyond imagination's wildest portraiture.

In summertime, we often walk for exercise,
Through shaded, fern-filled, log-strewn Appalachian woods,
To grassy knolls from which we note your dwindled shape
Crawl serpent-like among large rocks; reluctantly
You drain sustaining underground capacities,
And yield your fresh identity to saline sea.

We'll come again in fall to see the treasured tints
Of aspen, beech, and cherry boughs, or chestnut arch
Midst multi-ochered maple leaves, or scattered larch,
And you will be more difficult to navigate,
Meandering from side to side in shallow state,
But we'll be intimate with your most hidden traits,
As our canoe has autumn rendezvous with you.

Now gradually we hear your pounding waterfalls,
And we must pay attention to those urgent calls,
That we may prove our steering art's dexterity
To find a proper downward rush among the rocks....
Too soon it is upon us and your laughter's roar
Surrounds our palpitating hearts' rapidity,
As we plow through your writhing foam's complexity.

And then we take our rest with you on broad deep pools,
Your thunder slowly fading as we drift and cool
Our flaming foreheads with full handcups of your deep
Refreshing store; it's time for lunch--that boulder there
Protruding from the bank will serve as perfect scene
For roasting wieners and for spreading our cuisine....
Above, the gliding hawks keep watch, and so we face
Aloft to wonder at their heaven-soaring grace.

It is not long till excitation stirs again;
Our paddles like enormous hands soon fondle your
Resilient physicality with coaxing strokes;
Our hearts respond as to a lover's passion-breaths,
More ardently when you cry out in ecstasy
Of sound and thrust through narrow funneled passageway,
Then shiver out at length to quivering expanse,
Where hundreds of your bottom rocks protrude above
Your dazzling surface light, as bright as eyes in love.

An

A-door-able

Shed

Takes

Shape

The day before the scheduled demolition of the grand
Victorian house was to take place, we got permission to
Remove the windows and the finely fashioned oaken doors.
It truly seemed to us appalling that a great iron ball
Impartially would smash down everything--the roof, the walls,
And all that was within, to indiscriminate debris;
While contemplating such contrary waste, it came to me
That with those singularly seasoned, master-crafted doors
And windows, we could build a most attractive shed-motel
To house our Wheel Horse tractor, and our garden tools as well.

Dismissing commentary on our purposes, which self-styled
Comics might have proudly thought were somewhat humorous,
We labored with all possible dispatch to beat the clock,
And it became a most exhausting task, especially
Removing with impunity the oakwood window frames....
At last, in evening hours, we undertook extraction of
The massive double doors from the front entranceway, and the
Artistic, over-transom, leaded-glass cathedral prize,
No doubt the major segment of our curious enterprise.

The size and patterns of the paneled doors and window panes
Determined the dimensions and unprecedented style
Of our new edifice. Remarkably, the double doors,
When opened, proved to be a perfect garden tractor width;
When closed, their glass and that of the cathedral overhead
Reflected lovely scenes of seasoned landscapes in day's light,
And soft or bright kaleidoscopic sunset hues when night
Would fall on our estate. Long since, we've grown accustomed to
Its beautiful facade, and frequently glance out at it
With pride through windows of our house that face that way, or fix
On it as we go out the door, or when we work outside,
And echo in our minds the words of one who visited
Our home and aptly said: "Oh, what an a-door-able shed!"

A Quartette

of Unordinary

Weddings

Uncounted times across the years, my wife and I were asked
To offer special wedding music at the marriages
Of former students, friends, or relatives; almost always
These took place inside a church and were conventional in form...
But when our own close progeny were ready to be wed,
They either tended to select unordinary settings,
Or shaped the ceremonies with their own propensities;
Although long steeped in beauties of traditional reprise,
We found inspiring elements in forms that they devised.

Our daughter chose as wedding site the front yard of our home,
Beside a flower-filled urn, just where a flagstone walkway turns
In toward the house; we placed the chairs for family and friends
So that they faced our spruce-fringed mountain scene, which had been such
A vital daily part of Kristan's youth; the mountain, blue
As her clear eyes, was softened by an intervening mist,
As Marjorie, at our piano near the front door screen,
Proceeded with a classic wedding prelude potpourri;
When my turn came, I stood close by the door and sang some songs
From Broadway musicals which Kristan dearly loved: "Around
The world I've searched for you", "I've often walked this street before",
And, lastly, "There were bells on the hill, but I never heard
Them ringing...I never heard them at all, till there was you."
Just when I came to these last words, the bells I'd brought back home
From all around the world, and hung outside on various trees,
Were stirred by sudden breeze to add dimension to that song;
While Marjorie was modulating to begin to play
The wedding march, I joined the bride and bridesmaids at the gate;
As we processed along the flagstone path toward where the groom
And minister were waiting to begin formalities...
And then again at intervals among the spoken words...
The tinkle-tinkle-tinkle of the tree-hung bells was heard.

For Katie, Kristan's bosom friend, our home became a kind
Of second home retreat; we'd also had her as a student
Several years, and so it seemed quite natural when we
Received a letter telling us she planned to marry soon,
And asking if our home could serve as their pre-nuptial base.
We marveled at the breadth of her originality,
As she created for their nuptials: invitation cards, hand-
Lettered and embellished artfully; clay sculptures that were
Perfect likenesses of bride and groom, to top their homemade
Wedding cake; and she designed and sewed her bridal gown, as
Well as an inventive jacket, of the same white fabric,
For her spouse-to-be....

       They dressed in our retreat, and then we
Chaperoned them in to Katie's aptly chosen church;
A college friend sang folk songs, meditatively;
Facing toward each other, the bride and groom then spoke the language
Of betrothal they themselves had penned; a festive picnic
In a public park sped that creative day to splendid end,
And then they spent their wedding night camping out with friends.

When Linda Bell, our artist-niece and long-time cherished friend,
Prepared to marry Greg, an architect, we weren't surprised
Their wedding plans included fine exceptionalities:
They chose as site an absolutely precious antique church
Of nineteenth century design, perfectly preserved inside
And out, just as it was long time ago, for now it's used
By Mercer County's preservationists of history.
One of their highly prized antiquities turned out to be
A finely crafted organ which the cultured bride and groom
Requested Marjorie to play; and it would be superb,
They said, if I would play my antique violin along
With her, perhaps for half an hour--a classic prelude
To their entry into lasting beauty of united love;
They also asked that Cesar Franck's ''Angelicus'' be sung
At the climactic moment of exchanging promises....
It all went off so feelingly, as though in candle glow of
Simpler times, with tested beauty of the place, the gowns,
The music, and especially the newlyweds; perhaps
It was uniquely meaningful for me because it was
The last of all the weddings at which Marjorie and I
Provided songs of love.... A short while afterwards, she died.

Most couples hope, when they start married life, that someday they
Will stumble into Paradise; but that's precisely where
Our son and Judy Anderson first joined their hands and hearts,
And planned their future as a mutual enterprise; they met
At Arizona State, where Erik taught and Judy was
A student seeking an advanced degree; the Paradise
Of which I speak is real--a valley north of Phoenix with that name,
Where Judy had a lovely home. It happened that her neighbor
Was a noted artist who'd designed the stained glass windows
For the chapel of a church quite near the famous Phoenix
Landmark mountain, Camelback; when the artist took them there
To see the glass, they fell in love with it, and all the rest:
The novel setting, and the outside rockwork aspect of
The chapel, as though it were connected to the background
Mountain's mass--the pure simplicity of the interior,
With frontal kneeling bench instead of altar, so that eyes
Would focus on the beauty of the floral glass below;
And the heaven-azured, sunburst-yellowed glass above;
They knew at once that it would be their wedding scene,
And in that tasteful seat of meditative beauty, the
Music of soft strings would fit in most harmoniously....
Thus when they processed toward the chapel's stained glass fantasy,
Three violinists graced the witness of their wedded unity;
And there was poetry read--a sonnet by Millay, which stirred
In me such deep response that I remember still the words
With which it closed: "Fare by my side that journey in the sun,
Else I must turn from the blossoming year, and walk in grief
The way that you have gone; let us go forth together
To the spring; love must be this if it be anything."

Uplifting Golf

to Lifelong Art

García Lorca, famous Spanish poet-dramatist,
Tragically a victim in the Spanish Civil War,
Began one of his lyric poems with these intriguing words:
"O green, how much I love you green…green wind…green boughs of trees.…"
Although they lead symbolically to other ends within
His frame, they serve quite well to introduce my accolade
To what has been for me a most aesthetic lifelong game:
Green fairways…boughs in tree-green breezes…verdant sheens…textured greens
Of every tone, made still more precious when October foliage
Turns to flame or saffron at the margins of those vibrant scenes.…

My entry into golf was at a very early age,
When as a callow lad I caddied at a nearby links,
Where we were granted time to play on Monday mornings up
Till noon. Barefooted, using but a single club at first,
I energetically set out with friends in partial light
At dawn, to gain the fullest measure of allotted time,
Hurrying from shot to shot, leaving in our scattered wakes
An interweaving pattern of meandering footprints through
The cool gauze blanket of a summer morning's heavy dew.

Those effervescent and experimental weekly ramblings
Over North Park's greens and fairways stirred in me intense desire
To hone and fortify what seemed innate ability
In what for many is an often disconcerting sport.
I wasn't satisfied to merely play on caddies' day,
But innovated private courses 'round our country home,
And in the valley farmland pastures that surrounded it.
Those myriad hours of practicing brought youthful triumphs...
Rich fulfillment on my school and college teams: ongoing
Recompense, including more than thirty years as teacher-coach,
And healthful exercise at tempo of adagio....

Still sparkle in recall those crystallized dramatic highs...
Like smoothly stroking in a curling putt of fifteen feet
To win the first of several county junior championships...
Or, four full decades afterwards, that solid lengthy iron
Across a steep ravine directly to the flag to gain
A second championship at Treasure Lake...or sharing with
My wife those annual couple victories.... And there was great
Excitement watching my young teams work up to dominance
In district play, or feeling pride when high school protégés
Rose up to fine distinction being champions on their own,
Or coped with wrenching losses without alibi or moan.

But golf for me has meant so much, much more than what derives
From competition's lure. Though playing all alone, there's feel
Of great "well-being" cracking out a drive quite straight and far,
Or crisply striking through an iron that spins close by the pin;
And there's unique perfection when a long putt's tracking true,
Then clicks into the cup. But even more fulfilling are:
The matchless feel of footsteps strolling over velvet lawns
When April rains bring spring revival from the grasp of frost...
The sensuous fragrance of the new-mown grass of summertime...
The beautiful perspectives standing on raised tidy tees,
Scanning where precisely I would like to send my ball, then
Moving through the shadow patterns of high overhanging boughs,
Which rest, or whimsically portray the range of verdant breeze,
Or frame with vivid greens or golds blue peace of distant scenes...

Pausing at the edge of brooks or lakes, despite the sometimes
Irritating aftermath of errant strokes, to keenly hear
The subtle music, or to see the art reflecting there...
Concentrating on the shot which hopefully will reach the green,
But even if it doesn't, taking time to see the beauty
Of arrangement which the architect in planning it conceived....
These are the reasons why this game's evolved to art for me.
Green fairways...boughs in tree-green breezes...verdant sheens...textured greens
Of every tone, made more artistic when October foliage
Turns to flame or saffron at the margins of those vibrant scenes....

Rhythms and Moods from Chosen Lands

Climbing Pyramids
(Mexico)

From the Moon to the Sun and Beyond

At Teotihuacán, "the place where ancient gods were born",
We climbed the steep cathedral cone designed to praise the Moon,
And, ling'ring there to catch our breath, we let our minds roam free,
Back over time-worn miles where sprawled a ghost metropolis,
Once paved and painted artfully millenniums ago:
Vast monumental pyramids, truncated, temple-topped—
Fine palaces where priests and nobles thrived midst muralled walls—
Plurality of artisans perfecting master works—
Carved altars where religious cults plied restlessly their work—
Expansions...alterations...mass destructions...tribes at odds;
Evolving cultures striving, conqu'ring, merging, changing gods....

Our minds replete with imaging such scope, we carefully
Descended to the open space long called "Street of the Dead"
(Whereon unnumbered graves of cryptic citizens were found),
And walked in silence half the length along that darksome way,
With will to scale the greatest unearthed pyramid of all--
That of the Sun, some seven hundred fifty feet in breadth,
Two hundred twenty tall. On its flat apex long ago
A temple, planned to praise the God of Life Provision, rose,
With crown of monolithic Sun God statue facing east.
We gazed with sense of wonder at volcanoes that had birthed
Supplies of stone, which civilizing people carried here
To shape the greatest early city of our hemisphere.

Reviewing what we'd learned, we marked the mile-off Citadel,
The temple of the Feathered Serpent Deity of Heavens;
A vast stone-walled enclosure wherein tides of history
Were shifted zealously: A lovely little pyramid,
Most consummately wreathed with images in bas-relief
Of life-force deities of Rain, and Earth, and Sky,
Was covered over by a new-made pyramid, and new
Insatiate deities of Fire and War were idolized
In rituals of self-destruction, which unhappily
Required the blood of human sacrifice inexorably.

Ascending to the Temple of the Serpent

Chichén-itzá, unwrapped from seven centuries of sleep
Beneath lush Nature's tropical virescent coverlet
By patient archeologists, lured us to appraise its charm.
Evoking ghostly scenes of ancient Mayan majesty,
With feel of present time submerged in timelessness, we stood
Before the resurrected Castle's limestone symetry,
Then climbed the ninety northern steps that rose a hundred feet.
Two giant feathered serpent heads protruded at the base,
Their mottled bodies forming balustrades both left and right
Up to the temple's entrance where, aloft on either side,
The fear-inducing emblems of their rattled tails reside.

We sensed the heartbeat of the maiden to be sacrificed--
The fragrance of the incense as she started on her way
From top of terraced pyramid, then down the ninety stairs,
Along a quarter mile of dead-end avenue, and then,
To pacify and gain the God of Rain's assistance,
The priests would hurl her to the dark depths of the sacred
cistern.

From sad awareness of those dismal past realities,
We went to find the Caracol, a round, stone, dome-topped tower
Where Mayan scientists a thousand years and more ago
Made careful observations of the sun and moon and stars;
Archaic stairways beckoned us up to the very site
Where rituals more pleasing to our tastes were carried out,
And where, with tools quite primitive, they searched and found the powers
To make a calendar of Time as accurate as ours.

A Mountaintop of Antique Artistry

Conclusively, we journeyed through the jungle to Uxmal,
Where Mayan architecture reached its greatest flowering.
Painstaking excavations, sortings, patient scholarship...
To trace the throb of long-lost life in cryptic hieroglyphs,
Had made for our appreciating eyes a fairyland
Of antique artistry: man, bird, and serpent effigies--
Relief-adorned banquettes--facades of golden limestone,
Their massive friezes intricately shaped and carved--
Were splendrous to behold, as light and shadows played across
Their elevated reach.

Our sense of beauty deeply stirred,
We went to mount the steepest pyramid that we'd yet found,
Appropriately named the Pyramid of the Magician;
Within its thrice-built, elevated levels were five shrines,
Where priestly rites to Chac, the God of Rain were carried out.
Employing hands and feet, as on a cliff, we slowly climbed
Its western side, and then, to find the very ultimate
Perspective of that mountaintop of old idolatry,
I scaled the last facade up to the top-most temple roof;
A haunting cloud, perhaps old Chac, had gathered in the east;
But still the miracle of sunlight sparkled overhead,
And touched with hint of warmth and life the sculptures of the dead.

A

Kaleidoscope

of

Time

and

Place

(Mexico)

Like Ghosts of Prayers Whispered Long Ago

Marsh Aztec priests defined their capital Tenochtitlán,
When they discovered in that lofty site the sign they sought--
An eagle on a cactus with a serpent in its beak.
They founded there, five hundred years ago, the grandest city
Of the western hemisphere, but could not know that it would
Someday grow, through all those centuries of conquest
And advance, into the largest city of the modern world....

Like errant Lilliputians in that vast metropolis,
We jeopardized our lives in midst of unruled traffic race,
With nervous hope that we would find a proper turn to lead
Us out of boistrous maze to scenes of calm antiquity.

In countryside at last, beyond a primitive stone cross,
We stepped back to the sixteenth century, through creaking doors
Of Acolmán's secluded, massive monastery church;
Our footsteps seemed to pulse in solemn old-world silence there,
Until a sexton rang an iron-toned bell, which stirred a flock
Of resting birds to rise and flutter 'round that nave's dim glow,
Like ghosts of prayers that hair-robed friars had whispered long ago.

A Place for Honeymooners

At Xochimilco, where old Aztec farmers grew their fruits
And vegetables, rapt honeymooners love to spend their time
On boats with names of girls arranged in floral lettering,
Drifting in dreamy fragrance past green, effervescent banks
Of floating islands decked with fresh-sprung flowers and silhouettes
Of stately trees, savoring serenades of Mariachi bands
That laze along on nearby boats to amplify romance.
At least that's how it used to be before the age of sprees,
And bumping boats, and frenzied vendors' shrill intensity.

Our first time there was like a lovely second honeymoon
On which we took along our children, with the hope that they'd
Assimilate the fabled beauty we had read about;
They chose a boat with ornate name; they grinned when eye-locked pairs
Would hold each other's hands and kiss; their faces beamed when we
Engaged musicians to perform old songs of Mexico:
Pearl-toothed marimba players, whose gourd-hung instrument jam-packed
Their boat, were poled along beside our own, while soulfully
Their velvet sticks finessed ethereal music such as we
Had never heard, and likely would not hear again nor see.

Birthplace of a Nation's Liberty

Fulfilling long anticipation, as professors of
Hispanic language, culture, and our Neighbor's history,
We made unhurried visit to the celebrated town
In central Mexico re-named Dolores-Hidalgo,
Where, one hundred fifty years before, a parish priest
Courageously had rung his church's bell to summon his
Parishioners to fight for freedom from the grasp of Spain.
Siesta-vacant streets, a plaza with old square-trimmed trees,
Unpeopled benches, and the padre's statue cast in bronze
Enabled us to visualize uninterruptedly
The brave and hope-inspired drama that had there transpired,
So long ago, to shape the currents of a nation's destiny.

Then suddenly siesta ended, and the streets filled up
With workers, vendors, housewives marketing, and vibrant crowds
Of energetic youngsters on their way to school—a burst
Of hopeful life unbridled and ongoing fruitfully—
Fulfillment of the Patriot's dream he did not live to see.

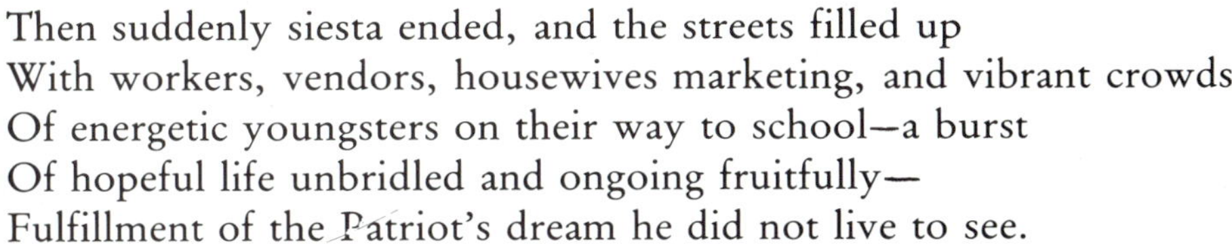

Where Some Long Dead Still Render Testament

Southeast from where Hidalgo rang his Independence Bell,
The town of Guanajuato, birthed to serve a silver mine,
Retains true aspects of an early Spanish colony,
Its thickly clustered base wedged into narrow canyon walls,
Where bridges picturesquely arch, and quaint old lamps of tin
Light staircase streets where facing balconies almost impinge.

Time seemed to slow its pace in that alive museum place,
As we meandered through the relics of a bygone age,
Not only well-preserved but still in use; reflectively
We climbed a steep-stepped way up to the curious Panteón,
A mausoleum-cemetery where the dead are packed
In crypts. Although we'd read about the "mummies" gathered there,
It still was shocking to descend a spiral stairs into
A vault with standing rows of bodies, notably preserved
By arid circumstance, their faces still inscribed with signs
Of their intense emotions at the moments of their deaths.
Not only were the buildings there a living monument;
The dead of yesteryear still spoke in visual testament.

A Solitary Trumpeter's

Unpeered Antiphonies

The Gulf's soft waves caressed the northeast shore of Yucatán
With gentle, teasing strokes, like urgings of our love that led
Our mellow matching steps along warm pliant sand, to choose
A small, surfside café for seafood lunch, with wine and views....

That's when the lonely trumpeter, who stood outside the door,
Intoned high, clear, supremely beautiful antiphonies,
Responding hauntingly to other players we couldn't see,
Unknowing that our souls would bear those notes eternally.

A Monument of History Day

Hillside Taxco, hung in white and red, is said to be
The oldest silver mining town in North America;
There De la Borda in the eighteenth century felt bound
To use his growing wealth to build the Santa Prisca Church
With fine-shaped gold relief, tile dome, and forty meter spires.
To help preserve the charming town's colonial integrity,
The government's decreed a "no new structures" policy.

Our "monument of history" day we wandered lazily
To fountained plazas, quaint old homes, and shops where silversmiths
With patient skill passed on their heritage of artistry;
Ascending then through tilted labyrinths of narrow, cobbled streets,
We stopped to chat with unspoiled children in their dulcet tongue,
And heard the wise unhurried words of old experienced folks,
Until we reached the city's highest lane and overlook;
Far, far below the precious church's double-towered array
Seemed like a tiny toy with which a wealthy child might play.

A Crystal Moment Graved in Memory

On Acapulco Bay we took a cruise to see the sun's
Bright disk turn gold, then primrose pink, before it disappeared
Into its own far-fading boulevard of filtered light;
When we had disembarked, we climbed up to the famous niche
Where divers plunge down forty meters to the swirling tide
That fills a narrow cove of sea but momentarily.

That torch-illuminated spectacle, hemmed in by night,
When high-poised diver touched his toes to beetling edge, then flew
Accelerating down toward rendezvous with shallow sea,
Remains a perfect crystal moment graved in memory.

Tenochtitlán at Christmastime

The Constitution Plaza was arranged inventively
With Christmas tableau scenes in colored lights "Cathedral high,"
And from that antique edifice, aglow with midnight mass,
Came swell of ageless organ pipes the Child to glorify.

In Alameda Park cute, bright-eyed children thrilled
To have their pictures taken with authentic Magi Kings
Apparelled lavishly; wee faces glowed with doubtless hope
That those three legendary sires their wished-for gifts would bring.

Garibaldi Square the finest Mariachi groups
ere gathered to display distinct originalities
f spangled Charro garmenture--of instruments and voice;
r mod'rate fee they'd serenade you with your song of choice.

he Guadalupe Church, first built where Juan Diego's flowers
ere said to turn, in his sarape, into Virgin face,
ad been replaced by ultramodern covered stadium
o house the hallowed image of the nation's patron saint;
nhappily, when we approached that famed basilica,
e found ourselves tight-packed in such a tourist multitude
hat humble, faithful worshipers, who crawled on pious knees
cross that vast expanse of asphalt leading to the shrine,
ere almost crushed in rush of "Navidad" festivity.

The marbled Palace of Fine Arts was perfect setting for
The opulent Ballet Folklórico's fast-paced romance
Of gorgeous beaus and maids, awhirl in dazzling rhapsodies,
Immortalizing graceful movements of the native dance.

The West's first-founded university bedazzled us
With vast symbolical mosaics on its new-made halls...
For lunch we took our students to the Sanborn House of Tiles,
A restaurant that's served the best of Mexican cuisine
For centuries...and then we walked the long historic way,
Beyond the monuments of Cuauhtemoc and Liberty,
Paid homage at the famed museum's Aztec Stone of Time,
And climbed up to the Castle of Chapultepec to see
Where ill-starred Maximilian and Carlota long ago
Looked out from palace luxury to far-off figured snow
Of high volcanoes, which the early Mexicans had named
Poetically "The Sleeping Lady" and "The Man Who Smokes."
Those distant gleaming beauties led me, mildly hypnotized,
To verbalize the tested wisdom of my aging eyes:
"They are the finest ornaments of all that I have seen
On holiday in Mexico for Christmas jubilee."

Glaciers and Gardens
(Canada)

I love to go to Canada
To climb its ice-draped peaks,
Then afterwards, sun-dried,
Toil-worn, I love to seek

Renewal in the fragrant shade
And fresh-sprung summer flowers,
Which always seem incomparable
In transient northern bowers.

In any case, I always laze
A day at Lake Louise,
To see the Iceland poppies blow
In concert with the breeze

That glides across the turquoise lake
From Mt. Victoria's face,
Ice-mantled to the very tip,
Where twice I traced its grace.

And many times from other peaks,
I've come back down to be
Restored in flesh and mind among
Banff's floral fragrancies.

Perhaps it is the contrast of
Frigidity with warmth...
Of striving to the edge of peril,
Then coming down unharmed...

That makes those gardens seem more fresh--
Perspectives seem more fair--
Just resting, breathing, seeing seem
As sweet as angel prayer.

Like Going Home
(Austria)

When first I went to Austria, it seemed as though it were
Like going home to sights and sounds significant to me
In years long past, perhaps to signposts of my ancestry;
Apparently those essences were never wholly lost
In all that intervened, but merely dimmed within my ken
Till proper season summoned them to re-emerge again:

Guest houses etched with flower-decked balconies or window trays--
Green rural scenes with spaced-out cottages and storage barns,
And haystacks neatly fashioned and arranged in patterned ranks--
Quaint villages that huddled close around wee churches, which
Were base for steeples worthy of cathedral shape and size--
And always overhead blue alp cathedrals framed the skies.

I walked Bergisel's ninety-meter ski-jump hill, which hovers
Over Innsbruck's burial ground, with sense it was a path
I'd trod before.... The matins bell at Thaur, which wakened me
Each morning with unparagoned harmonic overtones,
Massaged my soul as though it were designed for me alone.

Old Saltzburg had the aura of a dream I'd often dreamt,
But, waking, never found in actuality, until
I climbed to Hohensalzburg's old-world fortress overview,
And scanned the multicolored roofs and turrets of the place
Where Mozart first blessed music with his genius-tempered grace.
I stood entranced within his birth museum, pondering
The tiny violin which as a child he'd learned to play;
In tint and size it seemed a replica of that on which
I'd taught my son and daughter to perform at early age,
With hope that they might gain sufficient skill to someday be
Refined musicians spreading classic music's legacy.

Wherever I would venture there, I'd brim with ardent mix
Of disbelief and recognition that I'd finally unearthed
A realm where lovely music was exalted--was, in fact,
The common language of the city, put to daily use:
Smooth background harmonies of cello, flute, and violin
Accompanied each evening meal; I thrilled to see and hear
The Saltzburg Marionettes bring Mozart's "Magic Flute" to life;
Then, after strolling timelessly along white, flower-fringed walks,
Among tall founts and statues of the Palace Mirabell,
I joined an audience of kindred spirits to behold
The Vienna String Quartette finesse the best of music's gold.

Musicians, Glockenspiels, and Dancing in the Park
(Germany)

The first time that I sampled southern Germany--the land
Where my paternal ancestors worked out unpublished lives--
Was but a day's excursion out from Salzburg, Austria,
To scrutinize the gross extravagance of mad King Ludvig
Of Bavaria, who'd built the last of his flamboyant
Castles on an island in the middle of the lake Chiem-see.
This one was worked on seven years, but never finished, since
He drowned before he could enjoy it comprehensively;
In fact, in what might be the most elaborate of bedrooms
Ever made, he slumbered fewer than two dozen nights.
His palace floors were all inlaid in intricate designs;
Throughout the rooms most everything was fashioned with gold
And every fixture was of fragile, most fastidious   leaf,
Porcelain, in size and shape quite inconceivable.
But all that I've thus far described diminishes in scope
When one walks through the hundred-yard-long Hall of Mirrors,
In which hang incredible arrays of gleaming chandeliers;
On Saturdays, at night, two thousand candles burn and glow,
Reflecting to infinity the mirrors' perfect row.

While quite amazed at so much complex creativity,
I sensed such overthrust of unearned wealth could not evoke
For me true traces of my humble father's ancestry.
Although I knew they'd lived in Mannheim on the Rhine,
My climbing guide responsibilities in Europe's highest Alps
Have never left me ample time to probe those Rhineland roots;
But Munich, crossroads hub, as it appeared before and after
The sadistic and destructive scourge of Nazi idiosy,
Provided me a vivid, more traditional milieu
Of average German living styles and cultural displays.

Originating at the Hauptbahnhof, strategic base
Of modern Munich's multitude of merging railroad lines,
We pushed our luggage over sidewalks, using carriers
Resembling grocery carts, until we reached the Hotel Stachus.
Finding it to be quite near the famous beerhall, Lowenbrau,
We paused to sample mugs of what may be the world's best beer;
Then, feeling quite relaxed, we wandered past the sparkling spray
Of Karlplatz Fountains, and were soon caught up in thrall of
Famed Neuhauser Street, where flowers fill huge pots, and deck the
Window ledges of historic buildings--where, free from noise
Of automotive traffic, one can sit at outside tables
Slowly sipping apfelsaft, chatting dreamily--where amateur
Musicians base themselves on sidewalks or store entrances
To sing or yodel, or perhaps to play the Brahms Violin
Concerto, aided by taped background of great orchestras,
With hope of contributions from the lingering parade,
Or, at the least, encouragement from public accolade.

At far-famed Sporthaus Schuster, we purchased climbing boots,
Then went to rest before the Gothic Rathaus in the Marienplatz,
With frequent glances at the Frauenkirke's "onion towers,"
And jovial overtures to talk in "Deutsch" with native folks,
While waiting for the striking of the hour on Rathaus clock. . .
When all those precious, painted figures faithfully come out
The doors to frolic, dance, and make their circles merrily,
Accompanied by sweet-toned glockenspiel's clear cadency.

One Sunday afternoon we walked for hours on Munich's streets,
Past countless vibrant fountains, monuments, and flower arrays,
Observing handsome structures of Rococo, Renaissance,
Or Gothic architecture, which had been restored from the
Extensive bombing of the war. We sampled something of
Past royal dukedom pomp in the Bavarian Residenz,
Then lingered at the Deutsch Museum's unexcelled displays;
But even more we relished watching German "common folk",
Who toil assiduously all through the week, relaxing happily
Along the Isar River's sandy banks, their youngsters lost
In glee of water play…. Meandering on, we came upon
The English Garden Park, where, gathered 'round the Chinese Tower,
A multitude of picnickers were watching dancers clad
In native costumes skipping and cavorting to the music of
A captivating German band. That general "Frohlichkeit"--
"Great joyfulness"--was quite apparent everywhere we roamed.
Then as the evening shadows fell and lights began to glow,
We chanced upon the one and only Hofbräuhaus--an apt
Finale to our varied Sunday "Festlichkeit"; within
That celebrated hall a portly German band blew fast-paced tones,
As couples of all shapes and ages danced excitedly,
And rows of revelers, with liter mugs of beer in hand,
While swaying back and forth with mutual mirth, sang lustily.

Music Box Songs
(Switzerland)

Some fourteen years before, from Interlaken's shore,
I'd come the length of lake to Brienz by public boat,
To buy a dainty music box where they are made--
A special gift from Switzerland--a souvenir
Petite and sweet for one who could not be with me,
For I had gone to guide a climbing group that year.
From all that graceful art I chose a modest size
That played a gentle waltz with winsome tingling sounds,
Had lovely patterns, and was practical as well
For storing pins or rings along with music's spell....

Then, passing through Brienz again, on way with friends
To climb and film the peaks of Bernese Oberland,
We chanced to go into a shop where instantly
Another music box, more beautiful than all
I'd ever seen, attracted me spontaneously;
Its crafted cover was inlaid with Edelweiss
Surrounding ambered flute and horn and cello forms
So subtly made they gleamed with tasteful polished touch.
I turned it on and quickly felt its balanced tones
Caress my ears, and still more deeply touch my soul
As though some antique melodies from lineage past
Welled up in me to such exquisite rhapsody
That I was caught as if first love returned to me.

I went about the store and gazed at all the rest,
Then listened carefully to all that charmed my eyes,
But always I came back to check the first, confirmed
Repeatedly that none compared in looks or sound....
The price??...Alas, I could not think to purchase it!
Besides, for years we've had a music box at home
With pleasant shape and sound. We really don't need two.
It costs too much....My heart said yes; my purse said no.
I sadly left to focus on the Jungfrau snow.

But even with great projects to explore and do,
My mind kept bringing back that music box to view.
While lying in my bed at night in Grindelwald,
Or on the crowded train bound for the Jungfraujoch,
And even cutting steps into the mountain slope,
I'd hear its haunting music, "Where white lilacs bloom—"
I'd see its perfect inlays, with anxiety
That someone else might purchase it ere time
Would let me have a second chance to make it mine.

That week passed slowly as we filmed the Jungfrau climb;
We stopped to sample Interlaken's special charms;
But even then my secret thoughts devotedly
Returned across Brienzer Lake repeatedly....
When breathlessly I rushed into the shop at last,
My anxious eyes at once found refuge in the box--
It still was there! The salesgirl, noting my concern,
With voice as sparkling as the art she daily heard,
Spoke these perceptive words: "I knew that you'd return."

A Glimpse of Immortality

(Switzerland)

One Summer, after guiding climbs in many regions of
The Alps, I had a week of leisure time before my flight
Back home. Since we had finished with ascents of Eiger, Mönch,
And Jungfrau, I decided to remain right there to sift for
Truth and beauty in the restful, cultured atmosphere of
Interlaken--set ideally in between the Thuner
And Brienzer Lakes, with gorgeous mountains all about:
I walked among the gardens of the Kursaal frequently,
Passing by its floral clock, resting at the choicest spots,
Attending concerts of a chamber orchestra, late
Afternoons, and evenings too.... In morning hours I boated on
The lakes...examined consummately crafted woodwork art...
And made excursions up to postcard villages, like Mürren,
Poised at sheer cliff's edge, with sweeping scenes at every turn.

Perhaps the finest hour within that sweet abundance was
Absorbing a performance, in an outskirts forest,
Of the Friedrick Schiller drama, <u>Wilhelm Tell</u>. On a scale
As panoramic as the Passion Play at Oberammergau,
It held my interest and emotions in a ceaseless spell--
From the stunning opening cavalcade of villagers,
With cattle bearing mammoth clanging bells beneath their necks,
Striding noisily across the natural stage...through almost
Too heart-wrenching tension of the archer Tell being forced
To shoot an apple from his dear son's head to save his life...
To the redemptive climax when the evil instigator's
Heart was pierced by Tell's avenging arrow, symbolizing
Liberation of the Swiss from autocratic governing.

Still vibrant with the passion of that classic presentation,
No matter whether it was based in fact or fantasy,
I routed my return through Altdorf, Wilhelm Tell's hometown,
And found one of the finest monuments I've ever seen:
A choice bronze rendering of Tell, with ardent arm around
His son, and crossbow slung across his shoulder, standing by
A graceful tower painted with a mountain village scene;
A plaque beneath the painting phrased his immortality
In German words, which I was moved to translate into poetry:

"As long as mountains stand and cast their spell,
Good men will not forget the archer Tell."

Improvisions by the Sea
(Costa Rica)

We relished Costa Rica's freshly painted villages,
Its fragrant floriculture, and its clean lush countryside;
We sat aesthetically entranced within the gilded, bronzed
And marbled elegance of San José's rare opera house;
We braved the rapids of Reventazón (The Bursting Stream),
And even ventured up to where the newest lava flows
Still smoked and glowed on Arenal Volcano's ashen hulk;
But the portion of our second honeymoon that we most prized
Was visiting a wild, unspoiled, Pacific Ocean shore,
Whereon the ceaseless surging sea was as it used to be,
Its sandy margins flanked by virgin forest drapery.

We flew to Quepos on a plane of vintage World War Two
Which landed on a narrow, mowed-down strip of barley field,
Its wings near brushing in the tasseled tops of uncut grain;
A waiting van then quickly whisked us to the slow-paced town,
To lodge a night in bayside inn uncomplicatedly,
Where time was less important than the savor of the sea.

Next morning, ere we walked a country road to sylvan beach,
We tasted native food as well as folk philosophy
Within a quaint café by window picturing the bay;
As parting gift to close a most enlightening exchange,
The charming old proprietress sagaciously declared:
"In my long life I've always found that work's the best of prayers."

We walked steep, winding miles to find a natural preserve,
Where plaques with Spanish language truths were posted on the trees--
Succinct philosophy which self-styled sages wished to share
With every new adventurer who happened to walk there;
Among those forest maxims these intriguing words remain:
"Though ducks and swans are both derived from common ancestry,
The swans alone grow up to know the grace of artistry."

With that surprising thought reverberating in our minds,
Along with strong succession of climaxing waves, we went
To find the park, the only one that we have ever known
With entry walking waist-deep 'cross an inlet of the sea
From tide-shaped sand to far-off strand's luxuriant privacy.

It's called La Punta Catedral (Cathedral Point)--a kind
Of vegetation-decked Gibraltar Rock that rises up
Abruptly over massive white-capped swells on every side
Except where it connects with narrow strand of plants and sand.

Primeval forest covers it with peerless ancient trees,
Herculean in reach, their branches overhead enlaced
In mottled canopy where we could hear, and sometimes see,
Wild acrobatic spider monkeys play or scold with bursts
Of frantic chattering--with seige of downthrown buds and twigs;
Caressed by philodendron leaves and other tropic plants
Too numerous to specify, which crowded the damp earth
With unrelenting growth, we climbed up to a bird's nest view
That westward overlooked the cliff out to an island height,
Gainst which colossal breakers crested white in free delight.

Descending by the southward side through tangled fronds, we crossed
The narrow neck of land and had a glimpse of paradise:
A corridor of gently sloping, untramped beach, landlocked
By wall of jungle maze with green cathedrals at each end,
Which framed the westward gleaming image of a private sea.
A parrot startled us and brushed the shaded emerald
With scarlet flight; our hands entwined, we tracked the nestling sand,
And let our feet be teased by tumbling tropic foam; and finally
Our unclad flesh surrendered to the sensuality
Of ardent waves which fondled us with wild frivolity....

While walking back toward town, we chanced upon a rare hotel
Named Mariposa (Butterfly). Eight hundred feet above
The surf, it draped a hill that overlooked Cathedral Point,
Where we'd found life well-tuned, like Lost Horizon's Shangri-La
O'erlooked fulfillment in the Valley of the Pale Blue Moon.

It seemed the perfect place to end our ideal holiday;
From deck outside our room, from high veranda where we dined
To music of quartettes, our eyes and minds looked out
And slowly contemplated all the treasures that we'd found:
How Truth was prized by common folk, and written on the trees--
How Beauty frolicked with us in that chamber by the sea.

Burros I Have Loved
(Peru)

I've always felt great sympathy and admiration for
Our fellow creatures classified as birds and animals,
As each confronts the sometimes brutal world to which it's born;
I find I've learned a lot from them in paying careful heed
To their distinctive traits, and how they manage to survive.
Each keen observer prizes certain species over time
Which most intrigue…which prompts me here to highlight some
of mine:

Great Bengal tigers who portray their fearsome symetry
In silent statue watch, or stalking prey unflinchingly….
Alert rock pikas who inspire with ardent husbandry,
Storing bits of grass to face harsh winter's long frigidity….
Bright cardinal pairs whose scarlet pose flags hope's reality,
Mutually guarding while the hearty birds of winter feed….
Wee mint-green hummingbirds who hover incandescently,
Surpassing in sheer loveliness and quick dexterity….
Staunch Vicuñas, tiny, fine-fleeced camels of the Andes,
Who survive on tundra grass in cold thin air's severity….
Wild Lobo wolves, whose knowing gaze transects man's vanity,
Choose mates for life as humans try, but more successfully….
Nine German shepherds whom I loved, then buried 'neath a tree;
Nine best-of-friends who freely shared love's selfless legacy….

But now I must set down a private singularity:
I tend to fall in love with every burro that I see.
Perhaps the Spanish poet, Juan Jiménez, in his fine
And sensitive life story of his donkey friend, Platero,
Sowed the seeds of my affection, though it may have merely
Reinforced what was already there. In any case,
In Mexico, and Spain, and especially Perú, where I
Led many expeditions far into the Andes Range,
I found myself increasingly reloading, walking by
The side of, petting, frequently encouraging, admiring

The tenacity, endurance, resignation, patience,
And sure-footed capabilities of those intrepid,
Floppy-eared and furry-faced, soulful-eyed and shaggy tailed,
Load-carrying companions of wild, unforgiving trails.

To the amusement of the packers, I would often give
Their animals the names of poets, or musicians, or
Philosophers whom I have most esteemed; I'd tell a bit
About those noted personalities; it was a means
Of drawing close attention to the precious qualities
Of our brave beasts, each one with individualities
That should be recognized and treated with benignity.

I saved the name Platero till I really knew I'd found
The one that truly merited that prize. I recognized
At once the silv'ry countenance that I'd been waiting for,
When we arrived for rendezvous with our head porter and
His donkey train, beside the Llanganuco Canyon's
Lower Lake. It seemed like destiny he was assigned to be
The bearer of my personal possessions on that climbing
Expedition circling through the Cordillera Blanca
Range of north Perú. I scratched his fuzzy ears and head
At least a dozen times each day along the way; my heart
Leapt up to see him trot with apt security along
Steep trails; I'd call his name with real emotion in my voice
And think I'd see a hint of recognition in his eyes
As he'd go by. Sometimes, near camps, I'd go and sit
Beside him, as he nibbled on the meager tundra grass,
And slip him surreptitiously some goodies that I'd saved
For such communing hours. His lips were warm and friendly on
My hands in those sweet private sharings of our amity;
Then, lingering, I'd see within the shining depths of his
Large fearless eyes an image of my own identity.

A Tale of Two Pearls
(Japan)

At Toba in the cold sea's depth
A golden pearl was born
In the body of an oyster,
My lady to adorn.

A jeweler set it in a ring
Of exquisite design;
I took it home and put it on
Her hand, our love to bind.

It never left her finger as
The years rolled on to nine;
The pearl grew flawed from constant wear
And lost its lustrous shine.

Another year I happened through
Japan, while on my way
To climb the mountains of Nepal,
And had a leisure day....

Determined somehow to replace
My love's diminished prize,
With one as truly beautiful
And of the proper size,

I joined a group that went to see
How cultured pearls are made;
Each one received a number as
We entered the arcade.

When demonstrations were complete,
Three numbers were unfurled;
The persons holding them received
An oyster with a pearl.

The last one that they gave as prize
Was number twenty-nine;
It seemed quite inconceivable…
The number called was mine!

I spread the oyster and could see
Gold tint on this new prize;
And when the jeweler measured it,
It was the old pearl's size!

Where Buddha Is Reclining, Solid Gold, or Emerald (Thailand)

Before I ever had a chance to relish Thailand's charms
(En route to walk across Nepal and visit Everest),
I'd gathered concepts of that quite extraordinary land,
Derived in part from stamps collected as a boy, and then
From fascination with the self-biography of Anna,
Tutor of the children of that most compelling autocrat--
That charmingly susceptible old monarch of Siam.
The aging king, who valued learning with a passion--
Who inadvertently employed the future perfect tense
Instead of simple ones, was winsome to the "nth" degree,
And fired me with desire to test Siam's reality.

Lounging on the Oriental Hotel's famed veranda,
We savored Thailand-style cuisine, observing an array
Of neon signs reflecting on the River Chao Phraya,
Making rainbow ribbons dance upon the moving water,
While a pianist provided sentimental renderings
Like "Love Walked In", and "Moonlight Serenade", and
                                    "Memories"....

A restful sleep, and soon in early light we went to glide
Upon that very tide, beside the graceful pointed towers
And gold-leaf-gilded inlaid glass and porcelain and pearl
Of Wat Arun, the Temple of the Dawn, its ridge-pole horns
So set, presumably, that all approaching evil spirits
Would be caught, impaled upon those bird-bill spines. 'Twas easy
To imagine how impressive it would be to perceive
The very long and elaborately fashioned wooden
Royal barges, as they celebrate the very holy day
That marks the end of Buddhist Lent, when they process along
The water route that we were taking past the Wat Arun,
All colorful and gleaming in the early morning sun.

As we approached the building where those figured, high-bowed crafts
Are housed, I bought a quite distinctively adorned bronze bell
From an elfish urchin, raven-eyed and irresistible,
Who'd beat the other youngsters swimming toward our boat to ply
Their merchandise. Proceeding through a series of canals,
Observing scenery and culture of the river-folk
Who come and go throughout their lives along those water streets,
We paid a visit to the bustling Floating Market of
Bangkok--a kind of oriental Venice with a jam
Of boats where everything imaginable is bought or sold,
From everyday mundane to valuable, both new and old;
As souvenirs I bought a table set of polished brass,
With teakwood handles finely framed by craftsmen unsurpassed.

The next day was our Buddha day: in sequence we assayed
Wat Po, where the Reclining copper Buddha takes his rest,
And student monks in orange or yellow robes strive to be blessed;
Then Wat Traimat, to see the Buddha cast in solid gold
That weighs more than eight thousand pounds; and finally,
To Wat Pra Keo, Temple of the Buddha carved from jade,
Oft called The Emerald Buddha, the most revered of all,
Highlighted on a massive complex throne, inhabiting
A fine mosaic chapel at the entrance to the King's
Grand Palace grounds--a lavish, ornate complex of pagodas
Covered with the finest in-laid porcelain and glass designs--
The seat of royal luxury and gorgeous concubines.

Returning to the river and its maze of waterways,
We learned they also figure in the festival of Loy
Krathong, when, on the full moon night of the twelfth lunar month,
Almost every Thai throughout the land creates a cup
Using banana leaves, and floats it down a nearby stream,
Aglow with candle fixed and lit before the launch is made,
To carry off all sin and evil luck accumulated
In the passing of the year. Although originally
All cups were lotus-shaped, they now show creativity,
As each selects a shape to mark his self-identity--
Appropriate indeed, for "Thailand" means "Land of the Free".

The Long, Long Path of Prayer (Nepal)

The longest trek I ever felt compelled to take--
A pilgrimage from Kathmandu to Everest--
Began with climbing up four hundred hillside steps
To see the ancient Buddhist shrine, Swayámbu Nath.
There I observed the images of Buddha, Jesus,
And Mahatma Gandhi standing side by side
With those of various Hindu gods. Another day
I sought Patán, Nepal's artistic capital,
Renowned for wood and metal art and stone inlay,
And found within that Buddhist site, marked by emble
Stupas at the corners of the city, a fine
Stone Krishna temple, celebrating Hindu faith.
Two truths about the Nepalese were soon made clear:
At every turn religion seemed the central theme;
And tolerance of other faiths was deemed supreme.

I then set out on foot to cross the mystic land
That tilted upward toward the rooftop of the world
With features which till recently were not revealed.
For more than twenty days I crossed its north-south ridges,
Slowly toiling up through terraces where farmers
Bravely cultured grains on quite improbable terrain,
Or up through forests where tall rhododendrons grow...
Descending then to gorges...crossing rivers on
Precarious suspension bridges one foot wide...
Gaining once again an elevated pass,
Higher than the last...resting with long vistas toward
The sacred temples of the high white snow world, spread
Ahead, to lift the aching flesh and searching soul
To venture on...and on...to gain the longed-for goal.

And everywhere along the way were manifest
The multitudinous emblems of religious faith:
Mani-wall memorials beside the winding trails
Displaying silent rows of graven orisons;
Weathered lichened chortens keeping symboled vigil
And reminder at strategic solitary sites;
Prayer flags fluttering above the heads of travelers,
Topping with deep breaths high windblown passes;
Prayer wheels turning endlessly in rushing streams,
Or in the pious hands of some who journey by...
And often in the minds, and sometimes on the lips,
Of all who walk those far-flung mystic trails:
OM MANE PADME HUM. "Hail to the jewel within
The blesséd lotus flower...again...again...again...
On tongue, on stone, in wind, in glacial river flow...
Multiplying man's petitions to the deities
To earn a better incarnation...longingly...
Devotedly...tirelessly...everlastingly...

I'd read that ancient Varanasi, or Benares,
Which is currently its name, is the holiest of cities
Throughout India, religiously and intellectually.
My visit there of several days was confirmation in
The flesh of many grand anticipations stirred, when, as
A youth, I'd stretch out on the parlor floor and leaf my aunts'
Attractive leather-crafted Goddard Lectures set of books,
And read and ponder pictures of that far-off orient land,
Where cows, and Maharajas, and ascetics held command....

Some images were certainly up-dated, altered by
The sweep of revolutionary governmental change,
Made more distinct through living color media...but still,
To actually mingle in the crowded streets--to feel the throb
Of bustling daily life, where cows and camels, elephants,
And human carriers compete with cars and trucks for
Right-of-way--to breathe the mix of odors, ranging through
Extremes from human waste to pungent burning incense sticks--
Was far, far more instructive than mere media might predict.

I've read that throughout India's long history, the best
Of those important in the fields of learning and religion
Drew directly or in other ways upon the glory
Of this city, flanked on north and northeast sides by sacred
River, tributary of the mighty Ganges. Nearby,
At Sarnath, several centuries before the birth of Christ,
The Buddha gave his primal sermon, teaching man's direct

Where Agéd Pilgrims Come to Bathe and Die

(India)

Awareness of the cosmic being, initiating
Speculation on the nature of reality and
Knowledge--the problems of existence and of ultimate
Deliverance. Three hundred years of seeking truth ensued,
And then the Emperor Asoka built a stupa there,
Enshrining relics of the great Enlightened One's affairs.

Mahatma-Ghandi, also, left his mark upon this place
With novel concept for the Bharat Mata Temple, where
All willing worshippers may celebrate their native land
By walking 'round a floor-wide centerpiece, which is
A mammoth map in bas-relief of Mother India;
True affirmation that the heights of human thought have made
This city one of learning through the ages can be sensed
Within the campus of Benares University:
I was enthralled to read and view the "rules of life"
In words and drawings on the walls among the marbled halls
And inlaid balconies of Birla Temple; all the while
Musicians, playing horns and concertinas, jubileed
The chambers of the temple with inspiring melodies.

The city has the finest river frontage that can be,
With temples, mosques, palatial buildings, and six dozen ghat
That line the flowing water crescent for four miles or more;
There the devout of Hindu faith from every clime of India
Come down those steps to bathe themselves within the sacred
And many agéd pilgrims come a final time to die,   flood
And go direct to heaven, they believe.

                    At night, we rowed
Along the shore and passed close by Manikarníka Ghat,
The place where families cremate their own on funeral pyres
Of wood, the same for rich or poor; and then they beat the bones
With sticks, reducing them to lime within the ashen heap,
Before they push it all into the slowly moving flow,
With expectation they have sent them where they wished to go....

The Taj Mahal--So Lovely, but So Costly (India)

For just a few rare days my world became absorbed by domes
Of Moslem polished marble mausoleums, and fine
Contrasting reddish Sikri sandstone walls, wherein the shahs
Of northern India laid out the large dimensions of
Their lovelorn griefs or greatly bloated self-esteems, as their
Material wealth, however merited or gained, allowed
Indulgence to augment accustomed daily luxury,
To end of fancied, self-promoting immortality.

So was it Shah Jehán, a noted Mughal emperor,
Employed the finest architects of all of India
And Persia to conceive and build the splendent Taj Mahal
As worthy tomb for his belovéd wife, Mumtáz Mahál,
Engaging twenty thousand expert masons, inlayers,
Calligraphers (with best materials as requisite),
Devoting more than twenty arduous years refining it.

As countless visitors across the centuries have done,
I entered through the southern sandstone gate, and then began
Meandering around the garden grounds, resting here or there
To contemplate in meditative state the wondrous art
Of those unique designs, enhanced by changing light and shade
From viewpoints far or near, oft doubled in reflecting pools,
And flanked symetrically by matching mosques to east and west,
While north the Jumna River marked the bounds of timelessness.

In stocking feet I mounted to the pure white marble plinth
Which is its base, full seven meters thick, and entered through
The near facade to stand beneath a massive arch that soars
More than a hundred feet aloft above a chamber shaped
Octagonally, with walls embellished by pietra dura
And with patterns carved in low-relief. Behind carved marble
Perforated screens, studded well with precious jewels, were placed
The finely finished cenotaphs of Bégum and Jehán,
Beneath which they lie side by side in grasp of Death's cold hands.

Caught fast in silent wonderment in midst of such great craft
And beauty, born of lovelorn grief and egotistic need
For earthly immortality, I nonetheless could not
Suppress sad thoughts of all the hapless masses yearning to
Breathe free from hunger and despair, enslaved by poverty,
Denied all hope for gain which such great wealth might have decreed.

Another day I visited Sikandra, Akbar's tomb,
And Jama Masjit, moslem mosque at Sikri Fáthepur,

As well as what is sometimes called the "Baby Taj", the tomb
Of Itimád-ud-Dáulah, father of Janhángir's queen--
All exquisitely shaped and decorated at great cost,
With intricate inlaid designs which dazzle eye and mind
As much as almost anything composed by humankind.

My final day, I went to Agra's fort, Musámman Burj,
And climbed up on the balcony where aging Shah Jehán,
Imprisoned by his son, lived out his melancholy days
With poignant gaze through valley haze to where his cherished wife
Reposed beneath the gleaming marble Taj's house of death.
It's said he'd planned a duplicate, but all in black, where he'd
Abide, but earthly fates spelled out another destiny…
And now he lies beside his prized Mumtáz eternally.

"Heard melodies are sweet, but those unheard
  Are sweeter; therefore, ye soft pipes, play on;
Not to the sensual ear, but, more endeared,
  Pipe to the spirit ditties of no tone:
Fair youth, beneath the trees, thou canst not leave
Thy song, nor ever can those trees be bare;
  Bold lover, never, never canst thou kiss,
Though winning near the goal--yet, do not grieve;
  She cannot fade, though thou hast not thy bliss,
For ever wilt thou love, and she be fair!"
                    --John Keats "Ode on a Grecian Urn"

A Gauge of Great Ideas Here Was Formed
(Greece)

Returning from the Himalayas, back around the world,
I had my choice of routes through Athens, Istanbul, or Cairo
To assess, first-hand, important cultures merely read about.
I chose the first-named, for, in all my scans of history,
The classic age of Greece had greatest consequence for me
In theater...architecture...government...philosophy.

Awestruck, I stood beneath the massive pillars that remain
Of the Temple of Olympian Zeus, framing the Acropolis
Off to the west; it was amazing that old ruins could be
So beautiful--pearl marble shaped with such integrity--
Such stately concepts, stretching royal art's sublimity.

For one brief hour I sat among the semi-circle tiers
Of the grand Dionysian Amphitheater, hollowed out
From fortress rock to seat a multitude of witnesses,
When philosophic tragedies were held four times each year;
I gazed upon the statue-fronted stage, where fervent probes
Concerning man's predicament were eloquently phrased
By Aeschylus, Euripides, and Sophocles, who asked
Why man must be forever torn between the seeming
Incompatibles of good and evil. "Does man bring his
Suffering upon himself, or is it malice of the gods?
Is he the pawn of fate, or do the gods sit idly by
And wait for man to wreck himself through passion, greed,
                                        or lies?"

With such enigmas as "elusiveness of justice" or
"Accepting what cannot be altered" churning in my brain,
I wandered past the entrance Temple of Athena Nike
To appraise the restoration of the old Agora,
Where Socrates and other Greek philosophers held sway,
And argued on cosmologies and ethics every day.

Complexities of Roman overlayment made it hard
To ferret out the Greek originals, but in that place
I had as keen a sense of history's inexorable course
Of change as ever I have had--long years enriching life,
Then suddenly a violent force of nature or of man
Destroys the careful structures of an era's finest plans.

On this one site the gauge of much of occidental earth's
Oracular ideas, sculpture, architecture, science,
And government was first devised, discussed, put to the test....
As emblem of that marble age of creativity,
I focused on the forty-two-foot-high, octagonal
Creation of Andronicus called "Tower of the Winds":
Each side bore weather-beaten figures of wind's power; it's said
It once contained a weather vane, a sundial, and a water clock
For telling time on cloudy days; the conquering Turks, it seems
Left it unchanged, believing it to be the tomb of Socrates.

Three times I mounted the Acropolis, in morning, noon,
And evening light, and also gazed on it from several sides,
Below...far-off.... Its undisputed character as one
Of Earth's most haunting fortress shrines can surely not be missed
By anyone with any sense of art and history.
Despite millenniums of conquest, wreckage, bondage by
The Persians...Romans...Germans...Christians...crazed Crusaders...
The Parthenon, though blasted, decked as Catholic church   Turks...
With campanile, then made a Turkish mosque with minaret,
Maintained the matchless quality Athenian art had set.

As fitting climax to that sweet archaic holiday,
I spent the best museum-afternoon of all my life
Examining, close-up, details of the preserved array
Of statues of the gods and citizens of ancient Greece,
Created by the gifted portrait sculptors of that age.
Outside, I purchased from a vendor what might well have been
The largest, reddest apple ever grown, and supped on it
While climbing up a cone-shaped mountain-park, Likávittós,
To witness, from the lookout chapel crowning it, the sun
Become a crimson sky, the Parthenon a silhouette
Of history, and Athens, spread below in moonless night,
Turn mistily into a sable sea with sparkling lights.

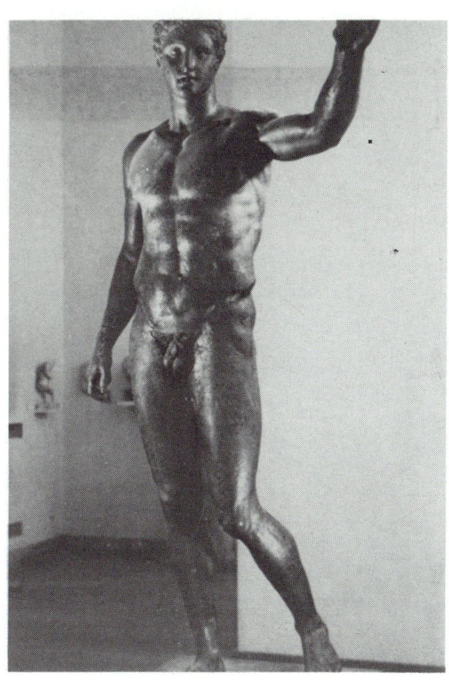

The Faces

of the Children

In my long search for truth and beauty all around the globe,
With first-hand looks at many of the grandest natural
And man-made wonders of the ancient and the modern world--
Through great metropoli, with priceless art and edifice,
And peaceful postcard villages, with ideal rural scenes,
To matchless outposts in the mountains of my dreams,
What's been most truly beautiful of all that I have seen
Has been the faces of the unspoiled children watching me.

With candid inquiry of eye or word, they'd stand their ground,
Endeavoring to fathom what must be the unknown world
From which I'd strangely come to pass through their remote terrain;
With courtesy they'd answer me, surprised to hear me speak
Their tongue, the Rembrandt candles of their steady eyes more bright
When animated, though quite beautiful in all degrees,
Unclouded by their common garb or harsh geography.

I've chanced upon them deep in Mexico...or after weeks
Of walking where there are no roads across remote Nepal...
In Austrian, or Japanese, or Spanish villages...
Or in the hinterland among the mountains of Peru....
There have been hundreds that I've not forgotten, passing by,
But some, by chance or destiny, engraved their faces more
Indelibly upon my quite susceptible heart's core.

While leading an exploratory trek up through Peru's
fantastic Blanca Range, in aftermath of one of the
most catastrophic earthquakes ever known, we chanced to make
our camp quite near an isolated hamlet, Santa Cruz,
where almost every building was destroyed, except the school.
The teacher asked me to address the children; I explained
our presence there; they sang and recited quite inspiringly;
and we gave gifts to purchase school supplies. Afterwards,
a darling child and her two dogs walked back to camp with me,
and, in the few days we remained, Cuidela came to be
my bosom pal...and evermore a precious memory.

Above Huaraz, in north Peru, there is an ancient ruin,
Uilcahuaín, six thousand years of age. So solidly
was it conceived that even the great earthquake that laid waste
the Santa Valley's homes in nineteen-seventy, did not
break loose one stone. I'd gone there several years
on warm-up hikes, but my most satisfying rendezvous
occurred when one keen lad with mammoth hat aspired to be
my guide. He knew more of its history than anyone
from whom I'd tried to garner facts, and spoke it all
with such pert earnestness and genuine sincerity
that I'd have loved to wrap him up and bring him home with me.

Wee, precious Loza, daughter of the man who watched our camp
In Mexico some thirty years ago, amused herself
Intriguingly, concocting games with rocks and flowers for hours
Upon the gritty drabness of her patio; just two feet tall,
Each part of her sweet body was a perfect miniature,
Her doll-size face aglow with smiles, pixie-like but pure.

Beyond Taksindu Pass, when I traversed across Nepal,
A girl, whose age and origin I could not guess, appeared
Mysteriously along the trail, and for an hour held hands
With me; with but few words, just warming touch of flesh
And charmed caress of eyes, we stepped along.... A gift of orange
A camera's click...a firmer clasp of hands...a final clinging look...
A fleeting wave...and she was gone.... Still haunted by that face,
I fancy she might well have been the object of my quest--
A princess from Pan's realm enrobed in ragged, homespun dress.

Preparing to walk through Peru's great Vilcabamba Range,
We rode a boxcar on a peasant train, which is the only
Means of travel down the Urubamba Valley to the
Trailhead at the isolated village, St. Teresa.
There we loaded animals with dunnage and equipment
To begin our week-long passage through high ice-encrusted towers.
Incredibly, what I remember most distinctively
From what would seem to be the most unique adventure of
A lifetime, are the faces of a lovely girl and boy,
Who suddenly appeared to earn themselves, unknowingly,
A portion of a passing mountaineer's biography.

A lot of children gathered 'round as we began to load
The line of horses for that premier Vilcabamba trek,
But one surpassing bonny girl with neck-length raven curls,
Apparelled in red sweater over floral-patterned dress,
Drew close and seemed to fix her pleasant, guileless, ebon eyes
On me alone. I spoke to her and soon was quite impressed
With her intelligence and quality of Spanish speech,
For often in the Andean hinterland the Quechua tongue
Alone is known. That stunning child had singled me as leader
Of the group, and asked me many questions as to where we'd
Traveled from, and why we wished to go into those realms
Of hanging ice, then listened to my answers with her face
A portrait of sheer wonderment and undiluted trust,
Yearning to behold the wide world's marvels one fine day,
Unconscious of the pristine beauty she for me portrayed.

As we approached our highest camp, before the highland pass
Close by the fluted ice of more than twenty-thousand-foot-high
Salcantay, we had to find a way across a mammoth swamp;
Just then a brilliant boy, remarkably polite, emerged,
In midst of all that vast expanse of thin air wilderness,
With offer of his services to guide us through the bog
The least boot-soaking way. Dear Juan Trujillo, nine years old,
A child of that unpeopled, starkly-sculpted Andean clime,
Exemplified what children everywhere might well be taught:
Awareness of environment--courage to face up to change--
Self-reliance, and willingness to aid at vital need,
Without demanding pay--to show respect and courtesy--
And every day go forth in quest of fresh discovery.

"Where will you go, my afternoon,
    That glints so still and swift away,
Blue-shaded like a ship of light
    Bound outward from a wimpled bay?"
                            --Edith Wyatt

Sevilla--City of Reflections (Spain)

Among the sundry splendors and exceptionalities
That I've experienced while exploring a variety
Of foreign nations, perhaps the most impressively
Anomalous was fathoming Seville in Holy Week.

Two times I guided groups of students there to see the rare
Processions through the streets of a hundred slowly
Moving floats depicting episodes of Jesus' Passion.
Confraternities of every parish had created
Their own versions of some aspect of the drama, from "Pilate's
Washing of His Hands" through "Christ's Last Agony upon the Cross."

It was, indeed, a stirring thing to stand among the throngs
That lined the narrow streets and watch the great unwieldly floats,
Which weigh four thousand pounds and more, move at tortoise pace,
Uplifted on the shoulders of some fifty men, who bore
Their awesome burden maybe half a block...until its tonnage
Ground them to fatigue. Immediately another group of
Pious parish laborers assumed their places underneath
The venerated icons, then strained to lift and carry
Them to fullest range of their combined capacities....

The jeweled "Madonnas" riding by wore gold or silver crowns,
And gold-embroidered blue or pure white grand-scale velvet gowns;
The floats were framed with polished woods, or gold-leaf paneling,
Blanketed with fresh white rose or red carnation drapery,
And outlined with tall gold or silver candelabra rows,
Which, lit at night, created a detached unearthly glow.

Preceding each and every creeping-halting tableau marched
A guard of uniformed musicians piping dirges on their
Trumpets, to the slow beat of the drummers; these were followed
By a fearsome troop of "penitentes", sandalled or bare-footed,
Holding flickering candles, faceless in their tall black cone-shaped
Hoods to symbolize Christ's passion and humility;
"Saetas" (mourning songs) were heard from wrought-iron balconies,
While "sidewalk penitents" consoled themselves with food and brandy.

On and on all week those dazzling floats and baleful hosts
Laboriously processed...but there were countless other lures
Seville held out to tempt and snare attentive visitants--
To entertain or to enlighten seekers such as us,
Within her labyrinth of tiny squares and twisting lanes,
At times so narrow lovers on their balconies could "kiss
Across the street".... Quite early on we went to climb the Moors'
Renowned Giralda Tower, on top of which the Christians built
A graceful belfry, sealing its transcendence over all
The spires of Spain.

Breathlessly we stood among the grand array
Of master bells (some twenty-five in all, from great to small),
Which toll their hourly signature on every common day,
Then every Easter ring a splendid signal serenade.

From that high choir we scanned the features of a city which
Survived more than two thousand years of spiritual as well
As worldly change, and gazed far down upon the maze of lesser towers
And fancy fenced-in roofs and domes of "the largest medieval
Church in all the world." Then down...down...down...we circled 'round
And entered through the Orange Grove Patio and Gate of Pardon
To a vast complexity of ornate naves and chapels...
Of tombs of kings and saints...of ecclesiastical treasures...
Of priceless brushed and sculpted masterpieces of the great
Creators of accumulating centuries...much too much for
Even Unitarians, or amateur historians,
Or faithful lovers of the arts to hope to comprehend
Within allotted time.... We concentrated on the Gothic
Choir-stalls and organ, surrounded by a handsomely carved screen...
Sought out the grave of King Alfonse the Wise...the rare old books
And manuscripts of the Columbus Library...and last,
The great bronze tomb which holds the bones of "The Discoverer,"
Whose bold adventures out across the unknown western sea
Restored Seville to eminence in trade prosperity.

Outside, perusing through the starkly whited, coolly shaded,
Time-defying quarters of this perfumed, amorous city,
With its wrought-iron balconies projecting overhead, we were
Seduced to visualize Friar Tirso de Molino's slick
Don Juan, the world's most infamous seducer, climbing up
To claim his thousandth conquest; we even thought we heard
The strains of Mozart's Giovanni, or Rosinni's Barber
Resonating through the mix of Holy Week festivity;
And as we paused beside the old-new university,
Converted from a factory where once cigars were rolled,
We fancied that we saw a dozen Carmens in the striking
Dark-eyed beauties passing by, for there Bizet discovered
Both the heroine and the setting for this masterpiece
Of Spanish dance, impassioned voice, and fatal jealousy....

A gripping spectacle of all the region's finest dancing
Was in store for us that evening in a theater-cabaret,
Which specialized in exhibitions of Flamenco and
The Cante Hondo of the Andalucian Gypsy heritage.
Our senses were intensely stirred and stretched to comprehend
Tall handsome graceful tight-clad men, creating complex
Rhythmic patterns in the clapping of their hands and the stamping
Of their feet, with vibrant damsels, dressed in dazzling
Ruffled wide-tiered gowns, whirling vigorously and clacking
Castenets, while high-pitched voices and endowed guitarists
Synchronized uncommon sounds and passionate narrations,
Accelerating by degrees up to a frenzied gaiety,
Which seemed at times to reach a wild unharnessed ecstasy,
And other times evolved to anguished cries of hopeless agony.

Next morning we appraised the lovely rooms and courtyards of
The old Alcázar, founded by the Moorish kings--later altered
By successive Christian monarchs--but still retaining much
Of the Mudéjar-Arab style, using oft-repeated
Geometric patterns or refined designs of flowers,
With inscriptions praising "Allah" in the art of inlaid tiles.
My favorite was a garden-patio, where almond trees
Were blooming full, reminding me once more of what I'd had
My Spanish students read--a tale set in this very palace:
It rarely snows in southern Spain, but in a February
Long ago a monarch's favored wife was very thrilled to see
This rare phenomenon occur, and afterwards bewailed
Before her husband that such beauty really ought to be
A part of every year. Not wanting his beloved to lack
A single thing that brought her joy, the king ingeniously
Conceived a way to satisfy her wish. Almond trees
Were planted in and all around the palace so that she
Could savor seeing petal snowflakes falling every spring.

One afternoon we walked among the fountains, colored tiles,
And flower-rimmed reflecting pools of the Delicias Garden
And María-Louisa Park, redesigned some years ago
To integrate the grand pavillions of the notable
Ibero-Panamerican Fair of which Seville was host.
Each Spanish-speaking country fashioned self-styled structures the
To house exhibits; later these became their embassies.
The Plaza de España was the "premio gordo" of
The scene, with its expansive semi-circular arcade
Designed to highlight towers resembling the renowned Giralda;
But even more amazing were incredibly complex
Mosaics, done in tile, of maps and some outstanding
Feature or historic episode of each and every
Province of Iberia. We contemplated every one,
Incredulous at what great minds and hands had done.

One final evening, promenading on the fabled banks
Of the calm Guadálquivír, we crossed San Telmo Bridge
To gain the eastern side, then ambled south until we found
An outside restaurant close by the water's edge, and just
Across the river from the emblematic Tower of Gold.
Feeling keenly the quintessence of romance, we relished the
Perfection of the setting and the savory Paella
(Vegetables and seafood mixed in rice) and Manzanilla
(Sevilla's wine of choice), reminiscing all the while
About the fascinating cornucopia of sites
And sounds of history, as well as past and present culture
We'd experienced that Holy Week in singular Seville.
We gazed across the river which has been an avenue
Of trade throughout the world, and focused on the gilded tower-
An outpost of the ramparts built to guard the harbor long
Ago.

Apparently a chain was fixed to it and stretched
Across the river to another tower, which must have stood
Nearby to where we dined. Aware our holiday in Spain
Would soon be ending, we felt a mist of bittersweet
Nostalgia cross our eyes, as the storied city's silver lights,
And the glowing image of its trademark Golden Tower,
Trembled in the moving water and in our recollections...
A vintage parting vision of that "City of Reflections."

Interlude on the Isle of Birds (Spain)

In Seville's Mari'a Luisa Park, we came upon a plaque with a stirring exhortation to protect our feathered friends. As we were reading it, we were startled by a unique sound and looked up to see a gorgeous peacock striking his most glorious sunburst mating pose.

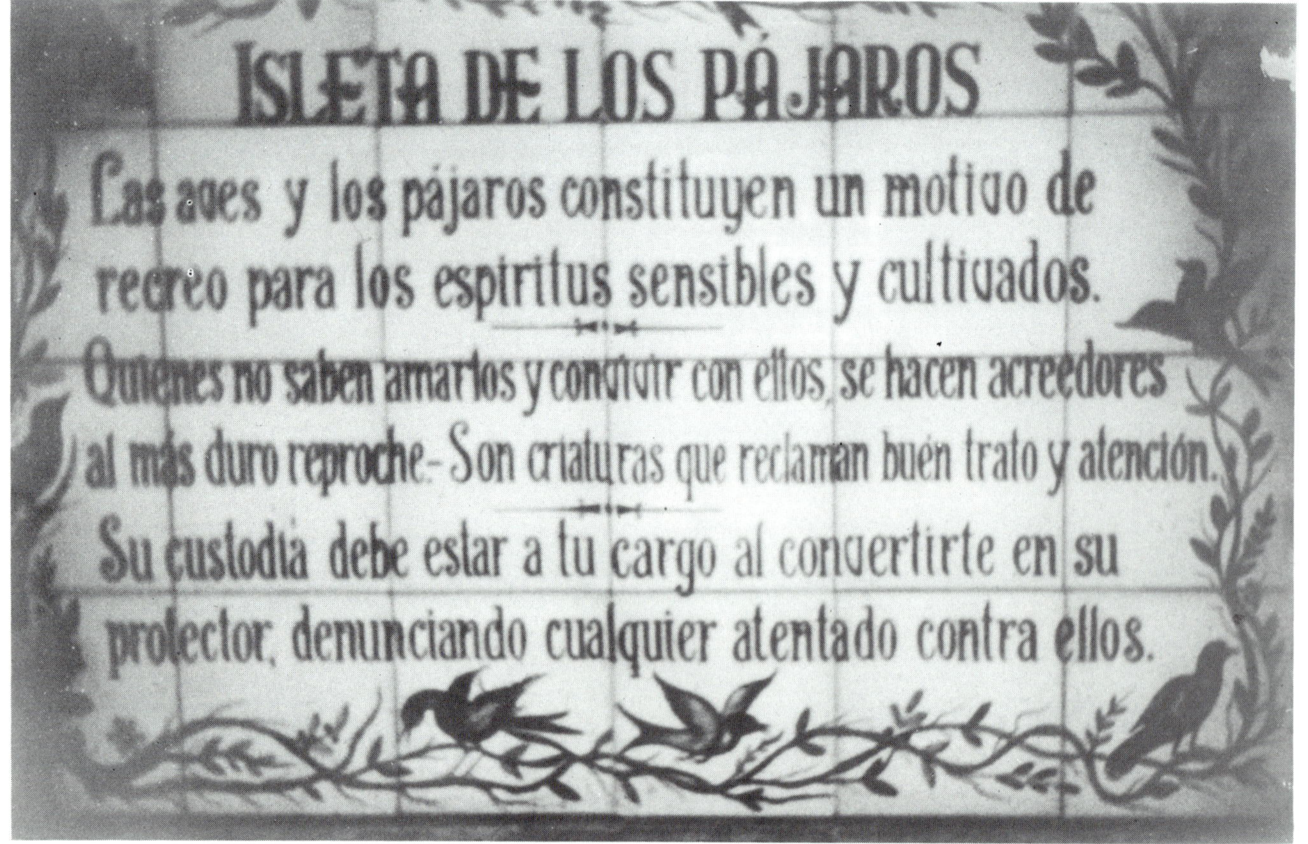

"Our feathered friends provide a recreational inspiration for sensitive and cultured spirits. Those who cannot find it in their hearts to love them and live with them deserve the harshest reproach. These dependent beings merit kind treatment and attention. You must be their custodians, repelling any assault against them."

(Japan)

Monumental

(Perú)

Odysseys

(Spain)

Roaming the Islands

of the Rising Sun

(Japan)

Drenching Flesh and Mind unto Satiety

Despite the understandable propensity of vet
Americans to caricature all Japanese with traits
Resembling those which their misguided leaders had displayed
In instigating the iniquities of World War Two,
I found myself quite captivated by the people
And their customs, when, in later years, I had a chance to
Be enlightened on a varied six-weeks odyssey
Through many regions of the Islands of the Rising Sun.
The slender, healthy, bright-eyed, and responsive human beings I
Encountered in the shops and on the sidewalks of the cities,
And in the villages and byways of the provinces,
Did not in any sense resemble war's revoltingly
Grotesque impressions of a ruthless enemy.

The service folk and steward at Atami-so (the small
Japan-style inn where we first stayed), quite near the Kábukízu
Theater in the Ginza Section of mid-Tokyo, were
Most sincerely courteous and helpful, as were the staffs
In all the charming ryokans where we were lodged in towns,
Or rural settings, or in mountain huts; sociable, but -
Mindful of my privacy, they unobtrusively conveyed
To me the grace and beauty of their oriental ways.

I was intrigued by customs such as taking off one's shoes
At the threshold of the inn, and replacing them with slippers
To ensure clean floors within...or soaking in the comfort of
Embellished baths, immersed up to the neck in liquid heat
To soothe tense psyches and tired muscles after taxing days...
Or sitting, pillowed on the floor, cross-legged in Buddha postu
Clad in nothing more than loosely-fitting cotton robes
They call "yukatas", eating supper meditatively
From little tables on which dainty covered dishes have
Been temptingly arranged...then afterwards, especially
On hot and humid summer nights, strolling through the towns
Apparelled only in those same unbinding coverings,
Refreshed from bottom up with nothing intervening.

Although the service and procedures in all ryokans
Were similar, each one played up some feature which distinguished
It from every other, such as entranceway, or garden,
Pond for fish, or meditation-corner of each room
Where one could contemplate aesthetic objects artfully
Arranged.... But for me the most rewarding of commodities
Were the hot spring tubs, each with a singularity of style,
Inventive in both structure and in patterns of its tiles.

Perhaps the most elaborate of all the dream-built pools
 I luxuriated in was the pride of Ayusato
Ryokan, in the scenic river town of Hitoyoshi,
On the Island of Kyushu. It was designed as a
Water-bottomed grotto, with stalactites hanging from
The ceiling, and with walls displaying variations of
Authentic cavern rocks and fancifully patterned
Tile mosaics. Investigatingly, I slowly waded
Through a series of uniquely-fashioned basins, each with
Water heated to a slightly higher temperature than that
Just left; there was a sense of exploration in rounding
Each new bend, and sampling hotter water in successive pools.
A pathway ledge, smooth-surfaced with a bright collage of tiles,
Allowed an exit any time the water might become
Too hot to stand; but, liking the keen sensuality
That trembled just this side the realm of pain, I persisted
There in simmering bliss, watching giant goldfish randomly
Creating mobile art within a huge aquarium,
Which framed the terminus of that compelling entity,
Designed to drench both flesh and mind unto satiety.

Uncommon Sounds

in

Unaccustomed Places

The music of traditional Japan can still be heard
In folk theatricals, court dances, or at festivals;
With chant-like narratives, accompanied by percussive music
Of the samisen, and gongs or drums, its somber, somewhat
Dissonant progression sounds quite tuneless when first heard by
Western ears. I found, however, that I grew to like its
Quaint and meditative strains the more I was exposed to it,
As we were entertained at old-style inns by serving maids,
At formal temple rituals, and even by a charming
Girl, kimona-clad, who rendered songs in high-pitched voice,
While all the while the rest of us, with drumming heartbeats,
Concentrated on the thrashing Kuma River Rapids,
Which we were boldly running in old-fashioned wooden boats,
A drama vastly heightened by her coloratura notes.

Concerto Grosso of an Empire's Past

antique architecture of Japan is well preserved
ughout the realm, in Buddhist temples, Shinto shrines, and
ed, multi-storied feudal castles. Distinguished by their
ing roofs, they range from rather simple thatch-topped frames,
ed by Shinto nature-worshippers, to quite imposing
dhist structures, similar to Chinese styles which vary
in size and in embellishment. Primarily of wood,
frequently have been destroyed by fire, and then rebuilt
erve as monuments of history.... Whatever road
ollowed in our exploration of Japan, it always
ed to lead to one of these, and then, inevitably,
neditative gardens which surrounded them with peace.

ed, so closely tied together were the edifice
garden that they seemed to be a part of one another;
sed and pondered this most notably in those designed
ouse the ancient ceremony of preparing tea;
had a feel of openness, to bring the outside in
best perspectives of judicious master gardening,
ch has been shaped and nursed to present beauty through the art
power of Man and Nature acting out their needed parts.

aku-ji, Kyoto's Gold Pavilion, was such a
ouse, built in thirteen ninety-seven by the ruling
ernor, then made a Buddhist temple at his death.
appily, in recent times, a malcontented priest
on fire, was sent to prison, and his sorrowing mother
committed suicide. Golden Temple, a novel by
ima, documents that melancholy tale.... I felt
rking tinge of pathos, thinking of the fragile thread
which both art and life are hung, even as I watched the
en image of that resurrected teahouse shimmer on
almost peaceful surface of the shrine's reflecting pond.

to, capital of old Japan, has been refined
a grand repository of the nation's art,
ious shrines, and palaces--the work of emperors,
ed craftsman, artists, priests, and poets for a thousand years.
mes, inevitably, those priceless heirlooms were
royed by fire, but always with fidelity renewed,
happily, preserved from bombing during World War Two.
ite of milling tourists, and a few incongruous
comitants of modern life, it was a place where I
ld fairly breathe the subtle substance of antiquity,
gather elements of minds that once sought harmony.

his antique Imperial Palace complex, in the
hin-den's historic Ceremonial Hall, each chosen
eror still comes for coronation. On these same grounds
antiquated high-roofed Residential Hall, scene of poetry
ivals in ages past, is kept in good repair
oster preservation of that rare vocation there.

Poetic were my thoughts, though unarticulated, as
I ambled over arch-shaped bridges or beside still ponds
Within the royal gardens…and later at the Heian Shrine,
Vermilion-tinted smaller version of the first Imperial
Palace of Kyoto, where white-garbed priests, and designated
Shinto virgins, dressed in scarlet skirts and snow-white blouses
(Symbolizing Shinto-valued cleanliness and purity),
Add their human loveliness to gardens flush with cherry
Blossoms, iris, and fine lotus blooms in season, and leaves
Of maple flame in fall, when couples choose that sacred place
As setting where they take their vows to live in wedded grace.

Sanju-san-gen-do, Hall of Thirty-three, was planned to have
That very number of auspicious spaces in between the
Pillars which uphold the sweeping roof of the longest wooden
Temple in the world. Conceived by Emperor Goshirakawa,
A pious devotee of the Tendai Buddhist sect in
Eleven sixty-four, he wished to spread the peace of Buddha
In his realm. Although I normally am less impressed with
Florid art than that which shows restraint, I must confess
To being overwhelmed with deep aesthetic sentiments
While passing through this temple, where the Mercy Goddess,
Is enshrined with a thousand portrait statue replicas,   Kwan-non
All standing as in choral ranks, with the exact benign
Expression of her countenance securely fixed on each
And every face. Superbly carved from wood, then covered with
Gold leaf, the saintly counterparts all have a dozen heads
In miniature above their own to multiply their wisdom, and
Some twenty pairs of hands in all directions so that they
May minister to those who suffer human miseries.
Outside, I felt a more exciting surge of sentiment,
Surveying the three-hundred-ninety-foot-long porch, on which
The archer-monks would test their skills to strike a target at
The other end. They must have shot with bows quite powerful
To send the arrows toward the distant mark with accuracy,
Yet keep their loft beneath the overhanging canopy.

Another day I walked the winding street where pottery
Is consummately made, then up a hundred forty-four
Ascending steps to enter Kiyomizu Shrine, where tufts
Of paper prayers were tied to trees by penitents. To cleanse
Their sins, they washed their hands in vats of sacred water ere
They entered through the torii, and, to gain long life, they drank

From three down-spouting springs nearby the towering central shrine.
I joined these rituals as good symbolic acts, and also
Struck gigantic gongs suspended overhead at altars,
Grasping with both hands the giant cords to swing the hammers
Forward, thus eliciting low trembling sounds. The shrine's
Most salient feature was a hundred-foot-high balcony,
Supported by a row of monstrous trunks of ancient trees,
Below which streamed the three blest waterfalls, perpetually.

A Hymn of Murmuring Solitude

I entered slowly through tall gates of sculpted hedge
On well-groomed gravel-bedded path, my crunching steps
Composing throaty bass clef counterpoint, beneath
High treble melody of full cicada rasp.
Ginkaku-ji Pavilion, treasured Silver Shrine,
Which Shogun Yoshimasa built as villa in
The fifteen century, was willed to be a Zen
Sect temple at his death. His wish to have the Goddess
Mercy's lacquered room upstairs encased in silver leaf
Was never carried out, though his intent is not
Forgotten in the temple's name. Enshrined downstairs
Sits Jizo, God of Children, his thousand statues
Stationed as battalions guarding Buddhist young.

Inside the Todu tearoom edifice, I stood
Before the forward-looking founder's wooden image,
Robed in monk apparel, and tried to visualize
What deep experience had caused a general
To choose the path of meditation as a way
To seek enlightenment, which could be used to foster
Good relationships in life. Intuitively
I felt profound respect for such a man, as I
Immersed my thoughts and flesh in murmuring solitude
Of garden scenes of plants and pools, resting quietly,
Meditating in the vein of Zen philosophy.

The trees were manicured with careful Nippon craft,
Spaced out along the paths to grant their welcome shades
By day, or muted silhouettes by night. I passed
The Ginsha-dan, the Sea of Silver Sand, furrowed
To resemble ripples on the surface of a
Chinese lake when quiet thoughts and cloudless moonlight
Blend to make them glimmer on a summer night,
Like truth surmised in eyes of patient eremites.

Stone Lanterns

of

Antiquity

Established as Japan's first capital in seven ten,
Nara even antedates Kyoto as a cradle
Of the arts and literature. It was a novel
Episode to walk along the paths of the largest park
In all Japan, twelve hundred fifty acres, and to feed
Some of the multitude of sacred deer who freely roam
Among large trees, nourished principally by rice-cakes sold to
Willing visitors at stations on the Deer Park grounds.

It seems quite fitting that the largest park should also hold
The largest bronze-cast Buddha in the world--The Daibutsu,
Which weighs at least four hundred fifty tons, and rises
Over fifty feet in height. The building which it now
Inhabits was designed and built around it after it
Was cast. Japan's next largest bell, which nonetheless is called
"The Great", some twelve feet high and weighing almost fifty tons,
Is also part of Nara's pride, as is the Kofukuji--
A five-floors-high pagoda of the classic twilight past.

But for me the most impressive segment of that stroll
Along the paths of Nara's storied past was the avenue
By which one must approach Kasuga Wakamiya Shrine;

It's lined with some two thousand ancient lanterns carved from stone,
Each fashioned by its sculptor to a vision of design
Just his alone. The nearby new vermilion temple, with its
Thousand metal lanterns, lit two times each year, and where
Two comely girls danced gracefully for us with fans and bells,
Was pleasing to my eyes and ears, but what my soul desired most
I had to conjure in the darksome depths of history--
Two thousand flames aglow in those stone lanterns of antiquity.

An Album
of
Oriental Novelties

Along the coast of Noto's "dragon's head" Peninsula,
I did a double take on seeing rising from the surf
Two monstrous rocks linked by a spiral cord--Atágoíwa,
Married Rocks, which locals had with whimsicality
Tied together on a spree of Shinto ingenuity.

Osaka Castle's ghostly splendors glimmered in the night
Like the features of an aging Nippon emperor,
Walking on a pathway lighted by a row of mossy
Lanterns, dreaming of past days of undiminished majesty.

At a private supper in Kyoto's Juni-danya,
Inn of Thirteen Steps, using chopsticks and a copper charcoal
Brazier filled with boiling water, each one dipped his own thin
Bite-size slice of octopus or Chinese vegetables
Into a self-concocted sauce's seasoned subtleties,
And slowly savored each and every singularity.

At Beppu Hot Springs we perceived a kind of Yellowstone
In miniature, with boiling pools of fiery garnet-hue,
Or liquid emerald, transparent to profound degree,
And mud volcanoes brownish-red, bubbling ominously...
At last we came upon a crowd, waiting near a geyser cone
Which soon would make display, and joined them, apprehensively,
For that volcanic shape was really not that far away...
In time, just as "Old Faithful", it spewed its scalding fountain
High into the air, but here we felt more intimately
How close we stride to inner Earth's compressed intensity.

After riding hot and crowded trains all day from Toba
Through Nagoya to Sagami Bay, we plunged into the
Mammoth curling breakers of a beach near Yugawara,
Where the sable-tinted sand added visual novelty
To wild freewheeling bodysurfing sensuality.

Entering the body of the Kamakura Buddha,
As though it were a temple of his soul, we climbed a stairway
In his back to pulpit-lookout, from which we could behold
The inside of his "third-eye" forehead, where a miniature
Image of himself was facing us in meditative pose--
His "brain child", so to speak, exuding magnanimity--
The centerpiece of Buddha's thought, discovered unexpectedly.

An absolutely captivating vendor on the shore
Of Lake Hakone, carved and painted wooden whistles shaped
Like warbler birds with mobile beaks, and could produce uncanny
Imitations of their natural songs quite realistically,
Dazzling all who happened by with his rare virtuosity.

Proceeding through the green cathedral avenues of giant
Cryptomeria trees, still thriving due to many centuries
Of careful husbandry, we marveled at the sacred Nikko
Precincts, where all the most elaborate splendors that the
Orient's best architects and artists could conceive were
Concentrated in such dazzling scope of ornate temples
That our senses would have frayed from over-stimulation,
If those extreme embellishments had not been sited midst
The peace of ancient trees, pure mountain lakes, and water falling
Endlessly in Nature's soul-pervading sanctuary.

A friend of mine, who happened to be Japanese, once said
To me: "You can't say 'perfect' till you've been to Nikko Shrine."
As overwhelming as those masterworks of ultimate art
May be, accompanied by the stirring music of the
Kegon Waterfall, I think I would have still refrained from
Saying "perfect" till I neared the end of our long journey
Through Japan. At Matsushima's Thousand East Coast Islands,
I left historic Hotel Kanko in the cool fresh pre-dawn
Lightlessness, to reach Shrine Island well before the break of day...
In solitary moonless darkness, almost breathless with
Expectancy, I strained to see a tiny prophesy
Of coming day dimly line what had to be the farthest
Surface visible of the great Pacific Sea; slowly
New unprecendented shades of peach and rose began to tint
The turning-cobalt sky and mirror bay, as evergreens
Nearby became defined in silhouette, and foreground isles
Began to prove their individual identities.
Profoundly moved by that transcendent natural beauty,
I whispered "perfect!" Another day of promise had begun.
"How right", I thought, "that it is called Land of the Rising Sun."

Along the Ancient Highways of the Setting Sun (Perú)

Although my expeditions to Perú were mainly to
Explore the high white roof of its fantastic storehouse of
Untrodden ice-draped peaks, I also eagerly seized every
Opportunity to learn as much as possible of
The dramatic history, and quite amazing cultures,
Of the often star-crossed actors in that Theater of the Sun,
Who rose to dominance but were themselves then overrun.

Four thousand years ago fine handicrafts and agriculture
Were developing along those arid coastal plains beside
The great Pacific Sea, as can be witnessed if one takes the time
To visit Lima's well-planned archaeology museums.
Finest fabrics and ceramics of incomparable
Workmanship, as well as flawless specimens of gold and
Silver bracelets, earrings, crowns, and breastplates, indicate the
Great good taste and talents of those craftsmen of antiquity.
There's also proof they practiced surgical technology,
And mummified their dead with complex strategies, for these,
In their dry tombs, retained remarkable integrity.

y most compelling hour in witnessing their science and art
'as contemplating the incredible collection of
Iochica "huacos" (portrait pottery), which Señor Lorca
athered privately for his exceptional museum.
stood amazed before the stark reality of row
'n row of ancient faces, each one shaped distinctively,
ot just in features, but in mood and personality,
s though they were the work of up-to-date photography;
nd there were realistic renderings of animals,
nd plants, and battle scenes, and every detailed aspect of
heir private, work, or recreational activities:
hey left no secret unexemplified--even making love:
our unbridled generation, with its videos
nd movies rated Triple X, assumes it's blazing new
ncharted paths in human sexual activities,
should appraise the frank "erotic" renderings displayed
that museum, and learn that everything it thinks is new
'as fancied by that ancient tribe, then sampled and pursued.

A Place

of

Towering Mysteries

From Puno, on the shore of mammoth Titicaca Lake,
The highest in the world, where steamships navigate between
Bolivia and south Perú, we first sought out the most
Elusive monuments throughout the Andean Mountain Chain--
The massive "chullpas"--random tombs of closely-fitted stones
In form of towers that ring Umayo Lake; according to
Tradition, the peninsula called Sillustani, which
Extends almost across the eastern portion of the lake,
Was used as burial-ground for unnamed kingdom chiefs.
We climbed a seldom-traveled path to stand in quiet awe
In midst of those occult, unprecedented specter shapes,
Musing, as they seemed to do, on far-extending scenes of
Treeless lakeside landscapes; a deep archaic mystery,
Like that of England's Stonehenge, wrapped itself around our though
And sensibilities; indeed, we tried to conjure up
An image of the beings who'd designed and found the means
To raise those finely-jointed, interlocking rocks into
Round, overhanging towers, with emblems left in bas-relief....
Among those most imposing, cryptic pedestals of death,
In the lonely, brooding silence of that site's austerity,
We absorbed our deepest ever sense of great antiquity.

Life among the Reeds of Titicaca

Within Chucuito Bay, the westernmost extension of
Great Titicaca Lake, survives a native culture that's
Distinct from any other in Peru, and quite detached
From even regional authority. In world apart,
The Urus Indians have based their whole existence on
The vast "totora" reed-beds in the shallow northern portions
Of the bay. The stems of these rare "tótaráles" harbor
Chambered air, enabling them to float extensively before they
Waterlog or rot and have to be replaced. Each family
Constructs a private islet and upon it a low hut,
With both its walls and roof homemade from these amazing stalks.
Quite naturally, those fisherfolk have also fashioned "balsas"--
Light "totora boats" with sails of tied-together stems as well.
On these not only do they fish, but also journey out
To gather rushes periodically, then tow them to
Their floating platforms to replace the parts that need renewed.

In spite of their ingenius adapation to the rare
Environment to which the chain of life has fated them,
Improbably the Urus have believed themselves to be
The most unworthy of all tribes that they themselves have seen.
That is implicit in their name, which in their tongue means "lice";
They say the lake has been created by their women's tears....
Learning these sad facts, and feeling that a lack of basic
Education was responsible, some missionaries from
The Seventh Day Adventist Church conceived a plan whereby
They would attach a floating schoolhouse to an islet which
Would be accessible, so that the children could be brought
And taught to read and write, and to depict their novel life
Through art.... Nearby they built a monument that is unique
In all the world--one made of those same stalks, and based upon
An Urus reed canoe. With deep emotion, I absorbed
The moving words inscribed thereon: "To study and to stir
Self-interest--to arouse the dormant instincts of the race."
And now the dark-eyed children sell small cane canoes and art
To visitors, and feel real self-esteem stir in their hearts.

Unfathomed Incan Walls Held Us Enthralled

In Cuzco, capital of the expanding Incan world
(Until Pizarro's band of ruthless Spanish conquerors
Arrived to vanquish it and make the natives slaves), there were
So many sites and facts of history to see and learn
That we were dazzled morning, noon, and night for many days;
The winnowing of years, however, isolates a few
Outstanding memories, which must suffice to illustrate
That brimful treasury. We had such vivid feel for both
The Incan and the Spanish prints of history, as we
Meandered up and down old streets, still paved with Incan stones;
And everywhere we noticed solid Incan walls were used
As firm foundations for the Spanish structures built on top.
This was quite apparent where the fated Church of Saint
Domingo had been raised upon the very bottom walls
Of the Incan Temple of the Sun, whose gold-leafed hall had
Housed a large, thick disk of gold--the symbol of their god.
The Spanish thought to purge the pagan site with Catholic church,
But in a sense the pagan gods returned for their revenge:
In 1950 an horrendous earthquake tumbled down
The Church of Saint Domingo into ugly rubble piles.
By the time we went to see, they had cleared it all away
And started reconstruction; we marveled that the Incan base
Had thoroughly survived the quake--all fitted rocks in place.

For days those superhuman Incan walls held us enthralled,
As we then ventured out from Cuzco to surrounding sites,
Each with distinctive features and intriguing names:

Tambomacháy, a small but monumental wall of fine
Cut stone, with trapezoidal niches and an underground
Fresh-water spring that issues in twin spouts—once seemingly
A royal residence, now often called "The Inca's Bath".
Kenko's tantalizing hilltop amphitheater, with its
Single semi-circle wall of throne-like seats that face
A phallic-like erected rock, and massive monolith
Behind, which teems with enigmatic carvings on its top,
The meaning of which still perplexes archaeologists.
Ollántaytámbo, probably the most artistic fortress
I have ever seen, whose hard red polished multi-angled stones
Weigh up to fifty tons, and fit so perfectly against
Each other that a knifeblade cannot be inserted in
The joints between. Beyond the seeming unattainable reality
Of moving such enormous rocks extensive distances,
And shaping myriad sizes so precisely, the masons
Even patterned outer surfaces in such a way that they
Add beauty to the shadings in the changing light of day.

A Panoramic Pageant of the Sun

The most impressive megalithic structure of them all,
Sacsáyhuamán, was built to safeguard Cuzco from the north,
With three-tiered zigzag fortress walls extending east and west
Two thousand feet. When first I came upon that awesome scene,
I walked alone, and felt as miniscule as Gulliver
When he was lifted in a Brobdingnagian's monstrous hand--
Too overwhelmed to comprehend the magnitude of what
I there beheld--a structure seemingly miraculous,
Considering they lacked the tools of modern science to shape those
Stones, and giant cranes to lift them into place. When I returned
Some nine years hence, to share it with my wife, and to confirm
I had not just imagined such grand scale, a multitude
Of several hundred thousand Urubamba native souls
Covered every hillside, and every fortress-lookout rock,
With the brightly colored patterns of their homespun blanket frocks.

It was the Festival of Inti Raymi, and the very day
On which the stately Pageant of the Sun was dramatized.
We found strategic seats, and watched attentively as
Smartly-suited armies staged mock battles. Then, to weirdly
Beautiful accompaniment of high-pitched native flutes,
A line of human carriers filed by in colorful
And proud parade, bearing first the giant disk of gold,
Inscribed symbolically with flames and rays; the reigning Inca
Followed on his wheelless carriage-throne, preceding
Several former Incas, mummified and fully robed, preserved
To have a part in celebrations such as this. Then passed
The blue-gowned Virgins of the Sun--young maids of special grace
And beauty, chosen from throughout the realm to be the wives
And concubines of royalty, as well as to attend
At sacred functions. When that impressive retinue
Had passed its solemn course, an innocent white llama braved
The high priest's sacrificial knife, and so, presumably,
The God of Light was satisfied, and that vast throng was free
To celebrate, and watch the native dancers make display
Of self-styled skills and costumes to complete that "sun-filled" day.

As twilight dimmed that super vibrant scene, we started to
Descend the headlong slope toward Cuzco when, quite suddenly,
We found ourselves swept downward in an inundation of
Stampeding human beings; obliged to join the speeding
Wave, we had to struggle just to stay afloat--like swimming
In a stream of fast-cascading water. Determinedly,
I clutched my wife with vice-like grip to keep her at my side,
Fearing, if we faltered, we might sink beneath the tide....

An Elevated Scale

of Human Craftsmanship

Amazingly, we surfaced in the Plaza Principal,
Where elegant facades of Spanish-style cathedrals had
Been fashioned some four hundred years before on sites
Then occupied by Incan palaces....We slipped into
The one the Jesuits had built, called Compañia de Jesús,
To catch our breath, and ponder all the patiently refined
Accomplishments that we had seen of both the Incan and
The Spanish architects and artisans.... We'd scrutinized
This grand interior previously, as well as those
Of other Cuzco churches and religious cloisters which
The Catholic orders had been moved to raise and to appoint
With zealous overplay of wealth and pious workmanship.
In one of these, by sixteen ninety-six, an unnamed craftsman
Had devoted most of his creative life to carving
An enormous cedar pulpit of elaborate design,
With realistic figures of the four evangelists,
The blest Redeemer carrying the cross, and intricate
Creations of angelic heads and sainthood effigies--
All sculpted to the highest gauge of human artistry.

When our pulsating chests had slowed to normal rate, we rose
And went out to the plaza, where at once we came upon
A vendor with a set of chessmen that were deftly carved
From ebony and ivory, all markers having guise
Of Incan characters, with subtle llama heads instead
Of horseheads serving as the knights, and model Incan walls
As rooks. It was the very gift I'd searched for nine years back
To give my son, but couldn't find. I'd asked some Cuzco friends
If one could be secured; they hadn't known, but all agreed
It was a fine idea native carvers ought to heed.

Savoring the Sacred Valley of the Incas

To end this canticle to what I've learned and sampled of
Peru's rare history and culture during several summers
Searching there, I must make mention of a journey through
The Urubamba-Vilcanota Valley, which I made
In nineteen sixty-three, the year when Belaúnde was
Elected president in what apparently had been
A free and open demonstration of democracy.
To be in what had been the Incas' favored haunt (which they
referred to as "The Sacred Valley") surrounded by high
Glacier-mantled mountains rising steeply on both sides, would be
Fulfilling anytime; but to explore it in the very
Year when finally the nation really seemed to break the yoke
Of persistent autocratic rule, on the very day
Which marks historically the country's independence from
Hispanic rule, I deemed a monumental privilege. There was
Celebration—dancing and parading everywhere--
Laughing, singing, drinking "chicha"--hope was in the air.

In picturesque Pisác, we watched young children marching by,
And mayors from surrounding villages in ornate garb,
Who'd come to Sunday mass and market with long staffs
(their emblems of authority) in hand. For lunch we purchased
Golden-crusted bread from a bakery whose ovens have
Continuously supplied such loaves since it was founded
In the sixteenth century. In the town of Urubamba,
I acquired from a local maker a "charango"--
A mandolinlike instrument, which I surmised my daughter
Might find interesting to learn to play. Later, as I rode
The train on down the valley, an elderly Peruvian
Removed it from my backpack, tuned the strings proficiently,
And entertained us with his store of haunting highland tunes...
Till we reached his destination...much too soon, much too soon.

Returning from that Sunday sojourn in the Sacred Valley,
We were nearing Cuzco just as night began to fall;
When we'd reached the plateau's rim, from which the train would make
Its steep descent into the valley via switchbacks,
We were suddenly astonished to behold the giant
Letters VIVA EL PERU (LONG LIVE PERU) flaming on
An open mountain slope beyond the city's southern side.
The marchers bearing torches in the region's great parade,
To mark Peru's most optimistic Independence Day,
Had gone to place their torches where all citizens could see
That hopeful shining emblem of their new democracy.

A Vital Harmony with Sun and Snow

In morning light I've traced and climbed the long-lost Incan trail
That surreptitiously ascends the almost vertical
Escarpment of the mountain Huayna Picchu (The Young Height);
I used as handholds shrubs, whose rain-drenched growth of centuries
Had quite obscured the pathway up the ever steepening face,
And then I came upon surprising stairs, which robust
Incan artisans had sculpted into green-patínaed cliffs,
Or tunneled up through solid rock where ceilings blocked the way;
Now I am poised atop the very highest prominence
Of this exotic fort, unique among the multitude
Of peaks I've ventured on--terrace-hung, improbably,
For fearless farmers to perform their life-sustaining
Acrobatic work, enjoying godlike bird's-eye views,
From buttressed lookouts with such constant verticality
No foe could hope to solve their inaccessibility.

Below lies silent roofless Machu Picchu (The Old Height),
The lost, then unearthed city of dead Incan kings and slaves,
Mesmerizing in its saddled posture of the past,
Where scholar-priests could tie the Sun to stones by shadows cast.
I keenly sense the slow and aching movement of the rocks
And soil--the massive human toil erecting stones to stars--
The strategies and purposeful constructions patiently
Pursued with alloy-strengthened tools, reshaping rocks
To fashion habitations, temples, terraces, and stairs--
The never-ending plantings, harvestings, replenishings,
Guided by the shadows which their god, the cycling Sun,
Never failed to cast upon the Intihuatana stone,
The grand divining instrument their genius had enthroned--
Profound, creative, bold, magnificent, enduring works,
Ample to fill to overflow evoking minds with awe,
And even hold the finest current scientists enthralled.

Faint sounds from Urubamba's rapids rise two thousand feet
To tease my sense, as long ago they rose to Quechua ears,
And I look down, as sentinel eyes once did on all three sides,
Through slow-paced seasons of mid-morning's shifting shade and light,
To watch that mammoth serpent slide around this citadel's
Precipitous sides, bound to flood the mighty Amazon,
But nourishing in passing this unrivaled outpost scene
With basic life-maintaining rock-effacing evergreen.
I lift my eyes to scan the verdure-mantled ring of peaks,
And higher still to gaze where glacier-hanging summits rise.
They are this land's premier providers; in the high thin air
They birth the nourishment of bush, of corn, of herb,
Of llama fur, of man...and the Sun, great God of Inca kings,
Blends its vital warmth with the snow peaks in the scheme of things.

A Real-life Sense

of

What We'd Taught

For years my wife and I had taught the language, history,
And culture of this fabled land, where Celts, Iberians, Greeks,
Phoenicians, Carthaginians, Romans, Visigoths, and Moors...
Then ultimately Catholic zealots...all aspired and had
Their days of sun and shade, and left distinctive imprints on
Its complicated tapestry. From books alone we'd tried
To bring it all to life.... Now, finally, we'd come to see
Firsthand the glory that was Spain...to speak the language
Of Cervantes in the heart of Mancha's stark terrain, where first
It stirred within the author's teeming brain...to send Quijote
Riding forth to right the wrongs that seemed Unrightable...where he
And his creation stretched the bounds of their mortality....

The Glory Wheel of Spain Was Axeled Here

In retrospect of wild and fearsome airport-hotel drive,
We walked along Madrid's broad avenue of Alcalá,
Past mix of modern edifice and monument, in search
Of features pictured in our texts, and recognized at once
The Fountain of Cibeles, Goddess of the Land, aloft in
Lion-drawn chariot--the emblem of the capital of Spain...
Eventually we funneled to the flower-decked Puerta de
El Sol (Door of the Sun), which is the heart of both the city and
The Realm. From that bright crux all distances are measured,
And each day at noon all passersby adjust their watches to
The proper time, as counted by the state's official clock,
Positioned in a small but quite conspicuous tower, which,
As Spaniards phrase it, "drops its golden ball" right on the hour.

That hub of many streets (as well as subways now) has witnessed
History-making episodes, such as the common people's
Grand heroic effort to repel invading forces
Of Napoleon on May Second, eighteen hundred seven;
A famous artist, Goya, sketched the French atrocities
Firsthand, so generations hence would know the facts; and so
That date is celebrated as Spain's Independence Day.
Although we were not there on New Year's Eve, I thought of an
Intriguing reading in a text I used to use, which told how
People would assemble there and try to eat twelve grapes, while
That defining clock portentously tolled out the midnight hour;
If they downed all, the coming year would bring them luck and
                                                        power.

Not far away, within the labyrinth of narrow streets
That indicate the old part of Madrid, we came upon
What's called Plaza Mayor, which in the eighteenth century
Was literally the "major square", where public spectacles
Like bullfights, jousts, and the parades of royalty were held.
Nowadays it is a lovely place to promenade and look
In shops in hot midsummer hours, because on every side
It has wide arcades fully shaded from the burning sun.
We rested under one of these, slow-sipping lemonade,
Conversing with a courteous civil guard who had invited
Us to share his outside table. We loved the clarity
With which he spoke "Castillian", and were charmed especially
At hearing "TH-sounding Cs", instead of the familiar
Andalusian "S-sounds" we had learned and used in class.
I must confess that, even as he talked, I thought of how
Spain's greatest nineteenth century novelist, Pérez Galdós,
Quite possibly had rested at this very place, alone,
Conceiving future novels from the human interaction
He observed...or, other times, with stimulating group of friends,
Whose liberal brains were at the forefront of that epoch's thought,
Questioning the merits of the way strait-laced society
Was functioning--confronting prevalent hypocrisy--
Bravely criticizing ignorant religious bigotry.

When our nice guard took leave, we braved more narrow streets...
and found
The Royal Palace grounds, then spent an afternoon attempting
To absorb the absolutely overwhelming luxury
In which most Spanish monarchs were accustomed to reside
In their exalted times. Each step within the entrance staircase
Had been fashioned from a single block of marble fifteen feet
In width, and each of more than forty rooms seemed to have been
Designed to win a prize for grandeur over all the rest.
Imposing paintings, such as "Hercules in Company
With Lady Friends", adorned the vaulted ceilings, from which hung
Incredibly elaborate chandeliers; rich-colored
Tapestries of intricate detail, or thick upholsteries
With silver thread embroideries, or velvet hangings
Decorated with the royal portraits, and enormous
Mirrors framed in bronze and marble garnished all the walls, while
Rugs and patterned hardwoods equally ornate bedecked the floors.
The room we found most interesting was that in which eccentric
Charles the Fourth had gathered every kind of clock that human
Ingenuity and riches could devise and fabricate:
Large and small, silver, gold, or porcelain....from every clime...
They all still function, though, amusingly, they do not chime
In unity, but each one at its own "eccentric" time....

All in all, such royal excess, though promoting art,
Was much too much for our poor senses to assimilate,
Or minds to comprehend, the egotism and the
Flagrant self-indulgence of the kings and queens of history,
While common people labored all their lives to pay for it,
Believing that their souls, if not their bodies, would survive
Life's gross inequities, if only they kept hope alive.

One fortunate concomitant of Spanish royalty's
Great wealth was that the kings became enamored of
The finest artists of the Spanish Golden Age, as well
As those of other nationalities, and their collections
Formed the basis for what many deem to be the premier
Art museum in the world--The Prado of Madrid....
Custodians were watering the grass when we arrived
And ambled slowly toward the columned, statue-studded front
Facade, perplexed by the apparent dearth of visitors;

Emotions surged on entering the inner corridor, as
I exclaimed, "Why there's the ancient statue, Dama d'Elche,
Found in Southeast Spain, which Salvador Dalí, the noted
Spanish artist, has declared to be most beautiful of all
The ladies of the world ." Quite soon we found ourselves completely
Captivated by the most refined of portraits ever framed:
Murillo and El Greco, on and on, with neither glass
Nor barrier to intervene...those faces by Ribera
And Velázquez where like living souls, so consummately
Captured and interpreted that we expected them
To move...perhaps to speak: "My name is Arquimedes," or
"Hello, I'm that immortal gentleman who holds his hand
Across his chest." The dark-haired duchess lying on her pillows
At either end of Goya's lengthy room, clothed in soft sheer silk
At left, and fully nude in similar voluptuous pose
At right, does not need words to come alive; she stirs the blood
In masculine veins to passion such as her fond lover
Must have felt when he bequeathed her double immortality--
One for the private mind, and one to fit the manners of society.

Although this famed museum overflows with masterworks,
There is but one that merited a room all by itself--
"The Maids of Honor" (Las Meninas), which Velázquez
Painted in the family chambers of King Philip IV:
Uniquely, in the background of this grand-scale portrait of
The members of the royal family, the artist chose
To paint an image of himself while painting them. A mirror
Just the stature of the framing has been set so that the
Fancier might view the scene precisely as the artist did
While painting it. With keen emotion I observed the bright
Red cross depicted on the painter's sable vest, for I
Had many times narrated to my Spanish students how
It came to be: It's said the king was so inspired when he
Saw the painting that he seized the artist's brush and painted
On the master's chest the emblem of the Order of the
Knights of Santiago, the patron saint of Spain, St. James,
Thus adding that prestigious honor to Velázquez' fame.

Another day we stretched our legs along the pathways of
Retiro Park's three hundred fifty acres of delightful open
Space of lawns, and lakes, and formal gardens; inhalingly
We strolled among the Rosaleda's heady fragrances,
Deep-bending here and there to taste in close caress the red
And pink and yellow blooms that seemed especially inviting;
We also loitered where the literary greats kept bronze
Or marble pose, and found Jacinto Benevente's tribute
Most appealing: This statue was an actor holding near
His face a mask such as were used in old-time stylized plays,
When characters were types instead of individuals.
The author's major work, The Bonds of Interest, a satire
On duality of human nature, uses those old names,
Like Harlequen, Polichinelle, and Columbine, but
Skillfully transforms the principals to vital human
Beings, who through the power of love and compromise, survive
The conflicts that inevitably are part of every life.
We must remove our masks as does the statue, artfully,
And pull the proper threads if we would find sufficiency.

We both were deeply moved by that symbolic rendering,
And went to rest and meditate beside a novel lake
Whose other shore presents a priceless columned monument
To mortal kings; we pondered it and its reflected visage
Trembling on the water's surface, philosophizing that,
Confronted with dual images, it's sometimes difficult
To tell which shows a false facade, and which one's face is real.
The evening promenade began, when all the Spanish take
Relaxing strolls before the supper meal--when couples have
A chance to court, old friends converse, or just sit quietly,
Observing all who pass, as we then did attentively,
Trying to imagine what satiric comedies...
What melodramas...what momentous human tragedies...
Were throbbing underneath those passing masks, potentially?

A Salient Centerpiece of Legacy

Leaving behind Madrid's unsettling rushing traffic games,
We loved the narrow cobbled winding lanes Toledo keeps
Behind her ancient Roman walls. When first we came upon
The panoramic northern view of it, it did resemble
In some ways our oft-seen textbook version of El Greco's
Painting in the sixteenth century, with single-towered
Cathedral and Alcázar still assuming prominence
On its more crowded ancient hilltop scene…. I normally
Esteem cathedrals of the natural world above those raised
In elegance by human hands, but of the artificial
Ones I've seen, Toledo's has remained my favorite.
Its mammoth high-arched Gothic columns, fluted vertically
In perfectly designed proportions, made it possible
That such great scale could demonstrate the touch of graceful art;
This also was apparent in its finely toned rosette,
And other muted splendors of its tasteful stained-glass renderings.
Its transom in the ceiling, where angelic figures seem
To rise in dazzling thrust of light, creates illusion of
A window unto heaven…. All the cardinals of Spain
Are buried in this preferential place, their scarlet caps
Suspended from the ceiling just above their tombs. More
Appealing to our tastes was the trumpet Organ of the
Emperor, with its celestial front of bas-relief and
Arab alabaster frieze around the choir. Apparently
It's played infrequently, reserved for Corpus Christi Day or
Other special times, such as attendance of a pope or king….
Proceeding up the hill, we came upon the lofty-walled
Alcázar, fortress of Toledo through the centuries;
Reduced to piles of rubble in the Spanish Civil War,
It's been restored and now serves both as a museum,
And, with its defenders buried there, as mausoleum.

El Greco's home was personal for us who've shared his life
And art with student minds; we almost felt we had been there
Before, when in his workshop we observed the small clay figures
That he'd shaped to test the light and shadings he would use on
Future canvas portraitures; face to face we scrutinized
His versions of the twelve apostles, fancying we saw
A blink of eye or twitch of lip on those created faces,
Each of them distinctive, but, admittedly, they all were
Rather like self-portraits of the artist done in different moods.
Upstairs a modernistic artist was at work, trying
To recapture on his canvas the mysterious magic
Of El Greco's painting called "St. Peter's Tears"; whisperingly
We wondered, as we roamed downstairs into the spacious
Dining room, if he had ever entertained Miguel Cervantes there?
It certainly was possible, for they were close in age,
And Cervantes' residence at times was very near.
They might have listened to musicians play "romances" while
They dined, or shared philosophies while sipping vintage wines;
Through different means both sought to elevate humanity,
Pursuing their ideals of truth and beauty...peerlessly.

The Trumpets of Glory

Then Called Us to Ride

We found it hard to leave that crowded fame-enshrouded hill,
And lingered for another day, inhaling history,
Before we crossed the still strong Roman Bridge that spans the
Tajo River's timeless flow, and drove into the countryside,
With sounds of distant drums and trumpets calling us to ride.
The olive groves stretched soldier-like across the rolling plain,
Until we came upon, above Consuegra's slow-paced charm,
A hill with several silhouettes of windmills just restored
Against the legendary vastness of La Mancha's sky,
Beneath which Don Quijote rode his steed to destiny
In face of overwhelming odds and brutish mockery.

And even farther under legend's luring canopy,
We steered our little car along strange seldom-traveled ways
To find Toboso, village where Aldonza's vulgar shade
Was shaped in our knight's brain to Dulcinea's fancied fame.
Siesta was apparent when we crept into the town,
For not a living soul was seen against the lime-white walls,
Until the courtly mayor rose and came to welcome us...
To share the rarest room of books that we have ever seen:
More than a thousand versions of Cervantes' masterpiece
In almost every written language that is known to man--
Thumbed copies sent by famous persons over many years--
Prime first editions--others of mere pigmy size, or huge--
One copied patiently in beautiful archaic script,
With clever complementing sketches facing every page--
A hallowed tribute from some monastery artist-sage.

Our minds replete with contemplation of this priceless store
Of literary artistry and fame, we slowly walked
Together over tidy streets of weathered cobblestones,
And read familiar maxims from Cervantes' mind and pen:
"A person's home's his castle", or perhaps, "The man
Who rises with the dawn has one more hour of life",
Inscribed on whitewashed buildings that we passed; the mayor bore
In hand an iron key as grand as any lantern light;
The weathered wooden door that fronted Dulcinea's house
Responded to its grating turn; we entered as had she,
For all was neatly kept as it had been so long ago,
Through all the countless ticks and tocks of Time's adagio.

When finally we'd seen and felt its time-glossed thrust enough,
We went out in the yard where sits a marble figure of
A Spanish writer who once came to visit as had we;
Enamored of its charm, he chose to live there all his life....
Although he never married, he was loved by everyone
So much that, at his death, his fellow townsmen paid
To have his statue cast and made a part of where he'd lived;
And on the marble base they thus his name immortalized:
"España was the real-life Dulcinea that he prized".

Bread and Wine

for

Soul and Flesh

Perhaps because few travelers are motivated to
Adventure off the major routes to seek Toboso out,
The mayor and his family accommodated us
As though we were celebrities, or long-time friends with whom
They had not visited in years. Taking leave of them with
Realization that we might not ever have a chance
To meet again was quite emotional. Their daughter cried;
My wife spontaneously removed her rhinestone necklace, and
Bequeathed it to the girl as emblem of our amity--
A sparkling tribute to their innate cordiality.

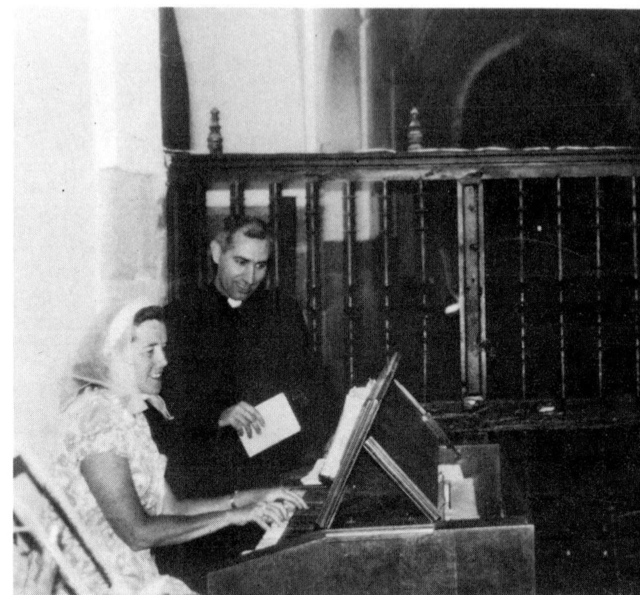

The mayor firmly recommended that, while heading south
Toward Córdoba, we must not fail to tour a vineyard and
Its winery at Valdepeñas, where, in his opinion,
They produce the finest wines in all of Spain. As an alluring
Lodging on the way, we chose Alcázar de San Juan,
Quite possibly the birthplace of Miguel Cervantes--
A village with a church eight hundred years of age,
A Roman tower, and empty wine vats in its public square....
When we stepped in the church, our ears and all the empty pews
Reverberated with a burst of organ harmonies,
As though a ghost of Bach were waiting there to pipe a hymn
Of welcome just for us; it stopped as we walked up the aisle,
And then a deep bass voice, as though from overhead, said:
"Buenos días. Bienvenidos." (Welcome.) A youthful priest
Was at the console of the tractor organ, smiling, beckoning...
In that medieval church, in the language of Cervantes,
A most exhilarating conversation then ensued.
We were amazed to hear exceedingly advanced ideas
Ably stated--that religion should concern itself with
Solving human problems of this world in which we find ourselves,
Rather than with worshipping a hoped-for heaven beyond the grave.
Learning that my wife had been an organist, he asked if
She would like to try their agéd instrument, and while she played,
That young-wise new-made Spanish friend and I sang hymns of prais
To "meetings of like minds" on "the very best of days."

uch stimulating chance encounters were the bread that fed
Our spirits throughout Spain, while crunchy golden-crusted rolls
And fruity wines, abundantly available at every
Noon and evening meal, satisfied our bodies' needs.
For lunch next day we visisted the Inn at Puerto Lápicé,
Where legend says Quijote first beheld a surly serving
Girl, Aldonza, transformed her in his upward-looking brain
To Lady Dulcinea, and placed her on a pedestal
As feminine ideal of beauty and nobility....
Once more we fueled our bodies with the fresh-baked golden bread
And the celebrated crimson blood of Manchan grapes...
And there was "spirit food" as well, encountering the bronze
And human figures there, and dream-quest ghosts that linger on....

By early afternoon, we scanned the endless vineyards that
Surrounded Valdepeñas, fountain of the wine of kings

And queens, and mayors and their townsmen, too. Once in the town,
We chose La Invencible as the winery that we
Would see, for seemingly the name implied the choicest of
The best of Spain. A retiree with weathered countenance
And winsome wit, José Fernández, came to welcome us
And be our guide; with typical beret on head and cup
In hand, and with his darling niece along as chaperon,
He led us deftly through the varied levels of a maze
Of giant vats three stories high, explaining in detail
Precisely how much each contained, and what degree of aging
Each had reached. The ritual before we left each section

Was that he would first remove the wicker cover of a vat,
Then reach inside to fill his cup with wine. He'd take a sip,
A glow of total rapture spreading on his ruddy face
To dramatize how good it was, then pass it round for each
Of us to sample, too; intently he would scrutinize
Our faces to assess each one's reaction. Always I
Would be the last to get the cup, still halfway filled, and was
Obliged to empty it for each new section's sequent test...
When we at last had reached the wine of greatest age and worth,
Beneath a thick formation of impenetrable rock,
I felt as though my feet had severed contact with the floor--
That I was floating more than walking when we reached the
                                        exit door.

A Poet's Dream
of Paradise

My feet were back on earth next day, but thoughts were far away
As we drew near to Córdoba, for I was thinking of
My Spanish students and the stories I had shared with them
About that charming city as it was a thousand years ago…
The Moors had crossed Gibraltar's Straits two hundred fifty years
Before, and in a mere six years were dominant in most
Of Spain. Fanatical and brutal Christian armies from
The northern provinces fought for centuries to take it back.
In fact, the life and culture which the Moors installed was far
Superior to any found in Europe in that age:
They honored honest merchants, were skilled in arts and crafts, and m
Importantly, were tolerant of other faiths and styles.
While many Christian rulers in the north of Spain couldn't
Even read or write, the Moors established universities
Where students studied law, philosophy, geography,
Astronomy, mathematics, medicine, and poetry….

One story that we used told how a Moorish Sultan sent
His doctors up to cure the Christian monarch of León,
Who had become so fat he couldn't walk. A student from
That austere province journeyed all the way to Córdoba,
Which in that epoch frequently was called "Pearl of the World".
It tells how he proceeds along a street where sweet intense
Aromas of fresh blooming roses and magnolias tease
His senses from behind fine wrought-iron lattices and walls
Of marble mansions. He pauses for a subtle moment
When he spies a lovely face behind a window's grating
Watching him, then ambles on romantically, approaching
The Mezquita (A moslem mosque as grand as any in
The Arab world), aware that every Friday on that path
Lush oriental rugs are spread before the Sultan comes
To pray. Our Christian student passes through "The Courtyard of the
Orange Trees", where worshippers are washing in a cleansing fountain
Prior to entering the mosque. He shares that goodly ritual,
Goes through the door, and finds himself afoot within a virtual
Forest of trunk-columns holding arches overhead,
Alternating crimson bricks with polished marble blocks.

ound the base of one of these, our student sees a group
scholars, lighted by a lamp refashioned from a Christian bell;
e youth is reading from a large attractive book a poet's
tasy of Paradise that every faithful follower
Islam can someday expect to see. It speaks of
er olive groves, a warming sun, clear lakelets brimmed
th lotus blooms, pervasive perfumes of a million flowers
fted by congenial zephyrs over private fresh retreats
ere women of surpassing loveliness await a poet-
tor who can stimulate their intellects as well as
the passions of romance.... The lector raised his eyes
d said to our young Christian: "We are reading what a poet
s the faithful may anticipate in Paradise."
ut why seek it in books?" our student asks. "Do you not realize
at living here is Córdoba you <u>are</u> in Paradise?"

PERSECUCION...DESTIERRO...MEDICINA...FILOSOFIA

	Though Córdoba's cathedral-mosque, with all its splendrous remnants	
	Of its Moorish-Catholic past was quite prodigious to explore,	
	Another singularity of that historic town	
Guía	Which curiously arrested our attention even more	*Libro*
	Was the haunting Jewish Quarter where the great physician	
	And philosopher, Maimónides, tutored by his father	
de	In astronomy and math, began his epic odyssey	*de*
	To ultimate medieval eminence in medicine	
Perplejos	And scholarship. Perhaps because his family was exiled	*Preceptos*
	By fanatical religionists, he labored long and hard	
	To leave a model legacy of written words and deeds,	
	Which wisely reconciled the "faith" of Hebrew orthodoxy	
	With "reason" stressed in Aristotle's Greek philosophy.	

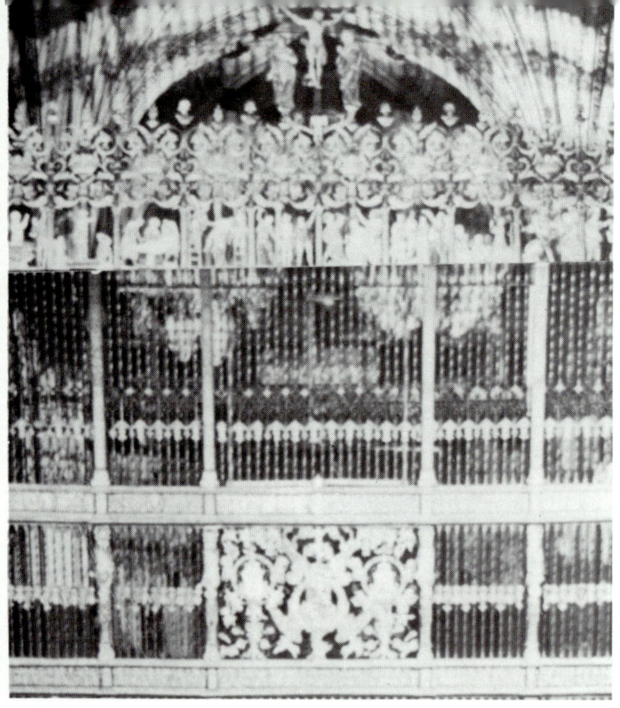

Our Quest for Truth and Beauty

Lingered Here

The "student from León" found paradise in Córdoba,
But we chose not to bind ourselves until our quest for truth
And beauty brought us to Granada's consummation of
The finest Moorish culture, nestled at the foot of the
Nevada (Snowy) Range in southern Spain, as a poet said:
"Like a teardrop on time's eyelid", though it's difficult to know
Whether it's a tear of joy or a tear of sorrow....
At that surpassing site, the armies of Spain's premier rulers,
Ferdinand and Isabel, in fourteen ninety-two,
Completed the expulsion of the Moors from Spanish soil,
After more than seven centuries of Islam dominance;
And, unbelievably, within that very place and year,
Columbus gained the blessing and assistance of the queen
To launch his little ships across the fearsome western sea's
Mysterious reach, and change the world's perspectives crucially.

The Catholic monarchs grew to love Granada's qualities
So much they chose it as their residence and final place;
When Isabella died, her husband had a lovely Gothic
Royal Chapel raised, whose entrance now is found within the
Grand cathedral. We stepped into the so-called "Christian heart"
Aware that overhead the royal emblem, "yoke and arrows",
Signifying "strength and union", were engraved. Gazing through
A wrought-iron screen, we pondered the reclining effigies, carved
From white Italian marble, and then, with solemn steps,
Descended stairs leading underneath to where the bodies
Of the history-making pair lie sealed in leaden coffins.
I must confess that, as I stood there contemplating death's
Irrevocable grasp, I pictured skeletons (the same
Return to bones and dust as commoners in earth), instead
Of noble bodies, in those royal boxes of the dead.

More beguiling to our instincts was the harmony of
Man and Nature we experienced when we roamed through the
Incomparable Alhambra--the "heart of beauty" fashioned by
The practiced artisans of pleasure-loving Moorish kings:

Intricately latticed windows looking <u>out</u> on spacious scenes,
Or <u>in</u> on patios with delicately carved arcades...
Aromatic oils to enhance one's steps through doorways...
Myrtle trees and fragrant flowers, bordering reflecting pools...
Lavender wisteria draping walls or barbered hedges...
And water everywhere, running down the bannisters,
Brimming basins, spouting from the mouths of carved-stone lions,
Devised to run perpetually by gravity alone.

Those lions were, in fact, the guardians of a central courtyard,
Positioned in between the "legal wife's abode" and
"The favorite concubine's retreat". We lingered there awhile,
Musing on that "kingly" living style...being overwhelmed
By such a maze of arch and lattice artistry...

We sauntered through another fountained courtyard to the perfumed
Arab baths, elaborately patterned with mosaics
On the floors and walls and ceilings; from balconies the sultan
Secretly assessed his harem while they took their baths.
We read that in a neighboring room naked women danced
Before the sultan and his wife, while blind musicians played,
Passionately imagining what <u>they</u> could not assay.

By noon we'd wandered past the cypress avenue and through
The blooming oleanders to the Summer Palace of
The Moorish Kings, where nature has been cultured to an even
More luxurious sensuality. We strolled and sat
In choice locations, contemplating deeply all that beauty
Through the afternoon and evening hours, breathing rose champagne,
Understanding fully why De Falla came back here again
To write his classic theme piece, "Night in the Garden of Spain",
And why our early writer Irving felt compelled to tell
The world about its wonders while residing in its spell.

"Give alms to this poor
blind beggar, for no pain
in life can be greater than
being blind in Granada."
(Translation of inscription below)

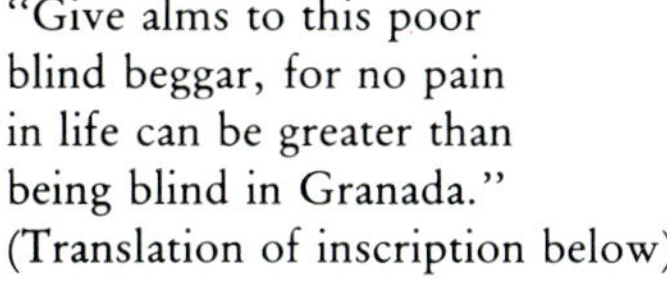

We drove our tiny car along the coast of southern Spain,
Descending winding ways through cliffs to compact strips of beach,
Then up sharp curves to widespread outlooks over sapphire seas,
Repeatedly, until some instinct brought us down to choose
As lodging for a night the small quaint fishing village of
La Rábita, quite picturesquely set in steep ravine,
With neat, red-roofed, white cottages and seascape scenes.

We found a charming inn beside the rhythmic pulse of surf,
With name to tantalize our "second-honeymooning" sense
Romantically: "Estrella de la Mar" (Star of the Sea);
The handsome Andalucian owner warmly welcomed us,
And led us up at once to corner room on topmost floor
With balconies and floor-to-ceiling windows on two sides—
For living pictures of the Mediterranean Sea's bright
Daytime scenes, or moonshine's mellow trembling boulevards at night.

We so much fell in love with it we stretched one night to three,
Took time to learn firsthand the villagers' noteworthy ways--
Learned that the men in pairs went out each night in tiny boats,
Returning after dawn to sell their catch to those who came
In trucks from Málaga, or other cities near that coast;
They'd spread their nets to dry, have breakfast with their families,
Then rest through daytime hours for another night at sea.

We talked at length with one of them beside his little boat;
Then it was time for him to sleep, he sent us with his son
To see his modest home and meet his wife and progeny;
They shared with us their wine and cheese with warm civility,
And then three daughters and the son hiked up with us to see
A round stone tower where visigoths once scanned medieval seas,
And Roman fort where Civil Guards now have their armory.
To crown the day we treated them to supper at the inn
In celebration of the new-sprung bond that made us kin....

In those few days affection rooted deep and stretched to years;
The middle daughter, Esperanza, often wrote to us with "hope"
That someday we would come again to Spain and visit them;
Alas, we were not free to go; the years slipped quickly by;
And then one day came shock of tragedy unthinkable:
A freakish inundation had befallen Rábita--
A writhing wall of water rushing down the steep ravine
Had crushed in span of minutes all the houses ruthlessly,
And swept those lovely fisherfolk abruptly out to sea....

Out of History into Legend

On the road to Cartagena near the Costa Blanca,
We found engrossing novelties at every turn and rise:
Still stable Roman bridges--villages and fortresses
That were the summits of steep hills--and rock formations rising
From the sea like fortresses. At Cuevas Almanzára
Natives dwelled ingeniously in caves with painted concrete fronts.
A Spanish couple whom we'd met while at Toledo had
Suggested that we stop to see the Roman fort and
Amphitheater at Sagunto near Valencia, where
Seven thousand citizens once sat and saw the violent
Passions of the plays of Seneca unfold. We wondered
If they watched them with the stoicism which the teacher-
Turned-philosopher-turned-playwright eloquently sought to
Advocate, and if they learned from those theatricals
To sublimate those violent passions in their private lives....
Indeed, it's difficult to understand why, if there is
A providence, the grossest ills befall good men and women...
And to accept all suffering as testing by the gods.
My wife and I, who at that very time were coping with
The burden of her cancer, pondered this as we ascended
To the highest parapet that bounded the old Roman fort;
Looking down upon that scene of ancient drama, and out
Across the city to the Mediterranean Sea,
We chose to focus on another thought of Seneca:
"Longevity is measured not in years, but in the use
We make of them, and in the qualities that they produce."

m viewpoint of that massive fortress wall, the surf of the
ncian Coast was visible, and we remembered that,
 far from there, The Cid, Spain's most exalted hero, was
uted to have won a battle after he was dead.
ems he had received a fatal arrow in his chest
 day before, and died within his fortress that same night.
en morning dawned, his wife commanded that her husband's body,
ssed in his full armor and with banner flying, be mounted
 his well-known horse, to ride out in the forefront of the
's defenders. The forces of the enemy, believing
 t The Cid had died, were so intimidated by his
emergence in the battle that they turned and fled.
 noble steed, unreined, continued to race on along
 distant curving shore beside the shining sea, till he
 s lost from sight. Thus did The Cid ride out of history
 d into legend...where he still rides on...unendingly...

Cathedral Spires and Citadels of Earth

Heading north and inland at the Ebro's outward flow,
We left awhile the fortresses and monuments of men
To lift our eyes and spirits to the hills, and farther still,
To range upon the highest ramparts of Spain's nature-fashioned
Fortresses, The Pyrenees...and then to feel the spiring
Skybound reach of majesty among the Picos de
Európa, the natural cathedrals of Cantabria.
In all they dwarfed in scope and mass the works of man we'd seen,
But in no sense did they debase his ingenuity...
Before we turned our pilgrimage back toward the heart of Spain,
We descended to the northern sea to witness primal
Creativity of early man, in earthbound caverns
Named the Cuevas Altamira. On the ceiling, well preserved,
Are images of animals so gracefully conceived
The cave's been called "The Sistine Chapel of Prehistory".

A Shadow of Man's

Yearned-for

Immortality

I'd long looked forward to a glimpse of Salamanca, for
I'd had some students go for studies at that old illustrious
University, and also I had used selections
In my classes from the writings of its two most famous
Mentors, Fray Luis León and Miguél de Únamuno--
The first, a mystic poet...the latter, a challenger
Of consciences.... How often I had wondered what it would
Be like to step into its antiquated courtyard,
And stand before the statue of León that graces it,
Recalling how he first addressed his students (after years
Imprisoned by the Inquisition) with the casual words:
"As we were saying yesterday...." How momentous then to
Turn and gaze upon the gilded friezework, eulogized with
Glowing eloquence by Unamuno in his love song to
The seat of learning which he'd served so well and long as guide--
As champion of the human right to freely think and act.
I thought I sensed a shadow of the immortality
He sought, somewhere between religious faith and scientific
Reasoning, because annihilation at one's death of
A carefully developed and experienced human soul
Seemed too illogical and tragic as its destined goal.

A Firm Grasp

of the

Distant Past

Although we'd scanned a hundred textbook images of Ávila,
It was an unforgettable experience to top a rise
And see the granite walls and turrets of that fortress city
For the first time in its full-scale physical reality.
The "highest city in Iberia", whose full name means
The City of the Knights, not only served as fortress for
High noblemen and warriors, but also as a bastion
For the saints; striving mystically toward the sublimity
Of unity with God, Teresa prayed, wrote, taught, and danced
Within these high grey walls...and with John of the Cross
Established Carmelitic disciplines in many convents
Throughout Old Castile. Even Avila's cathedral was
Constructed as a fortress-church, with a single access
From the outside world. We felt a firm grasp of antiquity,
Not only gazing at the city's unaccustomed outside
Aspect, but walking through its hushed and narrow cobbled streets
As well. No other town in all of Spain seemed so remote
From modern life--so like it must have been long time ago.

A Palace

for

a Vengeful God

The most austere of Spanish palaces, Escorial,
Was like an emblem of the somber, brooding character
Of Philip, legal son of Charles who was both the Holy
Roman Emperor and most predominant of Spanish kings,
When Spain was Lord of Europe and the Western Hemisphere.
His empire was so vast the sun could never set on that
Which he bequeathed to Philip, when he chose to abdicate
And round his final years sequestered in a monastery.
We keenly felt the melancholy temperament of Philip,
On arriving at that cold grey spectral building, with its
Unartistic walls and seven granite towers, which he'd planned
To serve "as palace for his God, and household for himself."
Some poet thought that God himself might well have trembled at
Its grandiose austerity. God also might have winced
At Philip's gross hypocrisy, for though he had a transom
In his bedroom, close beside the altar of Escorial's
Interior church, to hear each morning mass devoutly in his
Bed, and though he zealously approved the persecutions of
Non-Catholics in the Inquisition, he disguised himself
At night and sought the haunts and services of prostitutes.
He served a God severe and vengeful, not of mercy--
A God who was an image of his own harsh personage.
His policies were motivated by this one ideal:
The supremacy of Catholic faith. To press this cause
He signed (with but three words: "I the King ") an order for
His fleet to fight a holy war against the Turks, then taxed
His subjects to the bone to send his Great Armada north
To punish, unsuccessfully, Elizabeth of England.
He also spent much time and fortune on elaborate
Sepulchers for Spanish royalty down in the basement
Of his castle: red marble floors, green marble altar,
And black marble caskets--a pantheon for bones of men.
We found more interesting his simple bedroom furnishings,
Including but one simple chair of wood and canvas.
In that sparse atmosphere, staring at a skull on which was
Placed a golden crown, he displayed amazing courage through
Some fifty days of agony before he died of cancer.
Whatever may have caused the whims and incongruities
Of that licentious, pious, zealous personality,
He warped two hemispheres with his own iron-willed strategies.

The Valley

of

the Fallen

To feel a loss for words is not uncommon in the face
Of an impressive monument or work of peerless beauty,
But on entering The Valley of the Fallen, passing through
The four Juanelos columns standing as if guardians of
A wall of silence, I felt emotion that I truly
Cannot ever hope to fashion into phrases that I'd deem
As adequate. On the quiet rolling hillsides lay
The graves of both republicans and rebels who were killed
Irrationally and violently in the bloody combat of
The Spanish Civil War, which sometimes pitted brother
Against brother, and friends against each other. A towering cross,
Five hundred ten feet high, presides atop a central
Granite hill; to hear such measure stated is impressive,
But to gain its impact fully one must go up to its
Very base, where figures of the four Evangelists,
With emblems of their virtues, have been molded from gigantic
Blocks of granite glued together. Standing near a toenail
That's as large as one's own head bespeaks the monument's true size.
Below, a subterranean chapel has been hewn into

The rockbound mountain's base. On entering, we found that we
Were treading on the white stone surface of a vestibule,
Semi-circular in shape, toward massive black iron doors,
Above which we could see engravings of the life of Christ;
Proceeding through the polished marble high-arched corridor,
In the direction of the chapel at the far-off end,
Became a solemn promenade, as spirit-stirring as
Ever we had made. Perhaps it was the lateness of the hour
That left us utterly alone in that vast passageway...
In any case, that pure aloneness seemed to heighten our
Perceptions of its beauty, and to amplify to glory
The majestic music of an organ which resounded
From the walls and ceilings. On either side grand tapestries
Were hung, and carved in bas-relief at side-arched intervals
Were figures of symbolic mothers of the slain, covering
Their faces with their forearms, for they could not bear to look
Upon the grim atrocities--the useless loss of life--
The wrenching family sacrifices in that civil strife.
Within the chapel, dimly lit winged angels, bearing flares, and
Statues with their faces cloaked, kept vigil over empty pews,
In constant sorrow for the dead who lie beneath the foyer floor,
In hallway crypts, and in the soil of surrounding hills.
Upon the red-hued marble altar, as though it also had shed
Blood, a crucifix displayed Christ's head thrown back in agony,
That men were ever led to such destructive destiny.

A Perfect Place to End an Odyssey

How unforgettable the day we came upon Segovia,
Perhaps the most arresting and encompassing of all
The castle-fortress cities of Iberia, both in aspect
Drawing near, and then within, as virtual museum of
The shifting fates of royal politics, religious zeals,
And changing modes, spanning most of Spain's recorded history.
Every style of architecture--Roman, Romanesque, Gothic,
And then Renaissance--appeared in structures of importance.
Across the valley from the south, we stared and stared at the
Prodigious bright Cathedral, challenging the sky atop
The city's highest ground, its troupe of spires as sharp as beaks
Of hummingbirds turned vertically to feed on food from Heaven.
If Heaven is up, as some believe, that church's major tower
Must surely have appeared to local worshippers to reach
As close to it as any man-made structures then could reach.

The most outstanding work bequeathed to Spain from ancient times
The best preserved of all the Roman aquaducts, from that
Far view seemed like a giant railroad bridge joining distant hills;
In fact, it carried water twenty-seven hundred feet,
Supported by one hundred sixty arches, formed by massive
Uncemented granite blocks. Under its two tiers, we sensed
The crushing weight and near forbidding magnitude of raising
Such a framework so precisely that it could be used for
Two millennia, since Hadrian ruled Rome as emperor.

Spain's epitome of castles, The Alcázar, poised upon
A narrow crag, high above the conflux of two rivers
Like a skybound ship's sharp prow, seemed to us a vision from
Grimm's Fairy Tales. Though it was built by King Alfonse the Sixth,
We chose to think of his descendent there--Alphonse the Wise,
Burning candles long into the night, absorbed in his
Astronomy and literature...and once again the ghosts
Of Ferdinand and Isabel, inhabited those rooms,
For here the ideal queen received her crown of all Castile,
And Ferdinand was witness to Columbus' will, while they
Were based at this strategic place. We wandered dreamily
Throughout the rooms, where suits of armor kept a silent watch
From corners; we pondered and discussed the beds and thrones where
Monarchs agonized the destinies of men and empires;
And then we went exploring to the outmost sentry lookout
Of that most extraordinary ship of state and legacy;
The weathered walls and cliffs dropped sheerly down around our stance
And at their base the rivers merged their flows, as they had done
Through ages long before the kings and queens, and artisans,
And knights, and priests, and common folk at this pre-eminent site
Conceived their schemes and acted out their parts, then merged into

Time's everflowing stream…. It was, we knew with certainty
The perfect place to end our monumental odyssey.

An Elegy

"The hope I dreamed of was a dream,
Was but a dream.
And now I wake exceeding comfortless,
And worn, and old,
For a dream's sake
Lie still, lie still my breaking heart,
Lie still, my aching heart and sleep.
Life, and the world, and my own self
Are changed for a dream's sake.
                    Christina Rossetti

"To laugh often and much;
To win the respect of intelligent people
And the affection of children;
To earn the appreciation of honest critics
And to endure the betrayal of false friends;
To appreciate beauty;
To find the best in others;
To leave the world a bit better,
Whether by a healthy child, a garden patch,
Or a redeemed social condition;
To know even one life has breathed easier
Because you lived.
This is to have succeeded."
                    --Ralph Waldo Emerson

to Love

"How do I love thee? Let me count the ways.
I love thee to the depth and breadth and height
My soul can reach, when feeling out of sight
For the ends of being and ideal grace.
I love thee to the level of every day's
Most quiet need; by sun and candlelight,
I love thee freely, as men strive for right;
I love thee purely, as they turn from praise.
I love thee with the passion put to use
In my old griefs, and with my childhood's faith.
I love thee with a love I seemed to lose
With my lost saints--I love thee with the breath,
Smiles, tears, of all my life!--and, if God choose,
I shall but love thee better after death."
                              --Elizabeth Barrett Browning

What though the radiance which was once so bright
now forever taken from my sight;
ough nothing can bring back the hour
f splendor in the grass, of glory in the flower,
e will grieve not, rather find
rength in what remains behind...."
                              --William Wordsworth

O Aching Fragrance of Spring

O aching fragrance of spring, for you are gone,
And walk no more across the greening lawn,
Or through the door which framed your graceful for
For half a vibrant lifetime's rip'ning love.
Nor do the stolid stones which fringe the beds
Of flowers 'round our hilltop cottage home
Warm with your nearness now, as when you chose
To sit by them and dream, and slowly plan,
And sort the weeds from flowers for hours and days
To know this little kingdom we had shaped
Our youthful selves would safely persevere
And grow in seasoned beauty through the years.

Now you must be unseen where grass springs green
And all the flowers glow with private light,
In temperate sun, or under moonlit night,
Perceived in shadows with pervading ache,
Which holds deep ceaseless grip inside my breast
And will not let me know the boon of rest.
Alone I must toil on through daily chores
Which once were easy for our eager hands
And hearts, but now they seem futilities,
Though still I strive to harbour what we wrought
From briared field and quaking aspen copse,
With settled sentiment through sifting years,
Creating, sweating, planting seeds and trees,
Singing fair songs of goodlier things to be,
Fine-tuning life for artful harmony.

Madrigal of a Last Bright Day

That last bright day I brushed your gray-streaked hair,
Still vital, though the chemicals you took
To stay the dismal malady within
Had vanquished many cancer patients' hair;
I stroked to stir at least diluted joy
On your pale face, for still you strove to feel
Some remnant of past sensuality,
While bittersweetly breathing out the day--
A last pathetic grasp for happiness
At threshold of the enigmatic maze.

I left you in the sun close by the urn
With flowers, where, beside the flagstone turn
Of walk, our daughter had made marriage vows
In festive summertime two years before.
With parasol shading your face you lay,
Watching me cut the grass, petting the dogs,
And looking at the spruce-framed mountain view
As often in the twilight hour we'd do,
Or many times each day at work or play,
Never completely satisfied to say
We'd had enough of its intriguing joy.

That shimm'ring Sunday, with your tawny legs
Still warmed by sun, you asked to go inside....
Did you surmise your eyes had looked their last--
A final prize or token from the past
Of all the glimm'ring green and floral sites,
Of all the textured panoply's delights
We had created with our minds and hands,
Through twenty-seven years of steadfast plans?

I placed you on the lounge so that you could breathe
More easily, then, using the patchquilt
Your mother made from garments of the past,
I tucked you in with gently anxious hands.
How could I know it was the last embrace
Of loving legions we had freely shared
Through high romance of ardent, healthy years,
Or later tender times dispelling fears,
When Death's grim shade was ever reaching near?
Now stealthily he came in middle night,
Assuaging soundlessly your painful plight,
With me unknowing, tiny steps away--
With me so close, and yet so far away.

Then Came a Surge of Anguished Consciousness

Arising from oblivion of sleep,
I rushed to you at once to check your wraps.
The softest tints of dawn were on your face,
At rest in dauntless dignity and grace.
And then I sensed no breath; I spoke your name;
Incredulous, I kissed your paling lips;
Then came the surge of anguished consciousness
That you had slipped away into the night,
Into the starry night forevermore....

And then they came to take you from my sight,
Out through our gate in shadowed morning light,
And I was left disconsolate, alone,
Among the remnants of our earthbound home.

Immortal Overtones

of Elements

I had them make for you a box of pine,
Unvarnished and ungarnished, as a sign
Of closeness to simplicity of style,
Respecting Nature's forms as most worthwhile.
We had resolved to have our bodies burn
To basic elements of earth--return
At once to air around, not be encased
In vault beneath the ground, but ashes joined
To living grass and flowers, to leafy bowers
Of maple mass--to merge in roots of moss,
Or help to fashion fall's iridian gown,
As seasons make perennial cycles 'round.
These were our settled thoughts in lighter days,
When sparkling birdsong moved away the haze
Of early morning, and our minds were brave
Enough to face the prospect of the grave.

Accolade

at

Home

Heeding my wishes, though unorthodox,
They brought you in your close-to-nature-box,
Smelling of pine and cherry essences,
To lie near open hearth in final rest
Before the diamond window we loved best,
(Framing iris circle and valley view)
Where we had hoped to sit for length of time
Together, sharing well the life we knew,
But posing glad perspectives of a future, too.
"Grow old along with me, the best is yet to be,
The last of life for which the first was made."
This was the dream we dared to contemplate
Through cancerous seige upon our earthly state,
But now can never hope to postulate.

The Family in Sculpture, which I carved
Long time ago in living life-size clay
Then cast in matte-white setstone, kept its watch,
Reflectively on manteltop of pine,
As crowds of floral tributes soon embalmed
Your presence with fresh fragrances benign.
Firm friends arrived to kiss my shattered face;
Our students sat in circles on the floor,
As many passed in silence through the door
Of leaded glass, or wandered on the grass
To breathe the verdant atmosphere of spring,
Or scan the curious monument of rocks--
A thousand summit souvenirs I'd brought
To dignify our final resting spot
In maple copse. They'd read my "Mountain Psalm,"
Then come inside to praise your strength
Gainst rampant range of unjust suffering.
One friend expressed it lucidly for all
In citing how a pearl grows 'round a wound:
"You settled peace around internal pain,
Turning misfortune to inspiring gain."

Still Echo Here
the Drumbeats of Our Fate

In this new church you pioneered the first
Of all the sacred services of praise;
Your hands at console touched melodic strains
Of prelude to all future worshipping,
While few could guess the compass of distress
Within your breast that signal day before
I drove you to the Center by the lake,
Where doctors probed the cause and had to break
Our dream of far horizons with the words:
"A year to live." Too soon to stop and give
To death all laughter, all sweet flesh and breath,
All music from skilled hands through pulsing pipes,
All cultivated tastes, all sifted sights,
All cumulated wisdom's filtered lights....

Then, sublimating fear, you stretched that year
To five with will to live, with hope to give
It preciousness beyond the common scope.
Although it seemed that poignant genesis
In rebuilt church for us would be "farewell",
Eventually we shared again the swell
Of anthems thrilling to crescendoed ends,
And worship's silence, which sometimes transcend
Significance of words. Positioned near
Each other in the choir, we often turned
To savor mutual care, and feel content
Just being in that lovely privileged place,
Resplendent with such rare artistic grace:
Arched panes of glittering faceted glass--
Emerald, topaz, ruby, sapphire mass,
Patterned with sacred symbols--soon surpassed
The prized traditionals of the older church.
Behind us rose the rows of organ pipes,
Symbolic of the upreach of our souls
To raptured heights of music's aureoles.

Carillions in the Towers
of the Mind

We fashioned here so many well-cut jewels
Of pure delight: the weddings when you played,
Fluting the merriment of love, chiming
The organ pipes with close dexterity,
As I sang love songs glancing at your face
In blend of romance and solemnity.

And our recitals every Christmas Eve
When I played cello or the violin,
Mellow or sparkling as the case inspired,
And you accompanied with gladsome grace
Of apt arpeggios or rumbling bass--
Chaste, crystal moments time cannot efface.
Then those finales when the church was filled
With people holding candles in their hands,
And I from choir loft's unequaled view
Could see and feel the wondrousness of you,
Framed against mellow light's society,
Your hands moving across the shining keys,
And multitude of voices raising song
Of "Silent, Holy Night" among the throng,
The ancient warming wonder to prolong.

The Sounds

of Hymns Triumphant

Inevitably the clock ticked out its course.
We brought you one last time into this church
For celebration. Irrevocably
Within your box of scented pine you lay,
Covered with fragrant red carnation spray,
And all the pews were filled with saddened friends
Who loved your pleasant, graceful fortitude.
The organ soon began to sound the pipes
You loved, with other hands upon the keys
Remembering your favorite harmonies.
"Breathe on Me Breath of God" the choir sang,
And grief-assuaging words chimed in my mind
With soft caress as you were eulogized:
"She climbed the mounts of Beauty and of Truth,
With courage to the end." Then was recalled
The last of all the music we had played
And sung at services across the years:
"Above the hills of time the cross is gleaming,
Fair as the sun when night has turned to day...
Like echoes to sweet temple bells replying,
Our hearts make answer to a perfect love."
And finally, from your own notebook came
The ultimate of all the eloquence:
"To live with calm endurance every day,
To help someone less stalwart on the way,
Be grateful for the granted gift of life,
And death itself, for it gives weight to life."

"Oh, may I join the choir invisible
Of those immortal dead who live again
In minds made better by their presence...
That purest heaven,--be to other souls
The cup of strength in some great agony,
Enkindle generous ardor, feed pure love,
Beget the smiles that have no cruelty,
Be the sweet presence of a good diffused,
And in diffusion ever more intense!
So shall I join the choir invisible
Whose music is the gladness of the world."
          --George Eliot (Mary Ann Evans)

Modulation to a Darker Key

In dining room of newly structured style,
Where restful private moments we beguiled,
I sit through early morning in my chair
And know I cannot ever see you there
In yours again, watching the bluejay fly,
Or cardinal come near in gay attire
Against a winter landscape's frozen choir.
This was our place of light, rebuilt, improved
Less than a year ago; here you loved so
To sit and read, or dine, or watch the birds
Approach to see what morsels we had left
Within the little houses on the tree,
Which turned a final cycle in your eyes:
Replete with dark red apples in the fall,
Then bare, then architectured by the snow,
Before glad April summoned tender growth
To turn it all to blossomed elegance,
Like other apple trees one far-off spring,
When we were married in their blossoming.

We built it with full windows on three sides,
With ledges for the treasures of our trips
To foreign lands. Here we displayed, among
Pale pink and purple velvet violets,
Ivy, and hanging red geraniums,
A primitive plate carved on Andean slope,
Bronze statuettes of gods and goddesses,
Unusual rocks, and magic-sounding bells
Both placed and hung: from templed Thailand's
And far-off India's incensed palaces,   shores,
And Himalayan heights of quaint Nepal,
And Japanese enchanted garden shrines,
And Alpine villages of Switzerland,
And finest workmanship of sunlit Spain,
Or matchless patterns of Peruvian brain....
Alas, their charm now struggles to survive;
My cellos stand in corners silently,
Needing your background for my hands to glide
Alert with tuned vibrations at your side;
My violins are in their cases, too,
Black and unopened still for want of you
To move me to aesthetic enterprise.
O music in my clay, resound again
Within this home, and in the templed place
Where frequently we'd share such lifting grace.

Midway Through Adagio of Grie

Through our first years, I measured carefully
Each day and month and season wanting you,
For we were torn apart because of war.
The chasmed ache of needing you was bridged
By writing constantly each thought and act,
With aspiration for exalting time
Of our reunion at the struggle's end,
When soldiers would be going home in peace
To act out long-anticipated dreams
Of colleges, or cottages by streams.

Now once again I feel the gnawing pain,
Although more deep and constant than before,
For never will there be an open door,
Or expectation of a glad return,
Except in mute communion of the urn,
Or in some spectered heaven undiscerned.

Now, in reverse, I measure pensive days
And wistful weeks, with hopelessness of touch,
Or kiss, or asking your advice in what
I should or should not do in this or that,
Or hearing bubbling laughter and accounts
Of what was said or done in class at school,
Or passing by your room to feel the pride
And thrill your voice could gender deep inside,
Sensing the rapport your instruction stirred
In student minds--the awed esteem you earned
For courage, as you slowly walked the hall
In steady cadence to the final call.

With leaden heart through melancholy maze
I seek your gentleness, and face the days
And weeks, and then perhaps the rolling years
Of loneliness, of needing all your strength
And optimistic ways, throughout the length
Of what remains this side the mystic sea
Of death. The utmost consolation that I know
Is feeling in my grief with every breath
That part of you lives on within my mind,
And part of me has died and gone with you
To serve and be companion to you still--
So we are merged uniquely though we be
On either margin of a timeless sea.

Leaves pattern sunshine by our monument
Of stones brought home from summits of the world;
Soft beauty glows on scripted bronze, and brings
To life the sculpted features of your face;
And close around our private, final place,
The ashes of your mortal flesh revive
In elements of Nature's quickening:
O darling presence in the grass and moss,
Imbue me with acceptance of our loss.

A Few Sweet Notes That Fade at Summer's End

With you now only three months into death,
Returning from some weeks of mountain breath,
And visits to dear friends who knew our ways
On former trips in happy holidays,
Somewhat refreshed in spirit, but still sad
With haunting inner rasp of missing you,
I hastened home to reassume my lot
As keeper of our private Camelot....
When turning in the driveway quite alone,
I gladdened as I saw a light at home
And knew our son had come to welcome me
Back from my summer sojourn's alchemy....

But fragile threads of bittersweet return
Soon frayed again with other grave concern:
Tahoma, steadfast German shepherd friend
Of fourteen years was coming to his end,
Suffering sharp arthritic miseries;
Some massive ailment deep within him stole
Away the zest from all he loved to do;
Thus we were led in fellowship of care
To ease him from his agony, and share
Secluded grief of placing him in loam
Beneath a piney shelter near our home,
Among his predecessors on our hill:
Rusty, initial watchman of the yard,
Golden Thor, gentle giant and sightless bard,
And bright Denali, robust prodigy,
Who quickly mastered everything that we
Might wish, but vanished into mist one fall,
And nevermore replied to anxious call.

A Tribute to the Best of Friends

These are the pleasantries Tahoma loved:
To focus on the sounds of passing cars,
Or distant planes, or jump to catch a bee
Buzzing overhead, or lie in majesty
On porch like stately Metro-Goldwyn lion
As we came home, and only grant one sign
Of his regard, a slowly sweeping tail,
Except if we had been away a while,
Then to the gate he'd dash with splendid smile
And canine sounds of glee unlimited--
To slide his chin through blades of scentful grass
In June, or roll in summer ecstacy between
The feet of us he loved, in twilight scenes,
When we would sip our warming claret wines,
Facing the quiet sunsets through the pines.

His tireless avocation was to trace
With fine antennal ears and radar eyes
The movements of our pony Eboning;
Wheree'er he went, Tahoma held his scent
And scolded him in pasture or at fence,
Then looked at us to catch affirming sign
That we approved his watchful work's design.
On sultry summer days Tahoma lay
In sev'ral secret stations under arched
Forsythia, or sometimes he might squeeze
Through parapet protecting shrubs and flowers
To juniper's deep shade through midday hours.

We called him "Mr Perfect", for he was,
Of all the German shepherds we have had,
The most ideal in temperament and style,
Responsive, but with balanced dignity,
Keeping his individuality
Intact throughout his reign within our place;
And even in his hour of death his face
Was beautiful and placid, with a trace
Of understanding what our purpose was,
Stroking his fur and base of noble ears,
To ease his pain to death's assuaging rest,
With shelter of our love through his last breath.

Tahoma was of black and silver strain,
His smaller friend, Denali, black and gold.
They used to play and spar upon the lawn,
For hours and days with graceful moves go on,
"Dancing a gold and silver waltz," we'd say,
Marveling how they relished it each day.
Then came a time when old Tahoma could
Merely shuffle across familiar ground,
And vexed Denali never understood
Why his companion of the years now would
Ignore his overtures of canine play,
And nothing seemed to mend from day to day.

Thus ends the epic of their classic waltz--
The ballet master's form has disappeared,
And grieved Denali, more bewildered still,
Traces his scent, then circles 'round the hill,
Looking and listening all about the yard,
Expecting that Tahoma will emerge
From private lair beneath an arching surge
Of bush or pine, or from the shaded flowers,
Or scenic porch, where dark Denali waits,
Sorely perplexed by callous changing fates.

I Went Today

to Play

at Treasure Lake

I went today to play at Treasure Lake,
To walk the glimm'ring fairways of our past
Together there, and everywhere I stood
Remembering the magic which transpired
At edge of woods, or by aesthetic mounds
Around soft-textured greens and shapely traps,
And tranquil views from tees to hazy shades
Of blue on distant ridge beyond the range
Of golf or any man-made pastime game,
And flame of autumn 'round each private realm
Of hole, and dappled deer, or gay gray squirrels
Flowing through red leaves, climbing towering oaks,
Casting acorns down through transient cloaks
Of mottled birdsong close beside our trail....
O Love, although I may forever fail
To find your form in spring within a ring
Of greening trees, a summer day will bring
Your presence to me still; and pensively
I'll walk these fairways through the golden years,
Rememb'ring how you lived with pleasant grace,
And loved the beauties of this special place.

Still Burn the Fires Perennial

As Rembrandt tints of autumn flood my eyes,
Persistent embers deep within me rise:
You walk with me in rasping footsteps, through
The fallen maple mass on drying grass
Around our orchard yard, where moments pass
To hours and days, and now five plaintive months
Without your daily touch and winsome ways
Are merged in an expanding past--a blend
Of our perennials which must not end
In barren clay or fruitless elements.

Chrysanthymums around our sheltered home,
Which last year bloomed in gold and russet hues,
Are this year only white as new-formed snow.
I look on them in frame of emerald,
And shivers run my spine with quickened pace
To realize that in their slender stalks
Your ashes, which I scattered there in May,
Flow up to coronets of mystic white--
Displayed nobility of purest thought--
Ineffable miracle by Nature wrought.

Close by our burnished monument last June
I planted all your most-loved annual flowers,
To be custodians of the verdant hours:
Pastel petunias, ageratums, too,
And pink impatiens, favorites which you
Would plant each spring. And now I bring,
In midst of all the essences of fall,
The tested strength and permanence of bronze
And rocks to lock here in our chosen place
A lasting spell. How wondrous still to face
An oriole sky behind the spruce tree row,
Which marked our joint frontier so long ago
On autumn rambles only we can know!

A Monument in Sound

When bleak November turned our woodlet drear,
I searched within to hold the fading flame--
Some sparking bellows to reanimate
Your candent soul--some gift to celebrate
A legacy of beauty in your name.
Most apropos seemed tribute musical,
And so I purchased master-crafted bells,
Which frequently a practiced handbell choir
Now lifts in wordless anthems forcefully,
To new expanse of church's artistry.

Ring out bright bells with thrilling clarity!
Chime forth aesthetic glories in this place!
The loved ones we have lost will come again
Each time you fill this hall with beauty's grace.
Our spirits will renew in magic throb
Of cadenced strike and ringing harmonies,
Communicating through the length and breadth
And depth of all our private reveries.
Give us such meaning in your speechless songs
As lights the corridors of mystery,
Stretching beyond the limits of our minds,
Projecting hope for greater things to be.
Fill us with peals of consummating joy
Beyond the heartaches of mortality;
Tell us of strength and gentleness of heart
Which grace the reaches of life's entity.
So may our hearts make answer through the years
With constancy of love's remembered spell--
A wonderment in sound of ringing bells.

Out of the Fabric of Past Christmases

It's Christmas now within our hilltop house,
And for the second time a lighted tree
Stands by our floor-to-ceiling window panes
Quintupled in the row of high bowed glass,
Resplendent with select familiar forms
Of glist'ning globes and tiny tinselled bells,
And angels playing violins and horns.
Well-poised on podium of utmost branch,
The angel queen directs a choir of lights,
Recycled from those transitory sprites
Who blessed our watching other Christmas nights.

The baby grand, our first gift to ourselves
When we were wed, stands patiently near wall
Of books we hoped would once again enthrall;
The waiting keyboard needs your hands to bring
Some caroled charm of angels, shepherds, kings
To thrill again; but still I can ignite
Our children's Christmas candles which we flamed
This night only from early infancy,
In private ceremony to instill
Symbolic sense of continuity--
A source of inner warmth and light to fill
Unfolding dreams with meaning which might thrive
Through all their boundlessness of sep'rate lives.

The yule log remnant taken from the pile
Of still warm ashes out of last year's fire,
Whose embers glowed with special warming while
You still were with us, now will flare again
To touch the new yule log with crackling flame,
As haunting waves of recollecting frame
You still and fill the room with mix of glow
And grief. O teach my mind to nourish peace,
And from this heavy sadness find release,
In knowing that within our progeny
Resides some thread of immortality.

A Tapestry of Continuity

Erik came home to share this Christmas Eve;
He sought and brought and trimmed the Christmas tree
Then went with me to church's candlelight,
The service which you played last Christmas night

It made it meaningful for me to go
And play the violin again and know
Your gentle presence in the cradle songs
We played past Christmases in candle glow,
Encircled by poinsettias' scarlet row.
It was encouraging to realize
That you were present in his hazel eyes,
For physically he blends our wedded traits,
And mentally as well amalgamates
Your quickness and my scope, authenticates
Our hope to have our children seek the best,
Pursuing complex questions without rest,
Conditioning his body, too, in quest
Of some ideal design's identity.

On Christmas day I flew to Florida,
Where Kristan makes a life in Seminole,
Rising to cheerfulness, in spite of dole
Your death cast on their fresh-formed happiness,
In bright new home close by the splashing sea,
Where work and play evolve successfully,
And where you shared a summer's pleasantry--
Last transient season of tranquility,
Before the cancer launched its fatal spear
Inexorably down the bitter year.

Just as we flew together Christmas last,
The shadow of the plane leaped through the cast
Of clouds, now near, now far, to tantalize
My brooding mind, my effervescent eyes
Pleading to find the now lost paradise
Of you beside me through the shaded skies.

They met me at the airport with their care
Surrounding me, so poignantly aware
That we were four a year ago, but all,
Resolved to mask the underlying ache,
Were outwardly content beside the lake,
Fishing, or riding cycles through the park,
Reading in the sun, lying in the dark,
Working on the turf, running through the surf,

Sampling Chinese food, thinking in the dark....
And everywhere their optimistic ways
Projected as a beacon through the haze;
In their unfolding future I can see
A tapestry of continuity.

O Come My Love, Come Lead Me to the Fire

I've plowed once more the blowing, deep'ning snow
From our immense expanse of drive,
With glacial walls shaping perimeters,
And just a hint of picket fence above
Accumulating piles on either hand
Of wrought-iron gate and matching span, which holds
The tiny tower of frosted glass that glows
With welcome light above the gate each night—
And waiting on its graceful brace at right,
The great bronze bell we brought from Mexico
Half covered by high canopy of snow.

Even were I to ring it loud and clear,
You could not come to me with radiant tear,
Nor could you open wide the gate again
To let me in and lead me to the fire,
Except perhaps in recess of my brain,
My melancholy mind where mem'ries thrive,
You'd smile again, your laughter still survive
In vibrancies that thaw my frozen dreams.

It seems so futile to remove this snow,
To open space so I alone can go
And come. How much more meaningful when you

Were here to know the pride of all this work-
To know the snow removed, the road to go,
But first in tender snow-bound privacy
To fan the flames of trembling ecstacy,
To contemplate the storehouse of our years,
To recreate the things which brought us cheer
To recognize the import of a word,
A touch, a look, whose meaning no one else
Could know--a poised contentedness to go
Everywhere together, not ever tire--
O come, my love, come lead me to the fire.

The Reddening Maple Blush of Spring

The reddening maple blush is on the trees
Of winter silver, flushed by April breeze
Uniquely warm, and vibrant rising grass
More brightly green than ever seen before
Shines all about me in our corridor
Of earth; the facing pasture hill is still
More starkly green, now marked by length'ning shade,
And though the row of spruce beyond seems black,
I still can fancy towers of living green
Searching the northern sky for hint of hope.
My eyes and heart range west along the scope
Of boundary between their reach and sky
To where they dip, revealing distant mount,
With hue of lilac blue which you and I
Were wont to look upon untiringly.

Nearly a year has passed since last you viewed
This splendent scene, and now the daffodils
Are trembling in an April evening light
As brightly yellow as forsythia,
Whose starry bushes also hold sunlight
In all the corners of our hermitage
Of gently sloping yard, just where we chose
To plant them long ago, and row on row
Tall tulips 'round the house, and hyacinths,
Are blooming earlier this year as sign
That you in reborn beauty still will be
A part of each fresh spring's discovery.

And Gently Comes
a Calming May at Last

O darling presence in the grass and flowers,
There is so much alive that still is ours
To thrive through me....I've kept you fervently
In heart this spectrumed year; you walked with me
By woods and lake; no apples could I take
Or vegetables retrieve from garden plot,
But you were constantly within my thought--
Watering our treasured plants before the bow
Of diamond light in westward living room
(Surviving floral gifts from struggling times),
Framing with slow-paced life our artful urn,
Shining bronze of ultimate unity,
Watched over ever by uplifted face
Of statuesque Quijote, showing trace
Of great El Greco's heaven-stretching flow,
Dreaming a dream impossible to know.

At church memorial handbells now proclaim
A frequent, fitting tribute to your name,
And many winter twilights I may go
To play your music in the stain-glass glow,
And feel you quicken in my finger touch
Upon the organ keys, and keep as much
As possible the bittersweet resolve
To merge your force in mine--not let you die.

At school a scholarship renews each year
Your legacy to students who appear
To hold or strive for values you held dear.
A Treasure Lake Memorial Golfing Day
Will find your friends remembering you at play
Along a summer fairway's yesterday.

At home, now May, the lilac lavender
Is hanging lush beside our pasture gate;
Quite soon the dogwood which you prized will share
Its saintly blossoms with the temperate air;
And Eboning has wandered to the mares,
Grazing serenely, framed in valley scene
By keenly fragrant, blooming apple trees,
Where winter saw the tracking of our skis.

I drive your car which I've had painted new
In warming tones of dark metallic blue,
With love's deep-hued fidelity imbued
For future miles. And more assuaging news
I bring this spring about our children's lives:

Kristan gave birth to love's continuance--
A tiny April girl named Jenny Lynn,
Predicted for the day you died in May,
But anxious to be born, she could not wait
To give our wanting lives fresh happiness;
Then Erik earned his Ph. D. degree--
This coming August joins the faculty
At Arizona University,
In Tempe where the mountains ring the sand,
A dry but irrigated promised land.

A huge new German shepherd roams our yard;
(Retiring old Denali could not guard
The spacious premises with muted ears,
Nor give impassioned greeting through the years
As I come home from school or distant place.)
I call him "Wonder"; his attentive face
Show traits of all our shepherds; he awaits
My every move and word, then pleads to race
For sticks tenaciously with fervent grace.
This moment he is lying in cut grass
With head against our monument to pass
The time while I am writing to you here
Beneath a Maytime maple chandelier.

For school and home I had you cast in bronze
To resurrect your lips and eyes and hair,
And as I come into the silent house,
I feel your stable presence always there.
I stand beside our monument and know
I cannot ever from this haven go
And not return to kiss the greening grass
In spring, or autumn's tinted mass,
And love you still though decades pass....

In quiet country scene, or rushing city throng,
I sense your step, your warmth, your laughter,
                              or your song,
And even in darkest hours my seasoned soul
                                 can trace
The glow of inner splendor brightening your face.

Out of Death and Time,

"Try to remember the kind of September
When grass was green and grain was yellow.
Try to remember when life was so tender
That no one wept except the willow.
Try to remember when life was so tender
That love was an ember about to billow.

Deep in December it's nice to remember,
Although you know the snow will follow.
Deep in December it's nice to remember;
Without a hurt the heart is hollow.
Deep in December it's nice to remember;
The fire of September that made us mellow."
        --T. Jones, The Fantasticks

Concordance with New Melodies

"...Like beauty, my friend, 'tis all in the eyes of the beholder. Only wait and thou shalt see amazing sights."
   --Don Quijote, Man of La Mancha

"You are the promised kiss of springtime
That makes the lonely winter seem long;
You are the breathless hush of evening
That trembles on the brink of a lovely song;
You are the angel glow that lights the star;
The dearest things I know are what you are.
   --Oscar Hammerstein

Nocturne by the Sea

I run with naked feet on moistened sand
Where settling surf has surged up on the land,
And shades of twilight sky, and rocking sea,
And circling, gliding gulls accompany
My moving shape along the shining shore.

I wonder if these birds care I explore
Their realm? They flap and ride exultantly
On winsome wind above the churning sea,
As I pass by quite unimportantly.

Why do I run and heave the tidal air
Into my lungs and soul? And seek to see
Beyond the sabling sky what still might be,
As gropingly I plunge into the sea?

I only know that here suspense still runs,
As in the waves I sink and face the sun,
Tied to me still by wav'ring aureate bands,
Wherever I may breast it with my hands,
In reach for some new hope's serenity,
Before the final darkness settles over me.

Grandfather's Reverie

As the child plays I watch, remembering
Things she has no earthly way of knowing....
Toddling over insubstantial sand,
Speeding to grasp a seashell in her hand,
Chosen from scattered mass to be the best,
Then falling spellbound at the water's crest
To sit in sliding foam with gleeful zest,
Grasping her mother's stable, sun-bronzed knees,
Blond-silver hair caressed by soft sea breeze.

Beneath the shadow of your mother's gold,
O little girl my wife shall never hold!
O comely child my wife can never see!
Fashioning joy, assuaging agony,
Lifting blue eyes into my reverie,
Reaching love's hands up to the heart of me,
Bearing a torch of continuity,
Frolicking lightsomely by careless sea.

Intermezzo at Farnam Creek

"Shall I compare thee to a summer's day?
Thou art more lovely and more temperate..."
--William Shakespeare

Sunlight flooded Eva's face,
Shining through her hair,
Cumulating in her smile,
When I found her there....

Walking up a logging road,
Breathing mountain air,
Sharing freshened rhapsodies
That sprung from mutual care....

Rambling arm in arm through tall
Queen Anne's Lace supreme,
In a valley, near the rush
Of glacier-powered stream....

Each revealing private griefs
With tender candidness,
Scaling wild Canadian scenes
And our own wilderness....

Sunlight came along with Eve
Lucent in her eyes,
Blessing me with special warmth,
Which my eyes reprised.

A Twenty Minute Emperor

I went to climb Arapaho, alone,
In pensive aftermath of loved one's death,
To be among familiar mountain scenes
Where we had shared expansive happy breaths....

Returning down a paintbrush-bordered path,
I chanced upon a moving jubilee
Of wholesome female beauty such as I
Had never ever fancied I would see;

A smiling group of thirteen vibrant girls,
Each one potentially a beauty queen
In aspect and in grace, surrounded me
With quite disarming curiosity;

I learned they were a group of college friends,
Who'd chosen for a summer holiday
To sample strenuous mountain trails, and I
Was blessed as first to pass them on their way;

They wished to know where I had been, and why;
They scrutinized my climber's axe...my rope...
My weathered face; they touched my snow-white beard
And asked about my past...my future hopes;

The hidden substance of my errantry
With sparkling speed they charmingly unveiled,
Then drafted me to pose in midst of them,
Before I ambled down a lonely trail;

In sequence thirteen cameras appeared,
As they hugged 'round me on a patch of snow
And made me feel like Siam's aging king,
Whose ladies prayed he wouldn't have to go.

"Women...are the soul of man...
the radiance that lights his way."
--Don Quijote, Man of La Mancha

The Chimes of Love

Ring Clear Again

I did not think, through years assuaging grief,
When even summer skies seemed indigo,
That I could ever really love again,
For I had known a three-dimensioned glow
Of fullest flame for length of ample time.

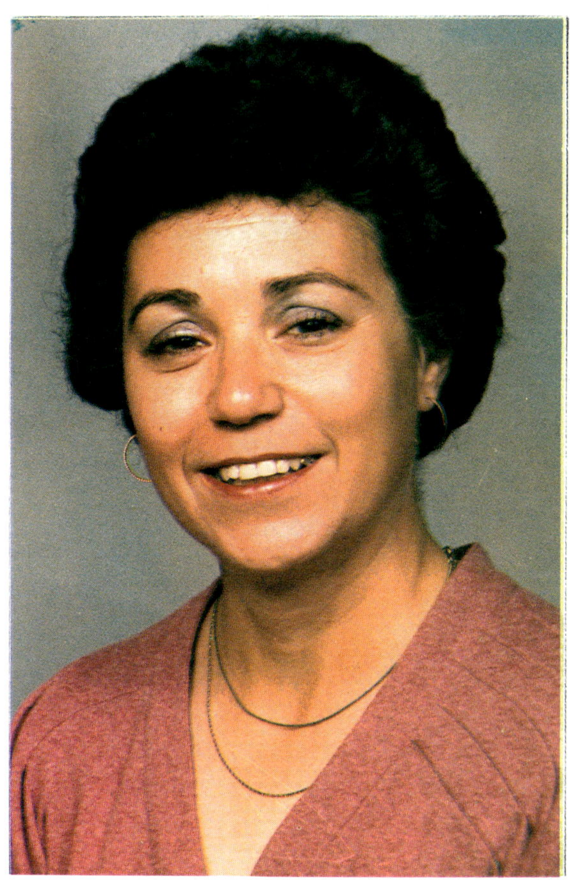

Confronting firefly darkness all around,
I almost passed a special sudden shine
That, as I turned, grew brighter still, until
It filled my earth with thrilling promise of
A second birth of absolute romance,
Touching my opening mind and captured eyes
With what I thought I'd nevermore surmise.

I saw your face that fated mountain night
Glow in the campfire circle's warming light;
I fathomed vibrant music in your voice
That prophesied: "You are my foremost choice."
Thus trusting intuition's instant grace,
Searching the tempting beauty of your face,
I spoke the words which launched our new career
Of happiness beyond the past frontier.

I saw myself as living out my days
Among accustomed scenes and well-known ways,
Not aimlessly meandering apart,
But helping student minds find culture's art--
Learn skills of language use, and summertimes
Teach kindred hearts to climb, see splendid views,
Have rendezvous with flowers—be for my part
Content with memories and private pain
To go and come--to love my children well,
And all those caring friends who shared my loss,
As well as new-made friends whose lives have crossed
My pathway as I've tracked a dimmer world.

We framed

Our Wedding

in a Highland Park

The Parthenon in Cheesman Park gleamed white as chalk
In morning sun, as through its columned shade we walked,
Then down the marble stairs in wedding promenade
To dulcet sounds of two violas' harmonies,
Befitting such a classic site's serenity.

Our dearest friends and families were waiting there
In smiling ranks, our love's acknowledgment to share,
In fragrance of a thousand roses fresh in June
Around the garden where we'd strolled one year before
When love was new with promise that there would be mo

The service, which we had conceived and framed ourselve
To share with all the deep commitment that we felt,
Reached highest eloquence in your well-chosen words:
"I offer you my trusting hand; will you take mine,
And truly love again beyond your lost design?"

Then I, my sight securely locked into your eyes,
Gave clear poetic witness to our enterprise:
"Above all others I have freely chosen you
To be my cherished wife, to share life's second part,
To be the trusted guardian of my tempered heart."

Again the music of soft strings encompassed us,
And as we sang our love's duet the mountains watched--
The mountains that had brought our separate paths to cro
They blessed our kiss, and then, before we turned away,
We thanked them with our eyes for that expansive day.

Our Tender Love

Fulfills

the Seasoned Years

I've found in you, my love, such seasoned grace,
Such depth of worthy self, waiting to give
To one endowed to recognize those rare
And precious treasures to their fullest range,
To savor and appreciate that wealth
Of mind, that comprehension of the shade
Of meaning to its finest textured tone,
That healthy openness that permeates
With probing honesty all spheres of thought,
As deep as earth, as broad as southern seas--
That tireless interest in each other's needs,
That freely-given tenderness that feeds
Our end-of-summer love and makes it bloom
With fragrance of a rose that springs in June--
That sensitivity to beauty's way,
That rainbow-splendored vision that we see,
As hand in hand we scan love's panoply
Across the years of our affinity.

Steep Snow

Arabesques

It was on STEAMBOAT SPRINGS' big northern hills that I first knew
The sensuous flake-white velvetry--the smooth fast cadency
Of skiing well-groomed Colorado snow; insatiably
My new-found fiancée and I drew playful, catch-up curls
On "Buddy's Run" and "Vagabond"--traced out the apogee
Of "High Noon's" circling ridge--felt "Heav'nly Daze" tranquility.

One blust'ry February day with snowflake swirls in air,
An eighty-year-old veteran of army skiing troop
And I, half frozen, rode the lift toward LOVELAND'S wind-whipped pass;
As I maneuvered cautiously across iron-crusted drifts,
My sly old friend's long skis shot down the fall line's polished glass;
His distant shape my target, I, too, shushed the mountain mass.

At SUNLIGHT, "best kept secret" of the Rocky Mountain Chain,
Our skis vibrated noisily as we made sliding turns
'Round "Sunburst's" elbowed paths of frozen filigree;
The sun still showed Mt. Sopris as we sped "East Ridge" that way,
Until a blizzard swallowed us in its white density,
And forced us to plow gropingly through cold obscurity.

We wanted ASPEN HIGHLANDS, but a frigid stormy day
Led us to BUTTERMILK, where sprightly, speeding youngsters jumped

And plowed the snow like colorful cavorting clowns; there we
Concocted pure delights, steering through dim-lighted, frosty
Chambers of close trees, or sliding banks diagonally
While swaying down "Red Rover's" rolls and smooth concavities.

The "Naked Lady's" curves enticed; high "Cliffside" we reprised
Along to "Upper Powderhorn", and then "Sheer Bliss" again;
But alpha and omega of our SNOWMASS holiday
Was running, from the top, "Green Cabin's" tilted knolls and bends,
Our tested skis now confident to carve through hillocked way,
In front of sweeping Ski Patrol to end a perfect day.

We loved the overlooking galleries of WINTER PARK,
And relished "Cheshire Cat's" fast-moving highland flings;
We gayly ski-danced "pas de deux" with smooth authority
Along high Lonesome Lift's side-winding trails; our last time there
We found new icing on the cake of those festivities—
On Vazquez Ridge's ideal "Stagecoach-Sundance" novelties.

The shaded steeps of MARY JANE are challenge for the best,
So we of upper moderate tastes approached with heedful skis,
Content with tempered knobs of "Sleeper", "Rainbow", "Arrowhead";
Then recently we made a marvelous discovery:
The backside of the mountain had been made a treasury
Of cruising trails that realized our fondest fantasies.

It took a while to fathom VAIL's complexity of lifts
And interlacing runs--its potpourri of disp'rate names;
We made our way to ridgetop Eagle's Nest eventually,
Then spent a charming afternoon in lonely Game Creek Bowl,
Experimenting with deep powder's changing subtleties,
Progressing toward refinement of new-found agilities.

Instead of being just a waiting place on way to heaven,
PURGATORY seemed the end itself: pearly, snow-draped pines
Were glist'ning gates to scenes of marbled mansions in the sky;
We rode soft rolling pathways to "Nirvana" and blue "Peace"--
Were tempted by fine "Zinfandel"--black "Hades" we apprised--
But in the end our wise old skis led us to "Paradise".

At TELLURIDE we were first down "Pandora" and "First Love",
Inscribing private signatures on sheets of down-like snow;
From every angle of that Alpine playground's drapery,
We looked, then looked again, at awe-inspiring mountain views,
Especially from "Polar Queen's" high-poised convexities,
But best of all from "See Forever's" spiral balconies.

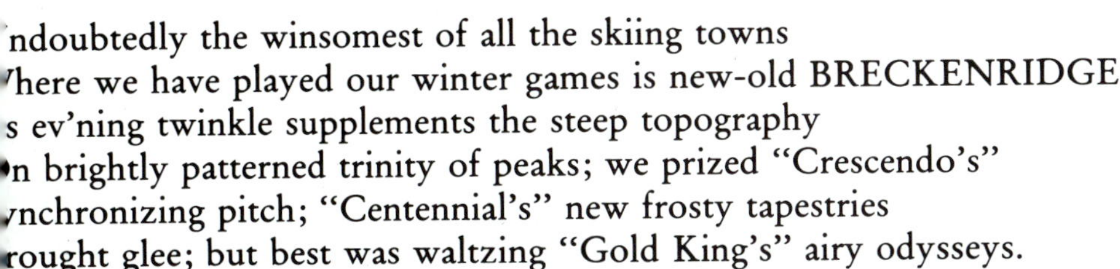

ndoubtedly the winsomest of all the skiing towns
Where we have played our winter games is new-old BRECKENRIDGE;
Its ev'ning twinkle supplements the steep topography
On brightly patterned trinity of peaks; we prized "Crescendo's"
Synchronizing pitch; "Centennial's" new frosty tapestries
Brought glee; but best was waltzing "Gold King's" airy odysseys.

On COPPER MOUNTAIN we
    embraced full gamut of this sport's
Wide range of alternates, from
    challenges to graceful moves,
Somehow surviving "Far East's"
    fearsome mogul jeopardy,
Exulting on "Collage" and
    "Encore's" long jewel necklaces,
Or rounding trees and undulations
    of "Soliloquy"
Like birds low-flying over
    favored meadows' pleasantries.

ARAPAHOE's the highest where our country's skiers ski,
Its setting sparsely forested, its basins topped by cliffs,
With feel of Europe's open Alpine slopes' frigidity;
But we, from corniced edge, engaged with zest its tracery,
Assiduously discovering "Lenawee's Face'ery--
Half-mooning mammoth shoulders in fast-gliding privacy.

There could not be more finely-shaped terrain for us to ski
Than KEYSTONE's pine-rimmed undulating trails: expansively
"Spring Dipper" poured us down to "Santa Fe" in cushioned sweeps,
Then over crystal mounds; "Wild Irishman" made poetry
Of our quick-flashing forms past angled surface brilliancies,
Like beams that dance across a giant diamond's panoply.

A Rash of Unrecorded Rainbows

terrible electric storm enveloped us as we
proached the western side of Trail Ridge Road. Our camper braved
wall of rain as dense as any I have ever seen,
les thick, aglow with overlapping, deaf'ning, angry light.
spiciously, the scary, almost overpowering
tensity abated, while we started to ascend
ng, steep-edged switchbacks, opposite the Never Summer Range.
mewhere up there, when we had gained the higher sidehill ground,
d were proceeding 'round a curve, a rainbow started
take shape, its iris arc arising from the still dark
ght-hand depths to full-formed splendor straight ahead. Continuing
ound the bend, my poet eyes in constant strife between
e winding road ahead and peerless beauty seldom seen,
e watched it hastily evaporate into the sky.

With comments such as
     "Wasn't that a marvel!" to describe
Our sentiments, we little
     guessed what Nature had in store
For us to see that day.
     Another rainbow soon appeared,
And then a rash of rainbows,
     doubles, triples, every time
We'd round a turn,
     another unbelievable display
Would dazzle us....But as we
     wound beneath that high arcade
Of rainbow arcs, whose mingled
     beauty took our breath away,
We sorely knew we'd used up
     all our film the previous day.

"Say that I was starved; that I was lost and weary;
That I was burned and blinded by the desert sun;
Footsore, thirsty, sick with strange diseases;
Lonely and wet and cold, but I kept my dream!
In vain shall any lesser lights be burning
For us who glimpsed the vision from afar.
We shall go down the road of unreturning,
Broken and spent, but faithful to a star."
An Epitaph - Everett Ruess

On Playing Don Quijote

The dream conceived beneath a broad La Mancha sky
Has crossed the seas and centuries to dignify
Man's wonderment--to beautify his upturned face--
To touch unique identity with poignant grace.

I sometimes dreamed that antique dream, portentously
To be a knight, to fight imposing odds, to see
A mission deep within take shape, to measure up
To fine ideals, with thirst to drink the bitter cup
Of injury, defeat, indignant ridicule,
Yet rise again and yet again to play the fool
In eyes of men, pursue an independent course
Whatever might befall, to heed the call to force
Against the evil ways, to find a destiny
Above the shattered ruins of actuality....

"Sancho, thou art a fat little bag
stuffed with proverbs."

"How long since we sallied forth?
...So soon shall I engage in brave
unequal combat!"

"Why do you do the ridiculous things you do?"

"I hope only to add some measure of grace
to the world...Whether I win or lose does
not matter...only that I follow the quest...
the mission of each true knight...
To dream the impossible dream,
To fight the unbeatable foe,
To bear with unbearable sorrow,
To run where the brave dare not go...."

And then she said: "I know you are the one to play
The part. You've climbed high mountains through untrodden ways;
You love to quote Elizabethan phrase; you taught
The language of Cervantes all your life; you fought
Malignant force against true language artistry--
The watered-down curriculum--and you could see
Potential beauty in your students' hearts; you led
Them into realms they knew not of, then slowly fed
Their groping, growing minds to fancy what could be
A multi-splendored quest into life's entity."

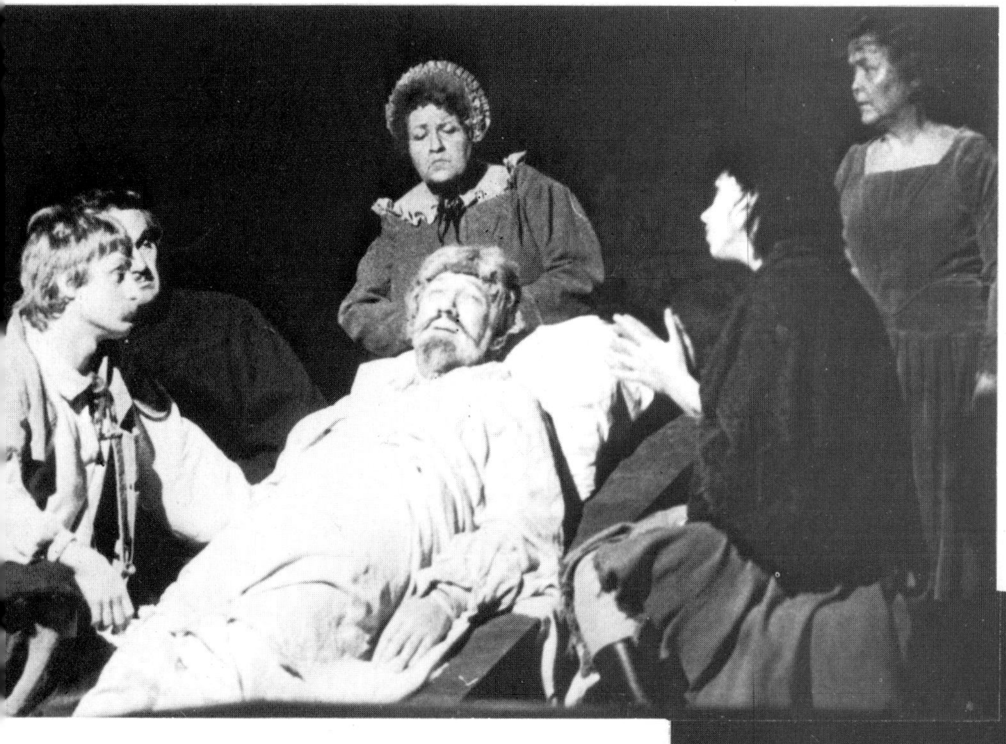

"Then...perhaps it was not a dream...
Not well? What is sickness to the
body of a knight-errant? What matter
wounds? For each time he falls he shall
rise again...Sancho! My armor! My sword!"

"Oh the trumpets of glory now call me to ride,
Yes, the trumpets are calling to me,
And wherever I ride, ever staunch at my side,
My squire and my lady shall be...."

Intrigued, inspired by such persuasive accolade
To search for truth within Quijote's masquerade,
I ventured curiously into the novelty
Of bearing sword and armor, and philosophy,
Upon a new-made stage. My music-tempered heart
Was tuned to kindred cadence as I learned the part.
Through skepticism's pain, and scarcity of praise,
I spoke poetic words and sang romantic phrase.

"I am I Don Quijote, the Lord of La Mancha;
My destiny calls and I go;
And the wild winds of fortune will carry
me onward, Oh whithersoever they blow."

Then, straining to insistence of a drumming pace,
With strident background tones that subtleties effaced,
I lost my voice. My flowering capacity
Could not be fully shown; unable to express
The fullest range my spirit sought, in sore distress,
My battered cords grown shrill before the curtain's rise,
I groped within to sublimate--to lift my eyes
Toward victory--to force my voice above the din
And throng--to don the Golden Helmet with a song,
Bring transformation into Dulcinea's soul,
And justify my faithful Sancho Panza's role--

"I have dreamed thee too long,
Never seen thee, or touched thee,
But know thee with all of my heart.
Half a prayer, half a song...
I see heaven when I see thee, Dulcinea,
And thy name is like a prayer an angel
Whispers...Dulcinea...Dulcinea."

Somehow to bravely face the ruthless spectral Knight
Of Mirrors' taunts, and gather strength again to fight
For love and stars--renew the quest, and though it seemed
Impossible, believe to be attainable, the dream....

"To right the unrightable wrong,
To love, pure and chaste, from afar,
To try, when your arms are too weary,
To reach the unreachable star...

And the world will be better for this,
That one man, scorned and covered with scars,
Still strove, with his last ounce of courage,
To reach the unreachable stars!"

The birds will not come back next year to last year's nest,
And I must travel on before I take my rest.
The pale horse bids me ride; the trumpets call me hence;
Wild winds of fortune bear me to my recompense.

A Song for All Winters

As I look out the window I can see
Meand'ring marks of our cross country skis
Enmeshed by sunlight with the patterned shades
Of leafless maples, picket fences, pines,
And wrought-iron gate's thin graceful curving lines;
Beyond, the sloping pasture's parklike glades
Are tracked as well, for when the flakes have laid
A proper blanket on our frozen land,
We cannot wait to take our poles in hand
And hitch our boots to long cross-country skis—
To slip into the glist'ring fields with ease
Of stride, and ride beside tall silent trees
Of snow-draped woods, or corniced drifts where winds
Have done wild work undisciplined....

Sometimes out there I think of romps long past,
And see our little children with us then--
My tying on their tiny skis again,
So primitive compared to what we have
Today for winter sport.

274

Back then we'd go
Adventuring together in fresh snow,
The four of us, our work shoes tied to boards
Of hickory, but still somehow explored
Ridged windblown scapes of winter wilderness,
Or intricate heaped chambers' tight access,
Where only we and creatures of the wild
Would make new tracks in surface undefiled.

The snow seemed deeper in that distant past,
But, whether that was so or no, the joy
Experienced in those years has never ceased,
Through countless winter snows that I have known,
Through every crystal landscape that I've skied,
Some solitary ones with muted zest,
But now again with gladder cadency,
In new-found kindred mate's fair company.

We glide together through the velvet white;
We stride in synchrony of movements bright;
We slide in barely audible reprise,
And relish each new scene's unique surprise;
With fresh perspectives where we so belong,
Our hearts exhilarate in throbbing song.

In the Realms of Titans

Gazing up at Rushmore's great quartette of granite presidents,
Henry Standing Bear, an Ogalala chief, was moved to tell
The sculptor, Korczak Ziolkowski, who'd helped to carve them,
That there ought to be a comparable monument that
Celebrates the native North Americans, "for we, too,
Have produced heroic history and leadership."
From that suggestion has evolved the grandest concept that
A sculptor ever has conceived--to shape a mountain some
Six hundred feet in height into a figure in the round
Of Crazy Horse, the great Sioux chief who routed Custer at
The Little Bighorn, and was then deceived and murdered by
Begrudging peers and "trusted" government authorities.

I learned about and visited the Black Hills site of this
Titanic enterprise quite early on, was deeply stirred by
Korczak and his wife--their infinite capacity to strive...
To improvise...and to believe in what to many seems
A fatuous fantasy. From time to time I'd go again
To scan and contemplate the slowly changing image on
The mountain...share its fascination with my family...
Then try to make its scope and meaning vivid for my classes,
With hope to stir a few to want to seek their own Parnassus.

Persisting fearlessly through ignorant local ridicule,
And vicious vandalism that destroyed his lifetime's art
(Including his renowned white marble bust of Paderewski),
This steadfast titan labored toward his dream throughout his life,
But will not ever see the shape of his colossal chief,
Mounted on a charging steed, tower complete above the Indian
University, which he envisioned and designed to be
Established at its base. His children may, for he's endowed
Them well; and I have hope that ours may someday see
That mammoth figure's full-hewn arm pointing a tragic answer
To the white man's taunting question: "Where are your lands now?"
I trust they'll comprehend the measure of the chief's reply:
"My lands are where my fellow warriors dead in battle lie."

"Search all your parks in all your cities,
You'll find no statues to committees."
--Unknown

The Needle Mountain Wilderness Revisited

"A book of verses underneath the bough,
A jug of wine, a loaf of bread--and thou
    Beside me singing in the wilderness--
Oh, wilderness were paradise enow!"
--Rubáiyát of Omar Khayyám (Fitzgerald)

Some twenty years before, our passage on the narrow gauge,
That hugs the canyon cliffs above the raging rapids of
The River of Lost Souls, was in an open baggage car,
Along with much equipment for a major climbing camp;
The train dropped us just opposite the mouth of No Name Creek,
Where, in the absence of a bridge, we had to pull the heavy loads
Across white churning water on a drooping cable rig
That almost touched the swells; and then we had to carve a trail
For horses to transport the gear to our remote base camp....
This time there were just two of us--my recent bride and I,
With tickets which we had to purchase months ahead of time,
Because round trips aboard the D. and R. G. Railroad from
Durango up to Silverton in summertime are now
Brimmed full with tourist trade;

the crowded train paused briefly at
A Forest Service bridge, where Needle Creek abundantly
Augments the rushing Animas, and just the two of us
Jumped off, strapped on our loads of gear and food to last ten days,
And paced into the Needle Range for pleasant lonesome miles
Of sweat, deep breaths of piney fragrances, long canteen rests
At scenic overlooks, and always, near or far, fresh songs
Of vibrant streams, asserting we were right where we belong.

In those ten days, we camped where'er we chose, sometimes in fields
Incomparably tinged with transient summer blooms--by lakes
Remote from humankind, reanimated with last winter's
Still persisting, slowly melting banks of settled snow--
Or balconies near granite walls, where phantom guards in towers
Of rock kept watch above our yellow tent's brief twilight hours....

We crossed high Twin Thumbs Pass, though heavy packs were difficult
To manage on the steep loose rock, heeled heedfully down long
Unstable talus slopes, then balanced over slippery slabs
Above Goose Lake to meadows lush with great variety
Of Alpine flowers; beside a waterfall, that I recall
Was clearly visible from our encampment decades past,
We huddled under ponchos, waiting out the customary
Thundershower of mountain afternoons, munching bits of lunch;
As soon as it was spent, we slipped down through thick firs right to
The site which long ago had been our camp, between the drinking
And the washing streams--the humble fountainheads of No Name Creek.
The place was hard to recognize, for floral meadows, where
Pack animals had grazed near scattered tents, had knee-deep grass;
The willows in the swamp where children played had risen, too--
So high they marred the valley view we'd grown accustomed to;
I showed Elaine where we had placed the cook and dining tents,
And where great campfires blazed with circled song accompaniment...

With sad reaffirmation that few things remain unchanged,
We chose to go on up into the narrow valley where
The sight of Knifepoint still had power to captivate
The climbing heart; we camped where we could gaze at it throughout
The supper hour, for I had hopes of scaling it again--
Of taking my new bride up there. Next morning dawned quite clear,

So we achieved fulfillment of that summit wish, and she
Experienced the tantalizing panorama of
The Needle Range, which I'd kept vivid in my mind for more
Than twenty years of mountain summiting around the world;
Then on descent, against the base of Knifepoint's buttresses,
I found and gave her, as bouquet, the bank of flowers
Remembered as the loveliest that ever blessed my eyes.

Replete with sharing mountain love, we moved our camp up to
An isolated tarn midst jagged peaks, and found that we
Were neighbors to uniquely friendly marmots who, with not
A hint of fear, stood very near, observing everything
We did, and seemed to understand when we would speak to them;
When finally we started 'round the lake to gain a high
And windy pass, beyond which reared the sabered Grenadiers,
The marmots trailed along for half a mile or more, as though
They didn't want us to depart their lonesome studio.

For several days we lazed and sampled life at Balsam Lake…
Till shrinking food supplies inspired us to the labor of
Traversing still another pass near thirteen thousand feet,
And pioneering down to make a final camp, that faced
The frontal armature of Vestal and sharp Arrow Peak;
We fancied we had ample time that last bright day to gain
The Elk Creek Trail, and amble down before the scheduled train
Would chug along the river, going south from Silverton;
How wrong we were! The designated time of rendezvous
Drew near, and still we seemed to have some distance to descend;
With real anxiety and quickened pace, our foodless packs
A burden still, we hastened on, quite breathless as we had
To strain uphill again two times to pass some canyon cliffs;
I had to run the final yards at frantic speed to reach
The tracks, in time to flag the fast approaching train to stop,
For missing it would force a hungry wait around the clock;
Exhaustedly, thankfully, we clambered on the last car's
Observation deck, slumping on the banister just as
The train began to move again. Gradually, wordlessly,
Fulfillingly, we settled to a restful reverie,
Watching tracks recede and river flow…relishing the rare
High lonely beauty that we'd had the will and strength to share.…

Harmonics

The Allegheny River runs its winding southwest course
Through checkerboard variety of rolling farms and woods
That thread the tapestry of western Pennsylvania hills,
Meandering 'round multitudes of random deep-cut bends
In quest of merger with Monongahela's northwest flow
Where old Fort Pitt sparked history two hundred years ago.

Among those myriad nameless curves is one that's touched my life
With great significance. Near Brady's Bend my first great love
Was born, knew childhood games, learned work on farm, excelled in
Took me romantically to see those scenes--to meet her folks, school
Returned to teach while I was gone to war, and finally,
In little country church nearby, joined married hands with me.

A favorite rendezvous for us in those unfolding years,
When brave youth urged our steps, was where the river turned
Almost unto itself, in long-persistent circuitry,
Through slow-paced eons scraping out a massive hill...until
We stood a thousand feet above its murm'ring fluency,
And looked down either side to muse its gleaming symetry.

Still Echoing

A legend says that narrow high-poised overlook was where
The famous Indian fighter, Samuel Brady, leaped to make
Escape from close-pursuing braves. Induced by legend's lure
And our romance, we made recurrent visits there to gaze,
Each time with fresh astonishment, from that high balcony
And hear unfailing overtones of Time's soliloquy.

Not long before my first love's death we stopped a final time;
Hang gliders had discovered it; we watched them run and launch
Into the air on currents high above the river's bend,
And then, against the farther landscape's patterned greens,
Full circle 'round in graceful deference to gravity,
Then slowly seek the other bank's less steep declivity.

Sad years walked by; I found my second love; we went to share
The quiet rhapsody that always trembled in the air
Around that chasmed river view; perhaps we'd also see
Hang gliders fly…. But no. The ramp where they had launched was closed,
And close beside it stood a rough-hewn monument, inscribed
With these affecting words: "He dared to go where eagles fly."

"As the fond mother when the day is o'er
Leads by the hand her little child to bed,
Half willing, half reluctant to be led,
And leaves his broken playthings on the floor,
Still gazing at them through the open door,
Nor wholly reassured and comforted
By promises of others in their stead,
Which, though more splendid, may not please him more;
So nature deals with us, and takes away
Our playthings one by one, and by the hand
Leads us to rest so gently, that we go
Scarce knowing if we wish to go or stay,
Being too full of sleep to understand
How far the unknown transcends the what we know."
--Henry Wadsworth Longfellow

In Praise of a Worthy Life

For nearly forty years he's waited here
Beneath the tangled turf of this high tier
Of antique hill—familiar childhood scene--
Historic site of early church, between
The graves of pioneers inscribed on stone
Long time ago, but slow through time obscure
Then joined by granite clear--familiar names:
My father's gentle face still clarifies....
And now you go to share his rest at last,
Your long-lost partner of the blooming past.

To us you seemed not young, but yet you were
Still steeped in summer season of your life,
With autumn but a distant prospect then,
And winter far beyond ingenuous ken....
How difficult to change familiar ways,
Bewildering to find the path, through maze,
To travel on, to cope alone, to grope
For meaning, wanting love--to rebuild hope,
Find independence, never burden be
To us your sons, though unprepared with skill
For gainful work: just early basic school,
And candor's bracing gift in fronting life's
Exigencies with boundless energy.

Remarkable how soon you found your way
In work at candy factory—new skills,
Fresh complement of friends, activities,

And ever optimistically you rose
Alone to meet the days successfully;
Sociable, but gossip free, you sought the best
In others, looked for bright'ning ways to live
Enthusiastically, adventure forth
To new experience or novel place,
And, undeterred by many suitors' pace,
Kept constantly in mind your life mate's face.

Through all, you cherished us your progeny,
With cheerful voice on phone or when we came,
Asked just to be with us in special times
Of holiday, or when the spring was flush
On our estate, or autumn tinged the hills
Beyond the gate....The seasons massed. You filled
Them up with love and gifts, and watched with pride
Our son and daughter grow, mature, and go
From home to make their own distinctive ways,
Then lived to see great grandchildren be born,
Form personalities, trade love and joy
With you in double force--for you and him
Who died long ere these treasured gains were made,
Who through your golden years in hidden shade
Has lain alone, but now alone no more.

Fifty Springs Too Soon

Conserving, keen, intense, creative Joe,
How can it be that you were marked to go
So suddenly, inexorably away?
Just when sweet spring is rising in the land
It is impossible to understand
Such grim, irrational caprice of fate:
That you by callous chance would be destroyed
Some fifty springs or more before you should,
Just when your April married love had made
A son to share the summer of your years--
Just at the prime of new, inventive work,
Your footsteps on the track of future source
Of energy, to harness nature's force--
Returning to revitalize your roots,
Explore old roads, savor familiar fruits
That grow among the early hills of home--
Just as we two approached the long-sought verge
Of merging our perceptions and our skills
In publication of your art, my words....

I look upon the delicate vignette
Of our high home you sketched one autumn hour
And left us as a seal of legacy, a dower
Of special sentiment you'd always feel
For our retreat. I turn, and through the glass
Of diamond windows see the hilltop grass--
The point of view you chose from which to pass
Your vision on to us, through waving pines,
Of pilgrimage to changing season's shades,
Instinct in russet maple glades once more,
Forsythia, and resurrecting grass,
And dazzling daffodils beside the door.

It is a monstrous, out-of-joint demise
Of kindred, caring spirit, such a friend,
With whom we fancied sharing through the years
Canoe trips, walks to "sudden presences",
Fertility of image-making minds,
Fine thrill of new designings, deep events,
Affectionate, aesthetic, probing ways
To know the essences of life....I may
Now only rage in grief, in stark dismay
Against such gods that senselessly deprive,
Or, gazing on our green and golden park
(Which you, in spring, as youthful lark
Could sing with colored pen and ardent heart)
Resolve to finish what we had conceived,
Find gratitude and peace in what was given,
Though brief, still deep, and keep it long as art.

Cylcing Country Roads

I used to run long distances to keep my body primed
Throughout the year, that I might meet demands of summer climbs
In rugged mountain wilderness; but after forty years
And more of bone and muscle overloads, of jolting leaps
Across a thousand boulder fields, deep chills from drenching storms,
And feet near-frosted from relentless touch of glacier ice,
Arthritis came to plague my joints, and numbness settled in my
Feet and legs, with threat to halt my lifelong enterprise
Of seeking Truth and Beauty where wild mountains pierce the sky.

It pained my hips too much to jog; yet there was need to keep
My muscles toned--my heart and lungs aerobically
Prepared--if still I wished to stay the course of extra miles
And years... In searching for at least a partial remedy,
We fixed upon my spouse's ten-speed bike, and purchased one for
A wise and meritorious choice: There were no painful jolts   me—
On hips while pedaling! For miles and hours I could go on.
No numbness crept into my legs when striving up steep hills,
Though once again my heart exulted in its exercise,
Propelling blood in healthful course through every artery
And vein, expanding lungs to reach for past proficiency,
Almost as well as when I ran to stretch sufficiency.

And there have been some unexpected boons to supplement
Conditioning, as we have sought expanding avenues
Whereon to wheel: In residential districts of our town,
Where otherwise we hardly would have gone to scrutinize,
We've found delight distinguishing, while riding by, fine homes
Where deft design of sash, of paint, of flowers, or shrubberies
Exemplify creative individualities.

A maze of country roads we'd never ventured on before
Engrave their narrow, winding, seldom-traveled asphalt bands
Into our ken, with charming, fresh perspectives at each bend--
Beyond each rise. Sometimes we smoothly roll beneath arcades
Of erubescent maple groves in flush of early spring,
Or cruise through dimly-lighted canopies of trees,
Exploring lanes which lead to camps where hunting men sojourn,
Or tracing tracks that fade into secluded glades or ferns.

We often coast into a photogenic vale, adorned
With farming structures freshly tinctured red, and Holstein cows
That briefly interrupt their grazing to appraise us with
Regard of mild surprise. The downhill levels out, inverts,
As we shift gears to ease the steep'ning climb, then stand at last
Upon the pedals to negotiate the stiffest rise,
Beyond which waits another peaceful scene to bless our eyes.

In Pennsylvania's June-time mountain flower jubilee,
We pedal mile on mile between pink laurel parapets....
October finds us paralleling lazy river roads,
Or circumnavigating dreamy mountain reservoirs,
Not only to awaken and rejuvenate our clay,
But to feed our souls with glory of a painted autumn day.

In Retrospect
of Colorado Friends

How poignant now to feel an era end--
To know that our incomparable friend,
So long our tempered reference and guide,
Has crossed the last untrackable divide....

Though all must someday die, we hoped to find
Exception that Louisa's fertile mind,
Replete with polished jewels of history,
So finely tuned in verbal artistry,
Would go on functioning unendingly,
Would go on telling us in winsome way
The fascinating facts of yesterday
Which she had gathered slowly, patiently,
Authentically, inimitably....

In time we must adjust our reverie,
Remembering she functions still if we
Reread the books which are her legacy,
If we her countless grateful friends retell
The special ways in which she wrought her spell,
Recall the many deeply-etched vignettes:
Slow walks through upland tundra flowerettes,
Fine talks while lunching midst tall columbine,
Beyond the Front Range Panorama line....

Charmed visits to the sources of her work:
Parched, tilted ruins where phantom figures lurk,
Torn remnants of old mines' mortality,
Tall, book-filled shelves researched painstakingly,
Historic sites, museums, pioneers
Through changing course of boldly carved careers,
In city where the plains and mountains meet,
Which she in tasteful Slices bittersweet
Laid out for us with love and skill complete.

In pensive mood I sing of private hearts'
Compounded harmony--a wistful song
Of Elwyn and Louisa: how we shared
Significant response to every care's
Revealing--much pleasantry of wit
At breakfastfests in upstairs kitchenette
By window filled with elm's high silhouette,
And morning walks through fresh museum park,
With joyful sounds of duck or meadowlark,
To panoramas, both inside and out--
The mountain world they knew so much about.

In many Colorado camps their tent
Was next to ours, with fair apportionment
Of mountain prospects gladdening our hours
In restday sun, or during tempest showers
A bit of brandy worked its warming charm
On kindred minds. One time we pitched our camp
Beside a Crestone stream where water music
Baptised every dream of what to climb.
There Elwyn in his sixties went with me
To mount the Crestone Needle by its face,
And at three quarters of a century
He climbed Teakettle's western walls with me.

They both embraced our little children, too,
On venturings, and taught them what they knew
Of birds and flowers, including them in plans
For happy hours in mountain wonderlands:
As first excursion in their Wagoneer,
They took us to Mt. Evans on a clear
Aesthetic day. Those hours will always stay
As time we can call perfect; on the way
We learned intriguing Colorado lore
And fortified our ken of Nature's store.

One Independence Day they soothed the grief
I felt at my first wife's untimely death
By taking me to their most prized retreat--
A privileged timbered cabin with a view
Across Grand Lake to Rocky Mountain hue.
We rocked for hours on quaintly-fashioned chairs
Before a rustic fireplace, where we shared
Remembrances, then went outside to see
Across the lake the town's festivity;
We stood near watery sounds, watching bright
High moving symetry of bursting light,
With spangling duplication on the lake,
And found some gleams of comfort in the wake.

Three years passed by; I fell in love again,
And my new lady charmed my dearest friends:
They helped with our fresh wedding in the flowers
Of Cheesman Park's high-vistaed classic bowers,
Arranged for our reception to take place
In Denver Women's Press Club's honored base,
Then took us to a last high mountain pass--
A wedding gift that cannot be surpassed,
As through the years we go remembering
The best of friends--the best of everything.

Fare-thee-wells

for Troubadours

Since first we found each other, then joined our lives to live
As one, even common days have had a background glow
Of loveliness, although we've had to spend most daily hours
Apart at routine work, whose substance flows into a cloud
Of fast forgetting. But we remember well those times
When happiness was not just background glow, but overflowed
From deep within, and all around, with magic harmony
Of ample time, and place, and circumstance--when everything
Combined to grant us spells of which a troubadour might sing.

Zion

How often I have thought of that bright day in Zion Park,
When we were moved to climb the steep-walled Angels Landing trail,
And you were brave enough to go with me along the edge
Of those sheer cliffs, up to the narrow summit balcony
Which overlooked the tinted canyon's long and deep extent,
And faced the higher Great White Throne's superb ascendency....
Entranced by all the vast rock beauty of that centerpiece
Of Nature's fantasy, we scarcely could persuade ourselves
To leave...until the burning sun had turned our thoughts down to
The cool assuagement of the Emerald Pool's secluded shade,
And rest beneath the Weeping Wall's refreshing palisade.

Hyner View

It's easy to evoke that hazy Indian summer day,
When on a holiday-extended weekend circle trip
To World's End Park and the Grand Canyon of our state, we made
A stop for lunch at Hyner View, perhaps the grandest one
In all the Allegheny Range. We found a cozy nest
At one end of the splendid manmade viewing wall, and sat,
With legs close-pressed, slow-relishing our crackers, cheese, and wine,
But even more the feast our eyes consumed of dulcet views
Both up and down the gently moving Susquehanna flow,
Deep-set between late autumn hues, still yielding pastel glow;
And then, before we left our pensive perch, we watched the grace
With which a brave hang glider soared above the mellow scene,
And rode the wind beyond the river to a tiny patch of green.

Acadia

Our mid-September holiday in Maine's Acadia
Is just as firmly founded in our consciousness as are
Its massive granite trademark domes deep-rooted in the sea;
From sweeping summits of those glacier-polished rarities,
We scanned in morning light the sparkling sapphire surface of
The northern ocean's reach, just we alone, incredibly,
In solitary wonderment, where summer visitors
Reputedly are legion, crowding every lookout scene;
In pleasant quietude we biked alone, along old
Carriage paths, around the mellow shine of land-locked Eagle Lake,

Then lingered by clear mottled pools of intertidal zones,
Astonished at tenacious little lives surviving there;
We rode the churning, rocking ocean in a lobster boat,
To feel close-up the power and vastness of the sea;
And last, to grant the troubadour a fitting ending for
His song, we climbed the "Precipice", inscribed ironically
As "Trail", to stand on Champlain Mountain's rare topography,
For one last lingering picture of that peerless seascape scene.

Do you remember that blest day in June, returning home from
Pittsburgh's airport, how it came to me spontaneously
That you would like to see what well may be the most unique
And loveliest of buildings at any university--
Pitt's forty story Gothic-styled Cathedral of the mind....
That was a day when watches didn't seem to come in play,
So lost were we in scrutinizing every lovely thing
We came upon--the language rooms, distinctively arranged
With furnishings portraying varied nationalities--
Fine stone-arched Stephen Foster shrine, with stained glass windows
Depicted themes of the composer's well-known melodies-- which
And Heinz celestial Gothic Chapel on the other side,
With patterned windows of transparent and translucent glass,
Which we examined in minute detail to understand
The symbolism of each color, figure, and design....

Cathedral of Learning

Our eyes and souls replete with beauty of man's fashioning,
We linked our loving hands, and turned our lazy steps across
The Schenley Bridge, and strolled to where the Phipps Conservatory
Beckoned us to see and breathe the beautiful creations
In which Man and Nature have combined their creativity;
When finally we'd seen and pondered every plant and flower,
We exited with thoughts of home, for surely this had been
Enough to nourish souls for many common days that lay
Ahead.... But then we heard intriguing music coming from
Carnegie-Mellon's campus hill, where scattered groups of folks
Were sitting on the slope, listening and picnicking;
"O well," we thought, "let's stretch our fertile day," and ambled up
To lounge awhile in fragrant shade, and dream, without a care,
Of glass and flower beauty, and cathedrals in the air....

Everglades

A different kind of mood and rhythm permeated our
receptive beings when we traveled south in wintertime
To see and feel The Everglades. Then myriad kinds of birds
Accumulate to feed and bathe at waterholes along the trails,
And rainy season swarms of insects are not apt to mar
A full contemplative immersion in its varied charms;
Our arms entwined, we lazed along the railed Anhinga Trail,
With frequent stops to watch, close-up, exotic birds, and fish,
And water snakes, and alligators whose enormous grins
And self-contented eyes teased us to guess their purposes;
Our knowledge and our sensitivity increased extensively,
As we took time to read each sign on every trail, and then
Intently search each scene for its intrinsic subtlety;

The novelties of hardwood hammocks, stunted cypress stands,
And mangrove nurseries all drew our heed, but when we stood
Upon the Pa-hay-okee Overlook, and gazed across
The vastness of that pathless, shallow, prairie riverbed,
Where sedges and a hundred grasses dominate the scene,
We sensed the fragile fabric of its durability....
Our minds and spirits overflowing with that wonderment,
As coda to those mysteries that Nature comprehends,
We ventured to Flamingo village for a twilight cruise,
Among the scattered keys and seabirds of south Florida Bay,
Till sunlight sank in sparkling waves to end a flawless day.

I've always loved the singing euphony of Indian names:
Connoquenessing...Tuscarora...Sinnemahoning....
The last one chimes a special music in our consciousness,
For in the park that holds that name, our troubadour
Composed a song trancendent in both words and melody;
Perhaps it was because we found there perfect medicine
For minds fatigued from stringent overload of summer school--
Of striving 'round the clock to meet unalterable goals
At vital crossroads in our lives....

Sinnemahoning

                    In any case, we found
Revitalizing rest in quiet camp, and drifting on
The moonstone lake in lone canoe, or through small, tall grass isles,
Where entry of the spreading stream roams out intriguingly,
Or close along the shoreline base of very steep, tree-covered
Mountainsides, where half a dozen times or more our silent
Drifting brought us near to eagle roosts, surprising them to
Lift their wings to thrilling flight before our quite astonished eyes....
We found a solitary shaded promontory, where
We lunched, and looked upon the full-length misty majesty
Of the steeply folded, mountain-barricaded reservoir,
Like statues solely granted breath to breathe the beautiful....

...nd last, we cycled side by side the finest asphalt track
...e've ever known--smoothly rolling, meandering along
... green-fringed way, through shadows of great sycamores or spruce,
...paced out so that between them always there were graceful scenes
...f cobalt mountains, fields where deer were grazing, or sensuous streams--
...o much in tune with Nature that it seemed the stuff of dreams.

Niagara

Idyllic, too, was music of our senior honeymoon,
Exploring, with a mid-October feel, Niagara Falls:
We strolled along the eastern brink the whole breath-taking way
Through Devils Hole and Whirlpool Parks, awestruck, at frequent stops,
To stare down on and listen to the surging water's thrust--
Grinding, twisting power that's raged for twenty thousand years
Or more to carve and break away the underlying shale
And sandstone base.... The wonder was the far-resounding roars
Of such coercive force could settle in responsive souls
As songs of peace; in trance of golden age, I reminisced
Past visits to this fascinating shrine of Nature's slow
Destructive creativity: time-shaded images of
Early childhood, clinging to my mother's hand at verge of
All that sound and fury; sweet springtime images of fresh
Young love's discovering; warm summer images of my
Small children clinging to my hands; and poignant images
Of walking here in aching aftermath of lifemate's death....

Your firm embracing presence quickly brought my thinking back to
Current blessedness, as we traversed Goat Island Bridge, with
Rushing rapids close beneath our feet, and soon experienced
The throbbing mass of falling water, intimately,
Merely yards away, our clothes and faces catching spray,
As though to bear away a sampling of its vibrancy;
Then, circling 'round the island to the panoramic edge
Of Horseshoe Falls, and back along the rim toward Rainbow Bridge,
We learned firsthand the origin of its name, as iris arcs
Appeared, dispelled, and reappeared three times within the gorge;
Convinced our blended steps were tracking treasure cache, we crossed
The Rainbow Bridge to Canada, absorbed, all afternoon,
The floral and cascading beauties of Victoria Park,
Then lucked into a real Hungarian restaurant, where we
Reenergized our mortal beings to satiety;
As violinists played romantic music liltingly,
Our eyes reprised: "The treasure is our sweet affinity."
How could we guess that special day had even more in store?
A consummate sunset at our camp on Lake Ontario's shore!

Yosemite
Our honeymoon ascent beside
Yosemite's great Falls,
To rest, entranced, just where it
starts its canyon-ranging plunge…

And then the soul-deep effervescency along unique
Mist Trail, with timeless pauses to absorb tranquility
Of rumbling waterfalls and ancient cedar groves, on way
To lunch at topmost edge of Half Dome's legendary cliff.

Another, and another, of those signal holidays,
When cups of exaltation overflowed, parade and gleam
Across the aging landscapes of my late-November brain:

A

White

Sand

Beach

A twilight run along the still uncluttered pristine beach
Of smooth white sand, on northwest Florida's southern-facing shore...

Torremolinos

A seafood supper high above Spain's southern coast, with sea
Of boundless Mediterranean blue our tablemate...

Bryce

Observing and exploring through the eons-sculpted maze
Of Bryce's natural art and architecture, a fairyland
Of salmon-textured vaults and spires the scheme and range
Of which, to even seasoned minds, seems unbelievable...

Ticonderoga

Our stepping hand in hand into the date-suspending spell
Of history that came alive, among the battlements
Of Fort Ticonderoga, scanning Lake Champlain for ghosts
Of alien ships, with antique background thrill of fife and drum...

Jefferson's Monticello

The special awe we felt communing with the genius soul
Of Thomas Jefferson at Monticello's graceful place,
Full-savoring that peerless "man of the milennium" --
Architect, inventor, horticulturist, musician,
Untiring student of all aspects of the human scene,
Articulator of man's instinct for democracy...

Bok's Singing Tower

And now I must select a fitting final fare-thee-well:
An afternoon of utter blending of the beautiful
In sight and sound, roaming through the wildlife sanctuary
Of Bok's Singing Tower...sitting in some pleasant bower...
Listening to celestial chimes...resting in aesthetic bliss...
Feeling, could we choose a heaven, that it would be this.

Good-bye, My Great Good Friend

Good-bye, my great good friend. Once more grief's pain
Pervades, as memory must bear the daily hours
That we refined in private love's reality
For ten full years, since first you leaped the picket fence
Into my lonely yard, to lick my weary hands
And lift my shattered heart up through the lightless gloom
Of double loss and woe. You could not phrase for me
Your own past hurtful sorrowing in search for love,
But clearly I could read it in your deep brown eyes
As, paw in hand, we quickly, firmly chose to drink
The bracing tonic of our mutual comforting.

It was a trail of "Wonder" how you came to me
From distant place; instinctively I named you that.
On second thought I might have called you "Wanderer"
Instead, for through those testing, first-acquainting months
You often left my yard to roam I know not where,
Perhaps to grow familiar with surrounding tracts,
Or else to search for canine immortality,
But then you would be back when I returned from work
To greet me with enthusiastic confidence
That this was "home" and would be final "resting place"
For you, just as it has been so inscribed for me.

One time I sadly wondered if you'd wandered on,
Through eight days tensely searching, yearning your return
In vain, till finally I found you spent and thin
Beyond a river's rapid snowmelt flow, enticed
Improbably by ill-matched female foxhound's charm.
I brought you back to reassume your destined role
As monarch of our ample grounds, then seized the thought
To bring a second German shepherd here to cheer
Your lonesome hours or days when I must be away.

th your inborn benevolence you greeted him
 friend, but Splendor, almost twin to you in size
d coloring, abjured your overtures of play,
gressively asserting his inured desire
 dominate with frequent, clandestine attacks;
u did not wish to fight, so let him have his way,
til one day from ambush, still unsatisfied,
 flung himself on you with vicious, snarling wrath.
is time you would not acquiesce; a massive power
)m deep within your gentle soul rose up and cried
nough!" You might have killed him had my pleading voice
t pierced the fury through to your ungrudging heart.
ch nemesis of noble rage had set it right--
ere could not be two emperors in one regime;
)ught another place where Splendor could aspire
 rule; henceforth you'd bear the scepter with impunity,
d stride our hilltop realm with proper dignity.

u gave me in those mending years pure love,
naltered when it alteration found," as wise
ll Shakespeare wrote in sonnet pledge to true love's range;
us when I brought a wife to share our country life
u kissed her hand as if it were a part of mine,
d, with tolerant twinkle in your watchful eyes,
 once became a kind, amused companion to
at funny, hairy, jumping Scottish terrier
 brought along and lodged in new-built house near yours.

truth we had not yet imagined fullest depth
 which regard could reach, until retirement brought
 home to you full-time. Then did I realize
 every move while working in the yard, your eyes
th tireless adoration fixed on naught but me--
e awesome magnet center of your universe.

Each morning when Elaine had left for work, I'd go
To give you drink, to scratch your ears, to rub your back,
To hug your waiting, grateful, vibrant, furry form;
And then I'd hurl the stick which you'd selected from
The large collection of your splintered toys, but not
Until you'd raised your paw as you had learned to do
For sign of readiness, your face a painter's dream
Of concentrated portraiture. A pen cannot
Describe such instant speed, such beauteous grace,
Such tracking, catching miracles as I beheld
Each day on grass or snow. When it was time for rest
You always knew if I had brought a bone as gift,
And winsomely would wait for it with right paw raised
Distinctively, then slowly choose a place to lie
And savor it--a haze of sylvan ancestry
Apparent in the pleasured distance of your eyes.

Unnumbered times I'd call to you from house or yard
Poetic variations of your given name,
And phrase my constant care in all the languages
I know, in conscious search for eloquence to match
The stirring oratory of your wordless love.

And still more frequently, from porch or window frame,
I'd watch your lovely classic majesty at rest
In grass, or poised upon your roof, responding to
Each sight and sound with silent, well-tuned symetry,
Or, of necessity at times, with deep bass tones,
Reacting to events around, or shaping them.

Especially you prized our little nature hikes--
To trace close-up the scents which normally you sensed
Far-off--to satisfy your innate passion to explore;
A week ago we made a festive jaunt around
To every niche and corner of our highland park;
You seemed so strong--so full of life with zest for more....
And now you lie beneath a pile of frozen snow,
Awaiting soft'ning warmth of spring when I must place
You under turf you came to know as home, and then,
My best of friends, I'll have to say good-bye again.

Return to Bilgers' Rocks

If a decade had elapsed since that upsetting day when,
er teeming years, I'd gone again to Bilgers' Rocks and seen
e broken glass and loathsome lewdness painted on the walls
sed to love to look upon and carefully explore.
en one fine day there was a notice that some neighbor folks,
ensed by all the desecration that the vandal gangs
d caused, were organizing to attempt to clean away
e trash...to devise a strategy to keep the thugs at bay...
use the grounds as picnic place where families could play.

ew months hence I had an invitation from a friend--
ormer student-teacher who'd become quite dedicated
preserving the environment. He'd devised a kind of
th day to be celebrated out at Bilgers' Rocks, which
ery youngster in the Fifth Grade of the local schools would
attending. The salient purpose was to stimulate
preciation of the beauty and uniqueness of
ose monumental, nature-patterned monoliths,
d also make the students deeply feel and clearly see
eir molestation as a monstrous immorality.

role was to describe for them the way it used to be
years long past (pristine and unprofaned), and to explain
w I had practiced there to qualify as climbing guide
r many a far-off major mountaineering enterprise.
so was obliged to give a demonstration how
safely climb and to descend those steeply-sculpted cliffs,
ose lichened surfaces are treacherous when soaked by rain.
e walls of major passages among the rocks were so
otesquely marred by broken glass and brainless smut that I
reswore performance there, and quickly led my crowd of
ergetic youngsters through some narrow passageways which
emembered well, and took them to an outpost site, removed
t far enough from the main course that orgy bands had not
yet discovered and corrupted it. I mounted to
ample ledge from which the upturned swarm of eager faces
uld observe and hear my explanations of the climbing gear
brought along. I showed them how to use it properly,
scended on the rope, and, to conclude the exercise,
cended up the face with safe technique; a loud applause
ploded as I gained the top edge of that precipice,
ll tinged with nought but mossy green of Nature's edifice.

ccess in making that hard climb with grace at seventy
as not as meaningful as seeing there below the sea
bright, ingenuous faces watching me attentively.
ared to hope that in the soil of those fertile brains
e seeds of our "respect-for-Nature" lessons would take hold--
at in the future they would feel the need to take the lead,
storing and preserving there a proper legacy.

I Feel Such Boundless Pride in You

I feel such boundless pride in you, my dear;
Not only have you sought to bring to me
Fulfillment through the tempered golden years,
And loving partnership's integrity,

But you have reached so deep within yourself
To persevere through life's exigencies--
To bravely deal with problems thrust your way
By others...with determined equity.

And then at fifty-five, to elevate
Already well-trained capabilities,
You studied nights and summers to secure
A second master's "state-of-arts" degree;

But even more amazing was that you
Maintained a perfect "four-point" average through
That maze of infinite complexities...
No wonder that I feel such pride in you.

WQED-FM, We Love You

At Christmastime we gave ourselves a new clock radio,
And in its broader range we made a great discovery:
Pure, soul-relaxing consonance of classic music sounds
Caressed our unexpecting ears with cadenced artistry.

We hardly could believe that, midst accustomed multitude
Of strident, thumping, jarring, screaming, crude cacophonies,
Which blast and screech at almost every movement of the dial
We chanced upon <u>one</u> source of master-crafted euphony.

With Pittsburgh's Classic Radio, so many miles away,
We now feel close affinity; each morning, happily,
We gently wake to philharmonic beauty, or the grace
Of string quartettes, or minuets, or choral harmonies.

ALL CLASSICAL--ALL DAY

SLEEPERS AWAK

Jules Massenet
MEDITATION (from Thäis)
Fritz Kreisler, violinist

Jean Sibelius
FINLANDIA
Berlin Philharmonic/Kara

Jakob Meyerbeer
O PARADISO (from L'Africana)
Jussi Bjoerling, tenor

Johannes Brahms
VIOLIN CONCERTO IN D MAJOR
David Oistrakh, violinist

Giuseppe Verdi
ERI TU (from A Masked Ball)
Leonard Warren, baritone

Peter Ilich Tchaikovsky
THE PATHETIQUE SYMPHONY
Boston Symphony/Koussevitzky

Franz von Suppe
POET AND PEASANT OVERTURE
Chicago Symphony/Solti

Antonio Vivaldi
CONCERTO FOR TWO LU
String Orchestra of Vienna

Ludvig von Beethoven
SERENADE IN D (string trio)
Heifetz/Primrose/Piatigorsky

George Frederick Handel
OBOE CONCERTO IN B FLAT
Paillard Chamber Orchestra

MORNING CONCERT

ST. PAUL SUNDAY MORNING

Arcangelo Corelli
SONATA NUMBER ONE
Academy of Ancient Music

CANTOS DE ESPANÃ
Chamber Orchestra of Madrid
Alfredo Kraus, tenor

Franz Schubert
THE TROUT QUINTET IN A MAJOR
The Hungarian String Quartette

To a Wild Rose

EDWARD MACDOWEL

LUNCH WITH AMADEUS AND FRIENDS

Claude Debussy
TWO ARABESQUES
New York Philharmonic/Metropoulos

PITTSBURGH SYMPHONY PLAYS WITH PASSION

Josef Haydn
QUARTET NUMBER 4 (Horseman)
Budapest String Quartette

Ponchielli
DANCE OF THE HOURS (La Gioconda)
NBC Symphony/Toscanini

Felix Mendelssohn
CONCERTO IN E MINOR
Isaac Stern, violinist

nn Strauss
E BEAUTIFUL BLUE DANUBE
na Boys Choir and Orchestra

ADVENTURES IN GOOD MUSIC
arl Haas

Edvard Grieg
PEER GYNT SUITE
Vox Symphony Orchestra

uggiero Leoncavallo
ROLOGUE (from Pagliacci)
awrence Tibbett, baritone

George Philipp Telemann
FOUR SONATAS FOR FLUTE AND CONTINUO
Baron/Kouguell/Conant

Wolfgang Amadeus Mozart
SERENADE (from Don Giovanni)
Ezio Pinza, bass

Antonín Dvorak
CONCERTO FOR CELLO IN B MINOR
Rostropovich/Royal Philharmonic

MIDDAY CLASSICS

Carreras, Domingo, Pavarotti
In concert with Zubin Mehta
at Rome's Baths of Caracalla

Manuel de Falla
THE THREE CORNERED HAT
Frubeck de Burgos, conductor

AFTERNOON CLASSICS

Richard Wagner
LIEBESNACHT (Tristan and Isolde)
Kirsten Flagstad/Lauritz Melchior

MY TRUE LOVE SINGS
The Robert Shaw Chorale

Giacomo Puccini
UN BEL DI (Madame Butterfly)
Victoria de los Angeles, soprano

SONGS OF LATIN AMERICA
The Roger Wagner Chorale

Johann Sebastian Bach
BRANDENBURG CONCERTOS
Academy of St. Martin-in-the-Fields

LISTENER'S CHOICE

Bizet-Borne
CARMEN FANTASY
James Galway, Flutist

Franz Liszt
LA CAMPANELLA
Vladamir Horowitz

B. Godard
BERCEAUSE (from Jocelyn)
Pablo Casals, cellist

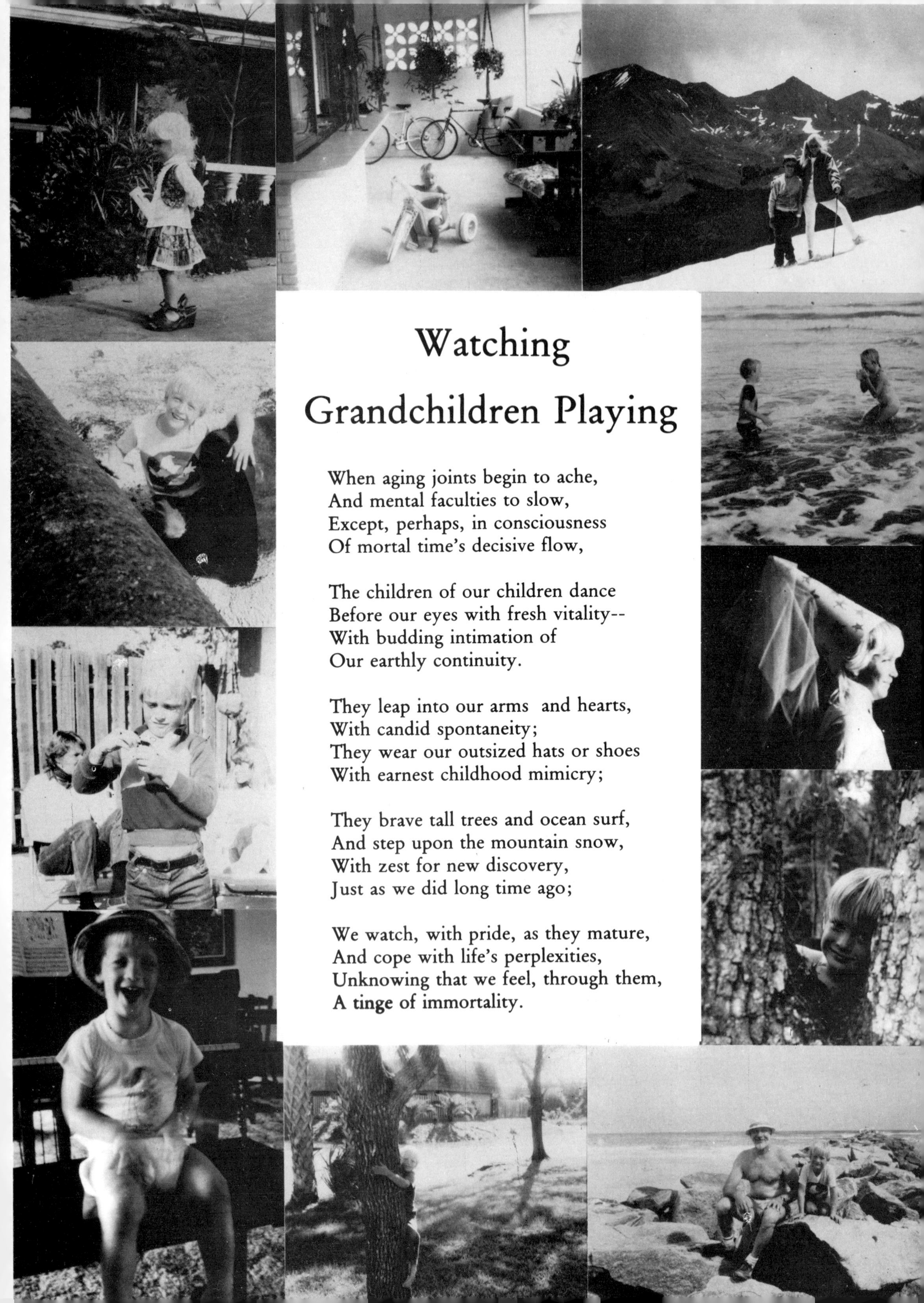

Watching

Grandchildren Playing

When aging joints begin to ache,
And mental faculties to slow,
Except, perhaps, in consciousness
Of mortal time's decisive flow,

The children of our children dance
Before our eyes with fresh vitality--
With budding intimation of
Our earthly continuity.

They leap into our arms and hearts,
With candid spontaneity;
They wear our outsized hats or shoes
With earnest childhood mimicry;

They brave tall trees and ocean surf,
And step upon the mountain snow,
With zest for new discovery,
Just as we did long time ago;

We watch, with pride, as they mature,
And cope with life's perplexities,
Unknowing that we feel, through them,
A tinge of immortality.

A Canticle of Sunsets

Another sunlit day is passing its last mile,
And briefly lingering, verging the obscure,
Flares in crimson splendor over dark'ning piles
And folds of mammoth mountain ridges standing sure,
Then, fading, travels on, but grants one goodnight smile
To me, in midst of almost fully shaded countryside,
Through barely parted lips of furthermost defile.

So has it been throughout my fixed or rambling life,
As I have watched in thrall of countless sunset spells…
From porch or lawn at hilltop home, where love clasps hands,
Or sometimes throbs with reawakened memories
Or stirring twilight dramas shared in years long past,
While building habitat with hope to make it last.…

So, also, has night's prelude magic often sparked
My gaze from myriad viewpoints all around the earth…
Beside still tropic lakes which finely duplicate
Each patterned nuance of a glowing, dust-hued sky…

round the World

From gleaming cruises on west-facing wavering bays,
Or walking near the breaker thrusts of ocean shores…
From solitary bivouacs on far Andean heights,
Or steep-stepped Himalayan terraces, or refuge hut
Verandas on Japan's or Europe's fabled Alps…
At sites of ancient ruins or cherished monuments
In Greece, or Spain, or India, or Mexico,
Where great events and architectures were conceived
And shaped by cultures that have long since ceased to be….

In all, whatever might have been the lookout place,
Before pervading darkness had the scene effaced,
Intuitively I seemed to sense and comprehend
The cosmic drift of natural beauty into truth,
And how my seeing-being functions in the flow,
As Nature wheels its cycles everlastingly:
Some days fly true as flawless arrows deftly arched
To strike the moving target of eternity.

A Toast to the Wonder of It All

First evening shadows stripe the land,
Then moving dust-clothed damask bands
Surprise as azure sky;
Carnelian rays
Marry my gaze
In ceremony high.

Magnetic eyes
Absorb the sky's
Rubescent overlay;
The life-source burns,
Vermillion turns
To ashes, covering day.

Last ember sparks ephemeral
Disperse into the night,
As eyes now gone celestial
Re-focus on the light
Of distal spangles shimmering
Within pervading black;
The charted stars,
Iron-tinted Mars,
And Earth are still on track.

Looking Up, Still Singing

My wife has given me the greatest gift of all--
Herself, but recently gave something that might be
Throughout my closing years a perfect medium
To lead me outward optimistically,
Still flushed with search for truth and beauty's harmony.

I turn my eight inch 'scope into the starry sphere
Of darkest night, when all the squadrons' ancient light
Responds to me with clarity of figures bright,
With constancy as man has watched through history,
And eons farther back through nebulosity,
Since light has traveled on to pinpoint in my eyes
And in my earthbound brain that quests for paradise.

The stars were fixed as ceiling by medieval clan--
Adornment for the chosen earth's unfolding plan;
Copernicus and Galileo fearlessly
Exposed the truth and faced religious bigotry....

Through many centuries of mankind's meager span
The moon was pictured with the features of a man;
We used our ingenuity to touch that place,
Now probe our neighbor planets as they speed through space,
Around a burning, blinding, sometimes warming star.

We've learned we're floating in the spiral Milky Way,
Our Sun a middling mass where legion giants play
Their parts, and nebulas give birth to bright new stars,
And old stars seek the center of the galaxy
Where even light dies into black hole gravity.

Then ever outward larger, stronger telescopes,
And other instruments surpassing their far sight,
Are patiently discovering phenomena
More deeply distant in that endless spacial night,
Confirming glimmerings, revealing new surprise
Of never dreamed of imagings in unimagined skies.

And in my private way I now may play a part,
As I look up, refining my perspective's art,
First tentatively to our cratered moon's details,
Then tracing banded Jupiter's pert satellites,
Or captivating Saturn's graceful rings--some nights
Confirming for myself Orion's Nebula,
Reflecting on Andromeda's great galaxy,
Or farther island universes' fainter light--
And with it all there comes mature serenity,
Though lost the comfort of sweet childhood's simple faith,
Accepting what I've learned of Truth and Beauty's reach
Although the lives we live on earth may prove to be
No more than island sojourns in infinity.

Remembered Beauty
Tints the Graying Mind

Remembered beauty kindly tints the graying mind,
And is a soothing balm that coats the wounded heart
When we are old, frost-fringed, and dreaming toward
The long, long sleep that lurks beyond the dimming light.

We should take time to sort the finest hours we've known,
And think on them again, before we have to go;
Although we may not ever know if there be waking,
Which humans have so yearned for since antiquity,
We can at least go bravely to that long deep sleep
Replete for dreams, contentedly aware that we
Have stretched the gift of life to fullest range, upon
This lighted grain within the dark totality
Which is our granted portion of eternity.

"Though I must give my breath
And my laughter all to death,
And my eyes through which joy came,
And my heart a wavering flame;
If all must leave me and go back
Along a blind and fearful track
So that you can make anew,
Fusing with intenser fire,
Something nearer your desire;
If my soul must go alone
Through a cold infinity,
Or even if it vanish, too,
Beauty, I have worshipped you."
                    --Sara Teasdale

"When you are old and gray and full of sleep,
And nodding by the fire, take down this book,
And slowly read, and dream of the soft look
Your eyes had once, and of their shadows deep;
How many loved your moments of glad grace,
And loved your beauty with love false or true;
But one man loved the pilgrim soul in you,
And loved the sorrows of your changing face.
And bending down beside the glowing bars
Murmur, a little sadly, how love fled
And paced upon the mountains overhead
And hid his face amid a crowd of stars."
--William B. Yeats

Notes and Identifications

FRONT COVER. The author portraying Don Quijote in the musical drama, <u>Man of La Mancha</u>, the premier production of the new Clearfield Arts Studio Theater on March 16, 1983. Don Quijote is shown proudly wearing a barber's tray, which he imagines to be the renowned Golden Helmet of Mambrino. (Mrs. J. Hess)

FRONT FLAP. Holding a child from the devastated Andean village of Santa Cruz, while leading an exploratory trip through Peru's Cordillera Blanca in the aftermath of the 1970 earthquake. 67,000 people were killed and 600,000 were left homeless. (F. Camphausen)

BACK COVER. Scene in the garden at Banff Springs National Park Headquarters, Banff, Alberta, Canada.

BACK FLAP. Resting after descending from the face of Longs Peak, Rocky Mountain National Park, Colorado, June 1980.

ii. (T) Spring at our poet's cottage which we built in 1951 on a hill above Clearfield, the county seat of Clearfield County, located on the West Branch of the Susquehanna River in the Allegheny Mountains of central Pennsylvania. In 1949, I accepted a teaching position in Spanish and English at the Clearfield Senior High School, hardly imagining that I would reside in this place all of my life. (MR) Autumn in our yard.

iii. (T) I first met Marjorie Ella Bell in September, 1942, when I entered Thiel, a small liberal arts college in northwestern Pennsylvania. A professor directed me to her because she had taken a Spanish literature course the previous year and had the textbook I needed. I was keenly impressed by her gracious helpfulness as a library assistant, and in a short while, we were mutually enveloped in a beautiful romance.

In February, 1943, when I was abruptly called away to serve in World War II, we became engaged. Apart, we exchanged daily letters. We were married in April, 1944, when I was granted a two-week furlough. Until I was discharged in 1946, she worked as a librarian and history teacher at East Brady High School. While I was securing my B.A. and M.A. degrees at Thiel College and Syracuse University, she worked in their libraries.

In 1949, we settled in Clearfield, Pennsylvania to teach, create a family, and live the fulfilling life which I've endeavored to reveal in the pages of this book. We remained totally committed to each other for 33 years, until her untimely death in 1977. (TL) Marjorie wearing a favorite dress made from silk which I brought back home from Japan in 1967. (TR) At the console in Clearfield's St. Paul's Episcopal Church, where she was the organist for several years.

(B) I met Elaine Sawyer of Lakewood, Colorado, while guiding for the Colorado Mountain Club at their summer climbing camp in the San Juan Mountains in 1979. She was then Head Teacher at the Day Care Center, a day treatment center for emotionally disturbed children at the University of Colorado Medical Center in Denver. We fell deeply in love, corresponded profusely during a year, and were married in the Rose Garden of Denver's Cheesman Park in June 1980. She moved to my home in Clearfield, where she taught briefly, and then became the librarian at the Philipsburg State General Hospital and the Central Pennsylvania School of Nursing. Currently, she is the librarian at the Clearfield Campus of Lock Haven University. The multi-splendored ways in which we have complemented and enriched each other's lives are the principal focus of the last part of this book. (BL) Coming down from an ascent of Longs Peak in Rocky Mountain National Park, one week before our wedding in June, 1980. (BR) During a visit to meet my daughter in Plantation, Florida, Christmas 1979.

vi. Capitol Peak and satellites, in Colorado's Elk Range, during an ascent of this, the state's most difficult 14,000′ peak in 1990.

vii. Meditating beside Balsam Lake while backpacking through the Grenadier Range of Southern Colorado in 1982.

1. My parents' home along the old Perry Highway in McCandless Township, Allegheny County, western Pennsylvania, as it appeared in the 1920's, shortly after my father had built it to fulfill his youthful dream of living in the country.

2. Espe Elementary School, located near Highland Stop where the old Harmony Tramway passed under the Perry Highway, ten miles north of Pittsburgh.

3. Caruso, Scotti, Shuman-Heinck: leading tenor, baritone and contralto during the Golden Age of Opera.

6 and 7. A first draft of this poem was written after reading James Hilton's novel, <u>Lost Horizon</u>, several times during my teen-age years. I took the picture across Snowmass Lake on a climb of Snowmass Peak in 1990. (Insert) Elementary school graduation portrait (8th grade).

8. (TL) Sinnemahoning State Park, central Pennsylvania, in April. (MR) Moshannon State Forest, near our home. (BR) Allegheny River near East Brady, Pennsylvania.

9. VIRTUOSA MAESTRA: Eminent teacher. Alas, I do not have a picture of my beloved Anna, except the one painted in my mind. This image has not faded in over 50 years.

10. Panorama near Home Camp, Pennsylvania. (Insert) Freshman portrait on entering Thiel College in 1942. After graduating from high school, I worked three years at service stations, cutting greens at the Highland Country Club, and as a sprayer of siding and roofing in the Pittsburgh area, saving for my college education.

11. Since I don't have a picture of my grandfather, I've used one of Fritz Kreisler, the great Viennese violinist, who was one of my idols, and who somewhat resembled my grandfather. It has been in my possession since I attended one of his recitals at Carnegie Hall in Pittsburgh at an early age. (MR) The great Spanish cellist, Pablo Casals, was another of my idols. I'll never forget watching him conduct his "Hymn to the United Nations" at age 95, playing his cello publicly for the last time. The picture is on the cover of an album which was a surprise gift from one of my advanced Spanish classes. It's one of my most cherished possessions because each member of the class inscribed the jacket with a personal note in Spanish. (BR) I first heard Leonard Warren's peerless voice during a Metropolitan Opera Audition of the Air in 1938. Overwhelmed by its rich beauty, I thought then that it was the most inspiring voice I'd ever heard, and I've never changed my mind. I was intrigued when I learned that noted critics such as Sigmund Spaeth and Olin Downs selected him as best baritone in their choice of ideal casts for great operas. Unfortunately, he died suddenly of a heart attack on the Met stage while climaxing one of his magnificent arias. Fortunately, I have several albums he recorded, and every so often I feel an overpowering need to feed my soul with his matchless renderings of "The Prologue" to <u>Pagliacci</u>, or "Eri Tu" from <u>The Masked Ball</u>, or "Di Provenza il Mar" from <u>La Traviata</u>.

12. (T) Belle Springs Golf Club near Lock Haven, Pennsylvania. (MR) Practicing on the neighboring Nixon Stoney Brook Farm, which I frequented throughout childhood. I caddied and played at Pittsburgh's North Park Course, and twice won the North Park and Allegheny County junior golf championships (Schlegel). (BL) Beneath the 20,000′ Andean mountain Salcantay in Peru's remote Vilcabamba Range during an expedition there, 30 years

ADDENDUM TO NOTES AND IDENTIFICATIONS

        During a careful reading of the bound book to make a final check for errata, I decided to include these additional clarifications. It may be convenient for the reader to use this separate sheet to mark progress through this section.

    DEDICATION PAGE: The setting of the picture at TR is St. Andrew's Episcopal Church, not St.Paul's.
    PAGE 16: Some letters in the verse at BR are obscured by the ink contrast of the organ pipes. I repeat here the complete text, along with clarifying notes:

        "I found you first among the walls of books,
        With recognition in your tender eyes
        That years before had bridged the frigid skies
        To fill my own with hope.(1) Instinctively
        I sensed your unadulterated warmth--
        Your quick intelligence in helping me
        To source my studies sought.... I soon forgot
        My tasks, so captive were my eyes to watch
        Your grace unfold; and then my lips were bold
        Enough to sing to you "The Evening Star" (2)
        On amphitheater stage, where first we kissed
        And cleared away all past forbidding mist."

    (1) These three lines refer to the last verse of the poem on p.15.
    (2) "The Evening Star" (O du mein holder Abendstern) is a love song from Wagner's opera Tannhauser, which I had memorized before entering college while studying "voice" and considering opera as a possible career.

    PAGE 43: SNOWBOUND PRIVACY refers to one of Whittier's greatest poems, "Snowbound", in which he crafted a superb line that I've never forgotten - "tumultuous privacy of storm."
    PAGE 45: (1) 1st verse, first line. Refers to James Russell Lowell's poem, "June", from The Vision of Sir Launfal:

            "And what is so rare as a day in June?
            Then, if ever, come perfect days;
            Then Heaven tries earth if it be in tune..."

    The remainder of the first verse refers to William Cullen Bryant's poem "To a Waterfowl", written in Plainfield, MA, to which Bryant had gone to inquire about a possible apprenticeship in law. Feeling very uncertain about his future, he observed a bird's unwavering flight across the sunset sky and was thus inspired to write:

        "He who from zone to zone guides through the boundless sky thy certain flight,
        In the long way that I must tread alone will lead my steps aright."

    I was so moved by this poem when I first read it that I committed it to memory.
    (2) GREAT BARRINGTON, MA is where he ended his early quest.
    (3) The final word in the 4th line should be "strode", instead of "rode".
    (4) The quote at the bottom right is the last verse of Bryant's poem, "Thanatopsis" (a meditation on death).
    PAGE 108: The picture at the top is at the ghost town of St. Elmo, up Chalk Creek Canyon, Sawatch Range, Colorado. The picture at the bottom is of the Gore Range in central Colorado.
    PAGE 126: First verse, line 9. The last word should be "rites".
    PAGE 140: Text, lines 5 and 6: "the long historic way" refers to Mexico's historic boulevard, Paseo de la Reforma, along which are found splendid monuments to (1) INDEPENDENCE (with figures of Father

(OVER)

Hidalgo and other leaders of Mexican independence at its base, and topped with a "winged victory" statue), and (2) CUAUHTEMOC, the last Aztec emperor, who endured unspeakable torture at the hands of the Spanish conquerors, but would not cooperate with them.

PAGE 162: PIETRA DURA: semi-precious stones. AKBAR, the grandfather of Shah Jehan, made Agra his capital.

PAGE 174: Third verse: FRIAR TIRSO DE MOLINO was a Spanish priest-author who wrote the story on which Mozart based his famous opera, Don Giovanni. Rosini's Barber of Seville was also set in Seville.

PAGE 175: CANTE HONDO means "deep song", which at times is like a wail of emotion.

PAGE 176: PREMIO GORDO means the "grand prize".

PAGE 198: Reverse the picture identification for this page. The 16th century bakery in Pisac is BR

PAGE 224: The picture at MR is of one of the lovely waterfalls found in the Pyrenees' Ordessa National Park.

PAGE 239: First verse, lines 10-11. The quote is from Robert Browning's poem, Rabbi Ben Ezra". Second verse, line 15, refers to my poem, "A Mountaineer's Psalm", which is inscribed on the bronze top of the monument I created from rocks brought back from mountain summits all over the world. The full text, also found on pages 357-361 of my book, A Lifelong Love Affair with Mountains, is given here:

> "When someday I have gone beyond the ring
> Of evergreens which guard the granite hill,
> And you seek out the upward way I went,
> You will find me still.
>
> Return the salutations of tall firs
> Which grace for centuries the alpine view,
> Retrieve from all the meadow mass one flower,
> And I shall come to you
>
> To stand where water makes its roar of peace,
> In amphitheaters hued with lichen glow,
> Or mark the frontier of the frozen world
> With steps on virgin snow.
>
> High in the chambers of steep mountain rock,
> Challenging the sky with ample height,
> At apex of some stunning pinnacle,
> The essence of my shade will greet your sight,
>
> For when I've gone forever to those vast
> Uncharted reaches that stretch on above,
> Yet shall I stay within the beautiful
> Of all that I have loved.

PAGE 241: Verse 2, last line. I'm suggesting that the glory of music may encircle our spirits somewhat like the halos of light which religious artists have painted around the visages of their sacred subjects.

PAGE 244: The note for this page on page 330 should read "Alaska's Mt. McKinley".

PAGE 252: TOP PICTURE: I placed half of Marjorie's ashes in the bronze urn. After my cremation, half of my ashes will be joined with hers. The rest will be scattered near the stone monument and in the flower beds around our home. The carved wooden statue of Don Quijote was purchased in La Mancha, Spain, during our meandering summer there in 1970. SECOND PICTURE: My desk at the back of my classroom, with statue and plaque at the right highlighting the memorial scholarship.

after entertaining that "dream of youth".

13. (T) Taken from a memorial plate. Located between Highland Stop and Pine Creek above the Perry Highway, the old church burned and a new one was built nearby. (B) Interior of the new church.

14 - 17. Illustrations on these pages are from old Thiel College catalogs and promotional booklets. DISSONANCE: Clashing sounds. (TL) Soldiers at basic training. (TR) Seal of Thiel College. (BR) Engraving of Diogenes seeking an honest man.

15. AUFWIEDERSEHEN: Till we meet again. (TL) Picture of my fiancee, which I carried while away during World War II. (R) Reproduction of tapestries created by the Thiel Women's Club, depicting Thiel scenes and themes: the Bell, Brother Martin's Walk, and the Alma Mater.

16. (T) Greenville Hall, the college's original building. (M) The library where I met Marjorie, who worked there as a student assistant for four years and as librarian for two more. (B) The chapel organ and the choir in which we both sang. In that era, all students were required to attend chapel service every morning. (BR) Ella Grace Hunton, Dean of Women and language professor, who became my mentor and our lifelong friend. She also composed Thiel's Alma Mater. A residence hall now honors her memory.

17. (ML) The outdoor amphitheater in Riverside Park, Greenville, Pennsylvania, where we first confessed our love for each other. She sat as the sole spectator in the top tier. I mounted the stage and sang to her "The Evening Star" from the opera "Tannhauser" in German. (BL) Faculty enroute to convocation. (BR) Front entrance to the Administration Building.

18. (T) The Greenville newspaper took this picture on the steps of Ridgeway Dining Hall as our group of 13 prepared to leave for the railroad station. (ML) Greenville Hall. (B) Vinoy Park Hotel on Tampa Bay, where I was based for basic military training in February 1943. (Sun News, St. Petersburg, Florida). While visiting my daughter in St. Petersburg in the 1970's, I noted that it was still standing, but unused, like a ghost of that era.

19. (T). St. Petersburg as it was in 1943. (B) The Don Cesar Hotel on the Gulf of Mexico. The Army used it as a hospital, but it was later restored to its former elegance and is still used.

20. Trinity Preparatory School in Pawling, New York, which Army Airways Communications System used as its cryptography school during World War II. (Wright). (B) Unidentified newspaper picture of Pawling Railway Station in 1943.

21. Crews of B-24 Liberator bombers were trained at Smyrna, Tennessee.

22. (T) Type of plane in which we flew from Nashville, TN to Brownsville, Texas. (B) Tampico Airport.

23. (T) Hidalgo Avenue, looking toward Tampico. (BL) The Mendive home as it looked in 1960, when I took my family there for a reunion with these Mexican friends. (BR) Vendor at Miramar Beach.

24. (T) Daily Hall, Marjorie's residence at Thiel, where, as initiation into the Sadhe Aleph Fraternity, I was obliged to sing a love song under her window. (B) Brother Martin's Walk. The name refers to Martin Luther; Thiel was founded by the Lutheran Church.

25. (TR) The Shenango River. (B) Miramar Beach near Tampico, where I frequently went on days off to swim or run.

26. The old East Brady High School. (Yearbook photo). Marjorie left college during the second semester of her senior year to teach history and to organize the school library, and continued to work there until the war was over. Fourteen months into my military service, I was granted a furlough. Without notifying her, I traveled via military transport plane to Brownsville, TX, then via railroad to Pittsburgh, and finally aboard the very slow East Brady local (rail line) up the Allegheny River Valley to where the train comes out of a long tunnel at Sarah Furnace, several miles upriver from East Brady. I walked down an unused track, up the hill, and into the school. No words exist to adequately describe the emotions of that unexpected reunion. (B) The bridge across the Allegheny River at East Brady.

27. (TR) The Mount Pleasant Church on the Chicora-Kittanning Road, where, within a week, we were married. We spent our brief honeymoon at a camp near Elliot State Park, and, even though it was just the end of April, we went swimming in the frigid mountain waters of Parker Dam. Incredibly, we were just a few miles up the road from Clearfield, which we did not visit at that time, but where the inscrutable fates would settle us within a few years for the rest of our lives. (BL) East Brady's main street as it appeared in the 1940's.

28 and 29. At Vernam Field, Jamaica, British West Indies, where our Air Force trained B-29 crews in 1945. One of those planes was soon destined to drop the A-bombs on Hiroshima and Nagasaki, forcing the Japanese to surrender.

30. (TL) In Kingston, Jamaica. (ML) Natives near our base. (BL) On top of Blue Mountain.

31. A collage of old Jamaican postcards showing typical scenes. (BL) Blue Mountain Peak.

32. (T) The Base Chapel, exterior and interior. (ML) Chaplain Mitchell and military car; author on boat to Goat Island. (BR) Scenes in Old Kingston.

33. Our gospel team, quartette, and some churches where we conducted services.

34. (T and L) Scenes at the leper colony Christmas party in Spanish Town. (B) Quartette singing at Bethany Church.

35. Collage of Jamaican postcards with typical scenes, which I sent to my wife in 1945. (BL) Hope Botanical Gardens near Kingston.

36. (MR) My father in his 30's. He died in his 50's of a heart attack while walking in a woods about a mile from home, above the pasture where I used to practice golf. The site was thick with laurel bushes (see picture at TL of p. 37). When he did not return home from work one night, a week-long community-wide search ensued until he was found. Military red tape delayed my homecoming from Jamaica until after his burial. His friend, the highly respected township constable, wrote an eloquent accolade in the community newspaper about the premature passing of this quiet, very constructive life. (BL) Site where Ole Bull, the famous Norwegian violinist, tried to found a colony and began construction of a castle in the 19th century. The colony failed, but the area became a state park.

37. The main entrance to Thiel College's Administration Building, which I re-entered in 1946 to complete my degree. (Thiel promotional material).

38. (ML) Shakespeare's statue in the old Thiel Library. (BL) With Mexican friends on the ascent of The Hat Mountain near El Mante, Mexico. (B) Entrance to Tampico's cemetery on All Saints' Day, 1943.

39. (BL) Rissell Gymnasium, where Thiel graduations were held in that era.

40. (T) Hall of Languages, Syracuse University (reproduction of a painting by Evelyn Schmidt).

41. Syracuse University campus, with the library on the right, where my wife worked while I earned my Master's degree.

42. Pictures from a scrapbook which we made up after a summer trip through New England: counterclockwise from top: Cullen Bryant cottage, Great Barrington, Massachusetts, now a museum tearoom; Housatonic River; Thoreau's Walden Pond; The Wayside, Concord, MA, where Nathaniel Hawthorne lived and worked; Thoreau's tombstone in Sleepy Hollow Cemetery, Concord; Orchard House, setting for Louisa M. Alcott's Little

<u>Women,</u>and Bronson Alcott's School of Philosophy, Concord. (Maynard)

43. (TL) John Greenleaf Whittier's home, and Quaker church, Amesbury, MA. (TR) Whittier's portrait (Whittier Home Association). (M) Cemetery and statue of Massasoit, friend and protector of the Pilgrims in Plymouth, MA. (B) Henry Wadsworth Longfellow's home and memorial statue, Cambridge, MA. He was of special interest to me because he was "Head of Languages" and "Spanish teacher" at Harvard. Soon I was to assume a similar, though considerably more modest, position at Clearfield Senior High School. The statue is the work of Daniel Chester French, Concord sculptor, who also executed the Minute Man statue (TL, p. 44) and many other notable works. His style set the standard for official American memorials for future decades.

44. (TR and BL) Concord Bridge and Ralph Waldo Emerson's home, Concord. (American Art Co.). (ML, MR, BR) Emerson's study, portrait and grave marker, Sleepy Hollow Cemetery (American Antiquarian Soc.). The boulder in the cemetery bears the inscription, "The passive master lent his hand to the vast soul that o'er him planned", from Emerson's poem, "The Problem".

Our visit to Emerson's home was especially memorable. The hostess was the very same lady who had come to live in the house as companion to Emerson's widow, Lydia. Incredibly, she was still alive and quite sharp mentally. When she learned that I had just been studying Emerson's writings, she granted me what apparrently was the rare privilege of sitting in Emerson's chair where he preferred to write.

45. (T) Looking out from the porch of William Cullen Bryant's homestead in central Massachusetts. (B) The fateful top of Monument Mountain.

46. Mossy stream near Ole Bull State Park, Pennsylvania.

47. (T) View from site of Ole Bull's Castle. (TR) Close-up of stream shown on p. 46. (BR) Waterfall in stream in Ohiopyle State Park, Pennsylvania.

48. (T) Taken on a walk near Pawling, NY. The original version of this poem written long ago was inspired by a picture which I had in my possession for many years, but could not locate in a recent search.

49. I have no pictures of that abandoned well on my wife's grandfather's farm near Kaylor, PA. I have used two similar ones taken at the Drake Well in Oil Creek State Park near Titusville, PA.

52. LEITMOTIFS: Themes associated with particular persons, situations, or ideas throughout music dramas. As this section deals primarily with family activities, most pictures are self-explanatory. I identify our two children here, and not with each piece or picture. Erik was born in 1950 and Kristan in 1952. In addition to the usual family activities, we also taught our children music, golf, skiing, and climbing. (T) From <u>Old Time Favorites</u> (Marks). (BR) <u>Carolers' Book in Song and Story</u> (Hall and McCreary).

53. Collage of family sharing: (TR) Backpacking into Mt. Jefferson in central Oregon, with Mt. Hood in the far-off background. Just below that, a visit to Lincoln's New Salem, Illinois. (BR) When Erik and Kristan were in high school, all four of us sang in the Trinity United Methodist Church choir in Clearfield.

55. SONATINAS IMPROMPTUS: Little spur-of-the-moment compositions.

56. ALLEGRO CON SPIRITO: Joyfully, with spirit.

57. TONE POEM: A composition intended to portray a particular story, scene or mood.

58. CHANSONETTE CELESTE: A little star song.

64. ROUNDELAY: A poem with a reiterated refrain.

65. (ML) The emblem of the German Alpine Club. (BL) Closeup of Switzerland's Matterhorn.

66. The Silver Spring Church and cemetery wall, near Mechanicsburg, PA. It is the oldest church west of the Susquehanna River. The cemetery has pre-revolutionary graves. A minister friend took that charge when he left Clearfield, and he and his wife invited us to visit them several times in fall.

70 - 73. We had German shepherd dogs at home when I was growing up, so Rusty. had it made when he showed up at our winterized tourist cabin at Pompey Center, NY, where we were living while I attended Syracuse University. We tried to find his owner through "lost and found" ads, but confessed relief when no one responded. When we settled in Clearfield, someone with a gorgeous female shepherd offered us the pick of the litter if we'd consent to mate her with Rusty. Thor, the most beautiful shepherd we'd ever seen was the result. Unfortunately, Thor developed cataracts in his second year. He miraculously navigated our two-acre yard with impunity, except when a bike or wheelbarrow was left in an unaccustomed place. These dogs, and the ones that followed, added a special glory to our hill

70. ALLEGRO GRAZIOSO: Lively and with graceful motion. (BL) Rusty loved to chase sticks, especially when cast out into water. He loved to swim so much that he would clandestinely leave the yard and go to a nearby strip mine pool to take a swim.

71. ANDANTE MAESTOSO: Slow and majestic.

72. Rusty accompanied us on our 1949 tour of New England in our 1948 Ford.

73. John Milton, the handsome English poet who wrote "Paradise Lost" and "Paradise Regained", eventually lost his sight.

74. The "friendly expert" was Willard Dominick, Supervisor of Art in the Clearfield schools, now retired. He is a marvelous painter, and, as a teacher, was very good at sowing the seeds of artistic ideas in his students for them to develop.

75. (T) The original exhibit. It was repeated several years later, and also elsewhere. (B) The models and their clay portraits.

76. Destruction of the great Peruvian earthquake of 1970. (TL) The large figure of Christ still stands on Yungay's Cemetery Hill, but the tombs around burst open. (TR) What remains of a residence. (B) The main plaza of Yungay, which was totally overrun by an avalanche from 22,208' Huascarán, burying 20,000 citizens.

77. Scenes at a typical strip mine operation near Clearfield.

78. (TL) The Trinity United Methodist Church Choir and the magnificent Möller organ, before the fire. (TR) Erik and the organist, Della Gallaher, practicing handbell presentation for Christmas Eve. (BR) The altar and Christ in Gethsemene window in the old church.

83. My mother faced the necessity of moving from the home she had helped my father build and had lived in for 50 years.

84. Denali sits at a birthday table.

85. (T) Bilger's Rocks as it used to be. (B) Same location now.

86. (BR) For me, the most moving verse of the consecrating poem inscribed on plaques around the burial ground at Gettysburg. In case it cannot be read from the picture, I'll give it here:

"On fame's eternal camping ground
Their silent tents are spread,
And glory guards with solemn round
The bivouac of the dead."

88. PERCUSSION: Drums, cymbals, etc.

91. Close-up of cicada. (Brooks)

92. CADENZA: A summary flourish just before the close of a composition; CACOPHONY: Dissonance, harsh discordance of sound. (B) Location of the Peruvian town of Ranrahirca, where 4,000 were buried in an avalanche that came down from North Huascarán in 1962.

93. ARPEGGIOS: Notes of a chord sounded in succession rather than simultaneously. Music example from <u>Cello Solos Series No. 40</u> (Amsco).

94. AEOLIAN HARP: A shallow oblong box with gut strings tuned in unison and vibrated by the wind. CREMONA

STRINGS: An allusion to the city in Italy where the greatest violins were made by Stradivarius, Guarnerius del Jesu, etc.

96. ETUDE: A musical lesson or study.

97. (T and B) Music examples from The Ditson Album of Cello Solos. (M) Christmas Eve in the rebuilt Trinity Church in Clearfield.

102. (TR) We bought the large bronze bell beside the gate in San Miguel de Allende, Mexico in 1960.

103. (R) Source of individual bells, L to R, T to B: Acadia National Park in Maine, Spain, Nepal, Peru, Tibet, India, Mexico.

104 and 105. CRESCENDO: An increase in sound. Pacific Ocean surf at Manuel Antonio Wilderness Beach, Costa Rica.

106. CAVATINA: A short air or song.

108. (T) Near the Gore Range in Central Colorado. (B) At ghost town of St. Elmo, up Chalk Creek Canyon, Sawatch Range CO.

109. (B) My classroom at the new Clearfield Senior High School. (BR) Some of my advanced students singing Spanish songs in our home, 1980.

110 and 111. Collages of my advanced classes from 1966 to 1982. Their bright glowing faces represent thousands that I had the privilege of teaching. For three and a half decades I devoted more time and effort to teaching than any other life activity. The countless complex challenges and rewards involved are not easliy put into song. Suffice it to say that I loved my students, especially the ones motivated to persist through the full series of four courses. My wife and I derived immense satisfaction from seeing many of them do remarkable things with their lives.

112. ODE: A lyric poem of exalted emotion, embracing varied elements and grand porportions, as does a presentation of a symphony orchestra. (T) Clearfield, looking north from Coal Hill Road. (B) On the West Branch of the Susquehanna River, toward the Market Street Bridge. Clearfield was originally the site of a Leni-Lenape Indian village, which was burned by enemy tribes in the 1750's. The first white settlers called the Indians "Delaware". The village had been called Chinklacamoose (various spellings), presumably because of the natural "clear fields" by the river in the vicinity. In the 19th century, the town became a center for lumbering. Huge timber rafts were constructed at various points upriver, and were transported downriver during the spring thaw and run-off, frequently supplemented by the opening of gathering dams to raise the flow high enough to float the massive hardwood and pine logs down the rock-strewn stream. During our use of the river for canoeing, we have seen the segments between Clearfield and Keating become a mecca for white water canoeists from all over the East during the high-water season.

122. Scenes in spring and fall at Treasure Lake. GREEN: For the Spanish, green, the color of spring, symbolizes hope.

123. (TL) We watch our son, Erik, win the men's championship at Clearfield-Curwensville Country Club, for the third time. He won his first at age 17. (TR) Pittsburgh North Golf Club, near Bakerstown, PA, where Richard Ulrich, my friend from childhood, and I would rendezvous every autumn, until his death in 1992. (BL) My wife, Marjorie, putting at the 18th green at the local country club, where we won the husband-wife championship eight times. (BR) Teeing off at the first hole at Treasure Lake in 1976, when I won my second championship there.

124. (TL) Hole number 5 on the Gold Course at Treasure Lake. (BL) Autumn scene at Hole 12 at Pittsburgh North. (TR) Desert Mountain Country Club, north of Chimney Rock, AZ, one of the courses developed by the company where Erik is employed. (BR) Course at Sedona, AZ.

125. Collage (LT to B) The Taj Mahal in Agra, India; poster, which translates "Work is the best prayer", in the restaurant of a small inn in the fishing village of Quepos on Costa Rica's Pacific coast; young horseman near Montemorelos, Mexico; alphorn player at Kleinescheidigg, Switzerland. (MT to B) Swiss lad leading herd of goats through the streets of Zermatt, Switzerland; Mexican lady carrying burden on head at Miramar, Mexico; Gayle Hartwig and Austrian friend, Rudi, bid me farewell with a serenade of favorite songs, Cortina d'Empezzo, Italy, 1976. (RT to B) Tenzing Norgay, who made the first ascent of Mt. Everest, and his wife, Daku, on the trail near Thyangboche, Nepal, 1969; the Acropolis and Parthenon, viewed at twilight from the veranda of the Orthodox church on top of Licavitos, the cone-shaped hill in the middle of Athens, Greece; Quechua children in the village of Musho, close to the glaciers of Huascarán, watching us prepare for our week-long ascent of Peru's highest mountain; musicians entertaining at the Hotel Monterrey, near Huaraz, Peru.

126. (T) View from the Pyramid of the Moon over "Street of the Dead" to the Pyramid of the Sun, Teotihuacán, Mexico. (BR) My wife, Elaine, and my Spanish students climbing the Pyramid of the Moon. It is thought that the foundations of these structures probably date back to thousands of years B.C.

127. (T) Group picture of 1982 Spanish students at Teotihuacán. (BL) Excavation shows how a pyramid honoring the gods of Fire and Water was constructed over one honoring Rain, Earth and Sky. (BR) My wife, Marjorie, before a rendering of Quetzalcoatl, the Feathered Serpent of the Aztecs.

128. (T) Nearing the Mayan-Toltec pyramid, the Castle of Kukulkan, Chichén-Itzá, Yucatán, Mexico. The Mayas were Amerindians who achieved high early civilization in Yucatán and Central America. The Toltecs laid the foundations for the advanced Aztec culture in Central Mexico. Kukulkan was considered the Giver of Life, Learning, and Wealth, and Lord of the Wind. The serpent (rattlesnake) was worshiped because he had the power to determine whether humans lived or died. (B) Sitting on the stairs of the Temple of the Serpent, looking down on the Temple of the Warriors.

129. (TL) Stone serpent heads projecting from structure at Chichén-Itzá. (TR) My wife standing on the brink of the Cenote (Sacred Pool), where maidens or young men were sacrificed to Chac, the God of Rain, during periods of drought.

130. Pyramid of the Magician, Uxmal, Yucatán, Mexico. (BL) Panorama after climbing it. (BR) Looking out at unexcavated pyramid, Uxmal.

131. (TR) The other side of the Pyramid of the Magician. (TL) Elaine near the top of the steep stairway. (B) The view looking down on the quadrangle of the Nunnery from the very top of the temple constructed on top of the pyramid. (B) The Nunnery, where the vestal virgins - keepers of the sacred fire - resided, had 88 intricately-adorned rooms.

133. The exterior facade of San Augustín Acolman Monastery. Note the bells at top of picture. (BR) The national emblem, showing the colors of the Mexican flag with an eagle perched on a cactus, holding a serpent in its beak, was presented to me by the officials of the Institute of Mexican Youth when I addressed them at their clubrooms in Mexico City in 1960.

134. Note how uncrowded Xochimilco was in 1960. When we took a group of students there in 1982, it was bank-to-bank boats. (TR) A sarape (blanket) vendor displays his wares.

135. The revolution against Spanish rule was initiated by Father Hidalgo in the little town of Dolores early in the 19th century. The brave priest was apprehended shortly afterward by the Spanish army and executed, but the revolution succeeded eventually under the leadership of other Mexican patriots. Hidalgo has been immortalized as the father of his country's liberty.

136. (MR) A corner of the wealthy part of the Panteón, where the deceased are left unmolested. There is another section for the poor, where the crypts may be used only for a time; eventually

the remains are removed and replaced by others.

We taught our Spanish classes much about Mexico, but we had special interest in Guanajuato. My advanced classes presented a play called Serenata en Guanajuato and also read a mystery novel, The Stolen Jewels, which climaxed among the mummies in the Panteón. While investigating this unique historic town, we became acquainted with two students who gave us a detailed tour and then insisted that we spend the night in one of their rooms at the University of Guanajuato. Knowledge of the host country's language and culture greatly enriched our experiences wherever we traveled. (ML) On the beach at Progreso, Yucatán. ANTIPHONY is a musical response of one choir or musician to another.

137. Another unusual experience we enjoyed in Taxco was attending a service in the Santa Prisca Church with a Catholic nun whom we met, and, at the end of the service, exchanging the kiss of peace with her and members of the congregation. Historic towns like Taxco have been designated "historical monuments" by the government and are to be kept as unchanged as possible. No modern construction is allowed. (BR) A cliff diver in flight (Mexican World).

138. Tenochtitlán is the Aztec name of what became Mexico City, Mexico's capital. The Zócalo (Constitution Square), the center of the city, lit up at Christmastime (Mexican World). (BL) The city's mammoth cathedral facing the Zócalo.

139. It is told that a peasant, Juan Diego, was walking on a hillside in Guadalupe, when suddenly the Virgin appeared and instructed him to tell the bishop to have a church constructed on the site. The bishop asked for a sign. The Virgin told Juan to pick the flowers on the hillside, wrap them in his sarape and take it to the bishop. When the latter opened the sarape, the Virgin's image replaced the flowers. The church was then constructed, and the Virgin of Guadalupe became the patron saint of Mexico. The exterior of the original church is in the middle of the collage and the interior of the new one at the bottom.

(BL) Due to the fact that Mexico City is constructed on the site of a sunken lake, heavy old structures such as the Palace of Fine Arts have sunk as the water level beneath the ground has gradually lowered. (Modern buildings are based on pilings driven deep into the subsoil to prevent this.) This theater has a world-famous glass curtain depicting the signal volcanoes, Popocateptl and Ixtacciuatl, The Man Who Smokes and The Lady Who Sleeps, visible from Mexico City. (BR) Dancers bedecked in the festive costumes of the Charro and China Poblana do the Jarabe Tapatío, the Mexican Hat Dance, in which, at the climactic moment, the man throws down his large hat and his partner dances around it (Mexican World).

140. (TL) Looking down from the mezzanine on Sanborn's elegant interior. It was constructed in the sixteenth century and has been in continous use since. (TM) The famous Aztec calendar stone is 12 feet in diameter and weighs 24 tons. It is a symbol of the sun's face, and its markings show that the Aztecs had extensive knowledge of astronomy, including how long it took the earth to revolve around the sun. (TR) A room in the Castle of Chapultepec with a portrait of the ill-fated Austrian archduke Maximillian, who was installed as Emperor of Mexico by Napoleon III and protected by the French army. Eventually Benito Juárez, a native leader who became one of Mexico's greatest presidents, caught Maximillian and had him executed. (BR) Exterior pillar and iron entranceway to Chapultepec Castle. (BL) Ixtacciuatl - the Sleeping Lady (head on left, breast in center, knees on right). Sadly, these ornaments are no longer as bright as when I first beheld them in 1943. Mexico City has become the largest city in the world, and the immense smog created by the unbridled motor traffic is usually so thick that the volcanoes are obscured.

141. (T) Views from near the summit of The President in Yoho National Park, Canada. (B) Scenes in the lovely gardens behind the headquarters of Banff National Park, Canada.

142. (TL) Scene near Arlberg Pass, Austria. (BL) Lovely Gasthaus and cemetery of church in the village of Thaur, where the most wondrous bell I've ever heard rang every morning. (R) Village of Heiligenblut (Heaven's Blood) with the Grossglockner (Great Bell), the highest peak in Austria, in the background. HARMONIC OVERTONES: The sounds produced by the division of a vibrating body into equal parts. Their presence, or absence, or relative intensity determines the quality of sound.

143. (T) The Vienna String Quartette performs in the Mirabell Palace, Salzburg, Austria. (ML) The Hohensalzburg Castle and mountains (Austrian Tourism). (B) View from Mirabell Palace Gardens toward the Castle.

144. GLOCKENSPIEL: Bells or bars tuned to the diatonic scale, played by hammers or keyboard.

145. APFELSAFT: Carbonated apple drink; FRAUENKIRKE: A church with distinctive towers in Munich; RATHAUS and MARIENPLATZ: Munich's town hall and plaza; HOFBRAUHAUS: The most renowned of German beerhalls; FESTLICHKEIT: Festivity. (TL) Glockenspiel on the Rathaus tower. (BL) The Glockenspielplatz on Neuhauser Street. I especially remember a delightful chat I had in German with an elderly lady resting there.

146. (TL) Floral clock in Kursaal Gardens, Interlaken, where I attended concerts. (BL) The inimitable music box, surrounded by the flowers of home.

147. (TL) Lovely entrance to the grounds of the Kursaal, Interlaken. (MR) The Wetterhorn, seen from Grindelwald, Switzerland.

148. (TR) San José's magnificent Opera House is modeled after the Paris Opera House. (MR) The wise old proprietress of the Pensión Isabel in Quepos, Costa Rica. (B) My wife, Elaine, ready to frolic in the splendid breakers of the Pacific Ocean in Manuel Antonio Nature Preserve. IMPROVISATION: Unwritten music played around a central theme.

150. (TR) The virgin forest on Punta Catedral (Cathedral Point), Costa Rica. (B) Looking down on Cathedral Point from the Mariposa Hotel.

151. (TL) Vicuña grazing on the agricultural terraces of the Inca ruins at Machu-Picchu, Peru. This native inhabitant of the high Andes has the finest wool in the world, but is now a protected species. (R, T to B) How frequently in winter I look up from my work to rest my eyes on the splendor of cardinals who habitually gather morsels in our back yard! This beautiful white German shepherd was companion to a miner at the Skytop Mine in Colorado's San Juan Mountains when I passed by on a climb. I snapped his picture because he looked exactly like the one I loved as a boy and lost when a sadistic neighbor poisoned him. Just below is a burro I petted while visiting the 6,000 year-old ruin at Huilcahuaín, Peru. The bottom one served as one of our pack animals in the Gore Range, Colorado. He was adorable, with unusually long furry hair on his forehead.

152. In 1971 "Platero" carried my possessions on rugged trails over 15,000' passes in Peru's White Range.

153. At Toba, the city in Japan where pearl culture originated, the divers are all women, trained from childhood to stay underwater for more than a minute. They tie themselves to a wooden tub and go down 15 meters to gather oysters, which have had bits of shell implanted so that pearls would form around them.

154. (T) A letter mailed home in November, 1969 from the old Oriental Hotel in Bangkok, before flying to Kathmandu for a month-long foot-journey through the ranges of Nepal up to the glaciers of Mt. Everest. It was the last word my family had from me until I returned home on Christmas Eve. An eight-page letter

I had left to be mailed at the desk of the historic Hotel Royale in Kathmandu never reached its destination. Oddly, a letter I mailed from the village of Those, which took five days by runner to reach Kathmadu, eventually did reach home, but not until after I had already returned. (MR) Beautiful Thai dancers perform on the grounds of the Oriental Hotel in Bangkok, Thailand.

155. Scene on the way to Bangkok's famous Floating Market. (TR) Children trying to sell bronze bells near the place where the royal barges are housed. (MR) Close-up of blooming lotus, central symbol of the Buddhist faith. (BR) The Solid Gold Budda at Wat Traimat.

156. (T) Entrance to the ancient Buddhist Shrine of the Four Hundred Steps, Kathmandu, Nepal. (BL) Krishna Hindu stone temple at Patán. (BR) Everest's incredible attendant peaks, Kangtega and Tamserku, seen from Buddhist temple in Namche Bazar, Nepal, largest Sherpa settlement south of the world's highest mountain.

157. (TL) Stupa (religious structure) on trail between Thyangboche Lamasery and Mt. Everest, looking back. (RT) Wearing a prayer scarf given me by Sirdar Ila Tsering, Sherpa leader, on leaving Namche Bazar to begin the long journey home. (RM) Suspension bridge over the Charnawati River; Sherpas and stupa near the sacred mountain Ama Dablam, "Mother's Charm Box". (BR) Finely wrought prayer stones in memorial wall along the trail.

158. ASOKA: One of the most benevolent rulers of antiquity, who encouraged non-violence and worked to establish the moral and physical well-being of his subjects. He had monolithic pillars constructed with historical inscriptions which are among the masterpieces of Indian art. (BL) Temple of Birla, University of Benares, India.

159. (T) Women washing clothes in the Sacred River, Benares. (ML) "Lessons of Life" inscribed on the walls of the Birla Temple. (M) Close-up of the exterior of the Birla Temple. (MR and BR) Purging mind and body at a ghat (stairway to the river). (BL) Manikarnika Ghat, where a funeral pyre can be noted just above the boat on the left. One night, we observed an immolation from a boat on the river.

161. The elaborately carved and inlaid entrance gate to the Taj Mahal, Agra, India.

162. (T) Natives visiting the Taj Mahal. (M) Detail of bas-relief and inlay.

163. (L) Exterior and interior detail of the "Baby Taj".

164. (T) The temple of Zeus, Athens, Greece with the Parthenon on the Acropolis beyond. (B) Stage front of the great amphitheater beneath the Acropolis.

165. (TR) The Philosophers' Wall on the old Greek Agora, center of ancient Athens. (BL) View from the Agora up to the Acropolis. (BR) Head of a Greek philosopher (Archaeological Museum).

166. (TL) Headless statue of Roman Emperor Hadrian, who was of Spanish origin. (TR) Agora, toward Tower of the Winds. (BR) Licavitos Hill from Parthenon.

167. (TL) The Parthenon lit by dawn. (BL) On the Acropolis at sunset. (T and BR) Statue of a youth from Anticythera, 340 B.C.; Pan, Eros, and Aphrodite. (Archeological Museum).

168. (T and ML) Young Japanese artists and mother and child, Ritsuren Park, Takamatsu, Japan. (BL) Delightful Spanish family who helped me find the way to the windmills being reconstructed above Consuegra, Spain. (BM) Child along trail in the Peruvian Andes. (BR) Girl at religious shrine in Kathmandu, Nepal.

169. (TL) Children who survived the great 1970 Peruvian earthquake. (TM) Child at the railway stop at Ollantaytambo, Peru. (TR) Colorful infant at the market in Juliaca, southern Peru. (MR) Interested children beside a newly rebuilt wall in the Andean village of Santa Cruz, also devasted by the 1970 earthquake. (BL) With a little girl and her twin white dogs, all of whom became my buddies at our campsite near the village in 1971. (BR) With my adorable little guide at the 6,000 year old ruins at Huilcahuaín, Peru.

170. (TR) A picture that I've cherished for 33 years, since I was privileged to watch this tiny child at simple play in Mexico. (ML) Enterprising Angel Quispu was earning a few coins posing at the great Inca ruin of Sacsayhuamán, above Cuzco, Peru, in 1963. (BL) The real-life Lo Tsen (Hilton's heroine in his Lost Horizon) who charmed me for an unforgettable hour along a remote trail in Nepal, then suddenly disappeared. (TR) With a group of students and their teacher who befriended us, in a park in San Luis Potosí, Mexico in 1968. (BR) Juan Ramírez (with book), a Peruvian teacher who became a dear friend over the years, took us to his school one day to observe his class. We loved the students' sincerity and courtesy.

171. (TL) Approaching 20,000' ice-mantled Salcantay on an exploration which I led through Peru's Vilcabamba Range, from Santa Teresa to Mollepata in 1972. (TR) The Peruvian town of Ranrahirca was buried by an avalanche in 1962, entombing most of the adult population. Many of the children, attending school in another town, survived. When we were passing their new school on a subsequent expedition, the children were all outside on lunch break, so we stopped to talk with them. Looking at those beautiful, happy faces, it was hard to realize that most of them were orphans.

172. (TL) The Gold Tower across the Guadalquivir River, with the Giralda Tower farther away to the right, Seville, Spain. (B) The hooded, masked "penitentes" who form escorts for the floats depicting Jesus' passions, which creep slowly through the streets of Seville during Holy Week.

173. (TL) The jeweled Macarena Madonna in blue velvet gown and golden crown, riding on the backs of her faithful worshipers. (TR) One of the Crucifixion floats. (MR) Close-up of another Christ on the Cross. (BR) Close-up of the Giralda Tower of Seville's cathedral - a converted Moorish mosque.

174. (M and BL) Carmen-like dancers and typical street in Seville (Spanish Tourism). (BR) The old tobacco factory, which Bizet used for his famous opera, Carmen. It is now part of the University of Seville.

175. (TR) An embroidered postcard depicting Flamenco dancers. I've had it in my possession since I started teaching in 1949 (Origin unknown). (BL) Exterior wall of Seville's palace. (BR) Interior patio of the palace in spring, with the almond trees in bloom.

176. (TR) Ceiling detail in Seville's palace. (LT) The Spanish Pavilion of the great Spanish-Panamerican Fair held several decades past (not to be confused with the elaborate 1992 World's Fair held in Seville). (M) Fabulous mosaic celebrating the city of Toledo. (BL) Mosaic dedicated to Don Quijote and Sancho. (BR) View from our outdoor restaurant across the Guadalquivir River to the Gold Tower. The tower was so named because ships returning from the New World were stopped at this point by the king's officials, who collected the king's portion of the cargo, especially its gold.

177. My wife, Elaine, and Clifford Rowles (my able successor when I retired from teaching), seated at the same location, when the three of us took a group of students to Spain in 1984.

179. (TL) Kinkaku-ji, The Gold Pavilion, Kyoto, Japan. (TR) Japanese musician (Yoshiwara). (ML) Girl with llamas at Sacsayhuamán Fortress, Peru, 1972. (MR) Exploring Sacsayhuamán walls. (BL) Roman aqueduct, Segovia, Spain. (BR) Statue of Don Quijote, at the well of the inn at Puerto Lápice, La Mancha, Spain.

180. (TR) At Aoi Shrine, Hitoyoshi, Kyushu, Japan, 1967.

(TL) Hostess at Kojo Ryokan, Hitoyoshi. (ML) Scene on Ginza sidewalk, Toyko. (BL) Supper at Atami-so Ryokan, Tokyo.

181. (TR and M) Typical entrance and room (Kanko Ryokan, Matsushima, Japan. (B) Distinctive baths at Ayusato Ryokan, Hitoyoshi, and the Atami-so, Tokyo.

182. (T) Dancers at the Kansei Ryokan, Beppu.

183. (TR) Old Imperial Palace gardens, Kyoto.

185. (TR) Kyomizu Temple, Kyoto.

190. (T) Peru's great "White Range", viewed from the "Black Range" on the family ranch of Cesar Morales, my Peruvian friend and helper on 5 climbing expeditions between 1963 and 1978. (BR) Display of portrait pottery (Lorca-Herrera Museum, Lima, Peru).

191. (TR) Peruvian portrait vase purchased in 1965. (B) Mother and baby llama along the road from Arequipa to Puno, Peru.

192. (BL) Detail of massive stonework on a Sillustani tower.

194. A herd of llamas passing before the mammoth, three-tiered fortress walls of Sacsayhuamán above Cuzco, Peru. (MR) Intact pre-Columbian Cuzco street. (BL) Still intact wall of the Temple of the Sun, Cuzco.

195. (RT and B) View of Ollantaytambo Fortress and prison, and detail of stonework. (BL) Kenko amphitheater above Cuzco.

196. (TL) Urubamba natives in holiday garb. Collage: (TL) Mock battle during Inti Raymi, Festival of the Sun at Sacsayhuamán Fortress. (TR) Procession of the Virgins of the Sun. (ML) The Inca (hereditary king) mounts the stage. (MR) Panorama of those attending. (BL) Native attire at the village of Pisac. (BR) Native dancers.

197. (TR) Close-up of the Inca being carried (McBride). (MR) Custodian activating bellows while my wife plays the organ in the historic colonial church at Andahualillas, Peru. (BR) At the Plaza de Armas, Cuzco, with the Jesuit church across the way.

198. (TR) Bakery in Pisac used continuously since the 16th century. (MR and B) Independence Day parades in the Sacred Valley of the Incas, 1963.

199. (T) The Indian market at Urubamba, where we bought food in 1972.

200. Machu Picchu, the Lost City of the Incas, discovered and uncovered in 1911 by an American teacher, senator and explorer, Hiram Bingham.

201. (ML) Intihuatana - the Stone Which Tied The Sun, telling the priests through its direction, angles and shadows, when and what their god, The Sun, decreed that they should do. (TR) Looking down on Machu Picchu from the heights of Huayna Picchu. (MR) The agriculture terraces from the residential district. (BR) Looking down from Huaynu Picchu on the Urubamba River, which drains into the Amazon and crosses South America.

202. The memorial to Miguel de Cervantes and the immortal characters he created, Don Quijote de La Mancha and Sancho Panza, in Plaza de España, Madrid, Spain.

203. (R, T to B) The Fountain of Cibeles, Madrid; the clock in Puerta del Sol, Madrid; Goya's portrait of the Tres de Mayo Uprising against French occupation troops by the common people of Madrid, and the execution of their leaders; refreshments in the Plaza Principal of Old Madrid.

204. Collage: (T and ML) Examples of the luxurious rooms in the Spanish National Palace (Spanish Tourism). (B) Approaching the Prado Museum, 1970.

205. (TL) La Dama de Elche. (TM) Ribera's "Arquimedes". (TR) Velázquez's "Man with His Hand on His Chest". (ML) Goya's "Self-Portrait". (B) Goya's "Maja Vestida" (dressed) and "Maja Desnuda" (naked). (all, Prado).

206. (L) El Greco's "Adoration of the Shepherds" and "Resurrection". (TR) Murillo's "Annunciation". (Prado). (BR) Lower portion of Velázquez's "Las Meninas" (Gran Hotel Velázquez).

208. (TL) Toledo from the south, showing the Alcázar. (TR) Puerta de Briagra, the north entrance to Toledo. (ML) Toledo's cathedral. (BL) The Transparente - "Window to Heaven".

209. (TL) Approaching El Greco's residence. (TM) El Greco's "St. Paul". (TR) El Greco's "St. Matthew". (El Greco's House, Toledo). (MR) Modern artist copying "St. Peter's Tears". (BL) El Greco's "Burial of Count Ordaz" (El Greco painted himself into this picture directly above the head of the priest holding the count's legs. But it seems that most of the faces in the painting bear a resemblance to the countenance of the painter). (BR) The interior of the rebuilt Alcázar, now a historical museum and mausoleum for the royalist cadets who died defending it.

210. (BL) 1622 edition of Don Quijote, flanked by the enormous key the mayor used to unlock Dulcinea's Palace. (BR) Handwritten copy of Don Quijote.

211. (TR) A quartette of old philosophers whom we happened upon in Consuegra. (BR) The memorial that townspeople of El Toboso erected behind Dulcinea's Palace to honor the writer, Frederico García Sánchez, who fell in love with Toboso, moved into Dulcinea's home and stayed all his life.

213. (BL) Tops of the huge Valdepeñas vats.

214. (TL) Tower of the Mesquita mosque, Córdoba, rebuilt as a Catholic cathedral.

215. (ML) A fragrant inundation of Wisteria. (TR) Portion of ornate ceiling and arch in the Mesquita.

216. (TL and M) Entrance to the Royal Chapel, and lead coffins of Ferdinand and Isabella, their daughter, and her husband. (TR) Looking toward the Sierra Nevada Range from the tower of the Alhambra, Granada, Spain. (BR) Reflecting pool in the Alhambra.

217. (BL) Getting directions from a wonderfully courteous guard in Granada. (TR) Detail of Alhambra arches (Zerkowitz). (BR) Patio of the Lions.

218. (BR) Unknown artist's rendition of the room where the sultan watched from a balcony as his ladies bathed. I had this picture in my files for bulletin board use from early years of teaching.

219. (T and BL) The Generalife, Summer Palace of the Caliphs (Moorish rulers of Spain from 711 to 1492), when Marjorie and I visited it in summer, 1970. (TR) The Generalife, wisteria-draped in spring, when Elaine and I took a group of students there in April, 1984. (BR) The inscription at the entrance to the Alhambra's tower, where a blind beggar once sat. References are to Manuel de Falla, most noted contemporary Spanish composer, and to Washington Irving, the first American author to gain fame abroad. He actually lived for a time in the Alhambra, researching and transcribing legends about it.

223. THE CID: A long epic poem recounts the heroic adventures of Rodrigo Díaz de Bivar, a Castilian nobleman born about 1040. Sometimes called "El Cid Campeador" (Lord Champion), he became a soldier of fortune, sometimes offering his services to the Christians and sometimes to the Moors. A marvelous movie starring Charleton Heston brought his story to life for many who otherwise would not have known it. I have learned that it is to be re-released soon.

224. (T) Pico de Gallinero (Top Gallery or Basket Peak) in the Pyrenees Mountains, Spain. (BL) Spain's Cantabrian coast. (BR) Prehistoric bison painted on cave ceiling (Cuevas de Altamira).

225. (TL) Statue of Fray Luis León, who was imprisoned for four years by the Inquisition for his liberal translation of The Song of Songs. (TR) The gilded facade of University of Salamanca. (BL) Student musicians. (BR) Miguel de Unamuno (Lazarillo). Unamuno details his personal striving to reconcile intellect and faith in his Of The Tragic Sense of Life in Human Beings and People - a book I eagerly read in its native language because of my own quest for reconciliation.

227. Charles V, grandson of Ferdinand and Isabella, inherited the Spanish dominions in 1516, and Austria and Burgundy (France) in 1519. As Holy Roman Emperor, in the Peace of Augsburg, 1555, he granted the German states the freedom to choose between Lutheranism and Catholicism. (MR) Portrait of Philip II (Tiziano).

229. (BL) Looking down the long corridor of the basilica in the chapel of the Valley of the Fallen. (BR) On the right, note the figure of the mother, covering her face.

230 - 231. Panorama on approaching Segovia in 1970, showing the cathedral on the left and the Roman aqueduct on the right.

232. Alcázar silhouette, throne room, and armor room (Spanish Tourism).

233. In 1984 I bushwacked along the stream's right bank to take this unique picture, looking steeply up at the Alcázar.

234 - 235. ELEGY: A contemplative, emotional composition commemorating the death of someone deeply loved or admired.

If, midway through the journey of my life, I could have been granted one thing above all others, it would have been to spend the golden years with my wife - to have lived out a leisurely Indian Summer, redoing contemplatively and savoringly the numerous things that brought us happiness…visiting dear friends and favorite places, discovering new ones, sharing fresh adventures.. But it was not to be. At age 47, in the mature flowering of her talents, when her considerable contributions to the lives of others were at their optimum, when, by any just standard, the lovely moderation of her physical living should have preserved a healthy body to house her beautiful spirit, she was suddenly stricken with cancer. The next eight years of our life were haunted and shaped by her struggle to overcome that dreaded disease. I suffered with her through the physical pain and mental anguish of operations, cobalt treatments, lung taps, nitrogen mustard injections, and weekly nauseating chemotherapy.

I am aware that there are many who have courageously faced similar shattering experiences. But after living intimately, inextricably, with one so bravely cheerful in the face of a devastating sequence of underserved suffering and bad luck, I felt a compelling need to record the way she faced it all, and the significance of her life to her family, students, associates, and friends.

As added preparation for reading understandingly "An Elegy to Love", I am including here a letter composed in the aftermath of Marjorie's death to inform our friends and loved ones residing far away.

Clearfield, PA
July 4, 1977

This is usually a happy time for us - school out, freedom to do the things anticipated, to accomplish special projects, etc., but this summer is very melancholy for me. I have the sad task of notifying friends in distant places that Marjorie's long struggle with cancer has come to an end. She died during the early morning of Monday, May 16, in our home. Throughout the winter we had made numerous trips to Erie for lung taps and injections of nitrogen mustard and tetracyclin which burned her pleural cavity, causing much coughing and pain. The fluid kept accumulating in spite of added drugs, making breathing more and more difficult. We had another tap scheduled for the day after she died, but her brave heart, which had won so many struggles over the last 8 years, suddenly stopped.

Two weeks before, we had been to Hamot Medical Center in Erie. The doctors did not seem unduly concerned and told us to come back after school was out in June. When Marjorie asked if she should resign her teaching position, they said not - that there wasn't any reason she shouldn't continue doing everything she had been doing. To help her breathing, they added an asthma medicine to her three cancer drugs, but it didn't work. That is why we scheduled a tap at the local hospital.

I had her brought to our home in a closed box of unfinished pine as she had requested. She wanted to be remembered as a person alive. She lay in front of the fireplace, near the large, new floor-to-ceiling bow window, which she dearly loved but was able to enjoy for merely a year. Hundreds of students, relatives and friends came to our home to express their love for Marjorie and their admiration for her grace and courage through the long struggle. My Spanish IV Class came and sat in a circle on the floor near her casket. It was a beautiful Spring week, and many walked around our grounds, looking at our monument of summit rocks and bronze, the flowers, and the view. We scheduled the memorial service at Trinity Church for Saturday afternoon, so that students, faculty, and relatives and friends from some distance could attend. The large church was filled. The organist used Marjorie's favorite stop combinations on the organ, and the minister used in his service some poetry and quotations we had found among Marjorie's papers. He also read the hymn "Above the Hills of Time" (Londonderry Air), the last music Marjorie and I had performed together, during a Lenten service in March.

Meanwhile, at school, our classes were disconsolate. Bertram Pritts, one of the vice-principals, and a close personal friend, delivered an eloquent eulogy which I am enclosing. I was told that there was absolute silence through the length and breadth of the vast building, and many students and faculty were in tears. She affected many lives. During the last two years she spoke to English classes on "Death and Dying" and had a tremendous impact on students. During the latter days when we walked slowly down the hall toward our rooms, I had the feeling that even the school toughs stepped back in respect as she went by.

It has been a desperate time for me, even though we had been facing the issue realistically for the last 5 years. That first awful morning, after I had discovered her, and they had come to take her away, I called Erik and Kristan. While waiting for them to arrive, I wrote down some of our favorite poems to have them made into a little booklet to give to those who would come to the home and church. I had to perform many shattering duties - picking her last dress (the pink brocade she made for Kristan's wedding); placing a pink ribbon on her hair, as she loved to wear it; going with her to Williamsport's Wildwood Cemetery for the cremation she had wanted, and waiting 5 hours to bring her ashes home…scattering them around our monument and in the flower beds; planting the garden alone for the first time. One of the most heart-rending was walking past her room at school, and finally into it to clean out her desk, deciding what to do with numerous things we had brought back from Mexico, Spain and Peru, the special displays we had arranged for her room. I found in her gradebook a beautiful poem by Tagore which crystallized how I feel.

I have periods of despair at no longer having her beautiful person at my side, especially when I look at the lovely improvements in our home, or when playing golf at Treasure Lake and realize how much she loved these things and had so little time to enjoy them. We did almost everything together. I miss her in all things, but I try to remember that her suffering is over, that she died in quiet dignity in our home, and that I must be grateful for 33 years of deep love for each other. I go about daily tasks with a knawing ache inside, but trying to face the future as bravely as I know Marjorie would be doing had I been killed on some far-off mountain. And there has been consolation in the appreciative letters from students and friends who loved her.

The Eulogy which Mr. Pritts spoke over closed-circiut television to the entire student body on Tuesday, May 17, 1977:

"I heard of Mrs. Filsinger's untimely death shortly after seven o'clock yesterday morning. Like all of you, I couldn't think of words to express my feelings. I have since talked to Mr. Filsinger and I feel today I can talk to you about Marj.

Did you ever wonder why life is so hard? Why does it hurt us so? One day it is as ferocious as a tiger; the next, as cruel as a cart wheel - it breaks our hearts and rolls on, leaving us crushed. In the last book of the Bible we are shown a vision of the City of Gold with its 12 gates; every gate a pearl. Do you know how pearls are made? If you were to ask one of your science teachers they would probably tell you something like this:

"A wound occurs in a shell, and a grain of sand, perhaps, gets embedded in the wound. At once all resources of repair are rushed to the place of hurt. Slowly, quietly the hurt is healed. At last, instead of a wound, we find a softly tinted pearl." In other words, the gates of pearl, by which we enter the City of Gold, are made of hurts, defeats, injuries and bitter disappointments of life.

If at times, life seemed too hard for Marj Filsinger, perhaps it was meant to be so - if only to turn her griefs into gems.

The natural reaction to pain, suffering, defeat is resentment, rebellion - but that turns defeat into disaster. When the worst came to Marj Filsinger, she not only made the best of it, but she looked to find the best in it.

Mrs. Filsinger was trying to tell us that those who do not know suffering, defeat, despair, do not know what life is. They only skim the surface and never learn that these give life meaning and worth.

Looking into the life of Marj Filsinger, whom we all admired for her worth and beauty of character, we find that she faced loss, difficulty, despair, and won out.

I think what Marj was trying to tell us is that life is not meant to be soft, smooth, sugary. It is meant to soften what is hard within us and to harden what is soft." Bert Pritts

The poem at the bottom of page 234 I also found in Marjorie's gradebook. It describes her philosophy so well that I requested that it be inscribed on the plaque given annually to the recipient of the Spanish Memorial Scholarship award, established at Clearfield Senior High School to honor her. I feel deeply grateful that, at my retirement, it was made a joint scholarship, honoring both of us.

237. MADRIGAL: Has several different meanings, including "a part song without instrumental accompaniment, often without contrapuntal imitation". I use it in the Elizabethan sense of "a short lyric poem of amatory character". In fact, there were many voices from the past participating in that song of a "last bright day". (TR) Two of our prized possessions appear on the dining room wall: a llama fur rug and a violin of native woods, both from Peru.

239. (MR) The last picture I took of Marjorie.

240. (TR) Trinity United Methodist Church, Clearfield, rebuilt after destruction by fire. CARILLONS: A set of bells played by hand or mechanically, or a mixture organ stop.

241. Reverend Carl Hill delivered a beautifully illustrated eulogy.

242. ADAGIO: Slow movement.

244. (MR) Denali invariably crossed his paws while lying down. We gave him the Indian name of Alaska's Mr. McKinley, which means "The Great One". (BR) Tahoma, whom we gave the Indian name of Mt. Rainier, "The Greatest of White Peaks", was quite ill when this was taken.

245. (TL) Eboning, the Welsh pony we purchased for Kristan in 1964, was then a dark grey roan, but he gradually turned white over the years.

254. (TR) With my daughter, Kristan, and grandchildren, Jennifer and Ryan, at their Plantation, FL home. (TL) September view from our home in 1971. (BL) October in our yard, 1984.

255. (TL and BR) My second wife, Elaine, shortly after she moved to my Clearfield home, August, 1980. (TR) Playing the part of Don Quijote at the Clearfield Arts Studio Theater, 1983. The part of Sancho Panza was played by one of my former Spanish students, Dudley Shimmel.

256. NOCTURNE: A night-piece - a quiet sentimental composition, usually in lyric form. I wrote this during a visit to my daughter on Florida's west coast, several months after my wife's death.

257. (R) Just about a year after Marjorie's death, my granddaughter was born. I wrote this piece for her when she was a toddler, printed it on a card, and glued colorful little shells around the edges to make it a special keepsake. (B) I met Eva while guiding at a climbing camp in Canada's Purcell Range in 1979. She had recently lost her mother and I my wife. Within those two weeks a special understanding nourished our spirits and drew us into a close friendship. INTERMEZZO: A Short movement connecting the larger movements of a symphony or sonata.

258. SIAM: A reference to the book, Anna and the King of Siam, which was adapted as the wonderful musical, The King and I, and also as a charming movie starring Yul Brunner and Deborah Kerr.

259. (ML) That Elaine Guldalian Sawyer and I met was something of a miracle. I was invited by Ardis Rohwer, a long-time Colorado Mountain Club friend, to guide at a summer climbing camp which she was leading in the San Juan Mountains of Colorado. I was already contracted to guide at two Iowa Mountaineers camps - one in Canada and one in the San Juans. The 5 days between those camps occurred in the middle of the CMC camp. By leaving the Canadian camp in the morning, flying from Calgary to Denver to Montrose, and rendezvousing with Ardis that same evening, I was able to spend three full days with the Colorado group. Elaine had registered for only one week and so was destined to leave the morning after my first day in camp. And she did not go on the climb I led my first day there.

At an evening campfire before my arrival, Ardis announced that I'd be coming. Apparently, some of my old friends expressed delight. The person sitting next to Elaine said something especially nice, so she had some pre-arrival curiosity about me. At any rate, the first time that I caught a glimpse of her was my second evening campfire. There were special festivities for those who would be leaving the next morning. Various presentations were made. I was asked to recite my poem about that area, "San Juan Idyll". Great campfire singing ensued. Gradually the campfire circle diminished, until there were only about a dozen left, including Elaine. It went on and on, so I said, "I know a good poem with which to end a campfire." The younger members ignored my words and sang another song. It was at that point that I heard Elaine's voice and saw her face for the first time. "I'd like to hear John's poem," said the sweet clear voice coming from that lovely face at 3 o'clock of the campfire's circle. "Last campfires never die, And you and I on separate ways to life's December, Will always dream by this last fire, And have this mountain to remember." - Clark Schurman.

"That's beautiful", said the fire-lit face with the bell-like voice. We all went to our tents. I lay awake in my sleeping bag, thinking about that glowing face - that intriguing voice. Next morning I saw her in the breakfast line and asked an old friend who she was. "A teacher in Denver...member of the club for a couple of years...a pleasant presence on the trail..." I washed my dishes, and started back to my tent to prepare for the day's climb. I couldn't get her out of my mind. Suddenly, we came face to face. Only five feet tall, she was carrying a huge duffel bag on her shoulder to the pile of bags to be packed out. I said, "You're Elaine." She replied, smiling, "Yes, and you're John." I almost went on, but a blessed intuition made me say, "You know, I have a feeling that ships are about to pass in the night." My pulse quickened when she admitted the same feeling. We went on to learn a bit about each other. I told her I'd be in Denver for a few days after guiding at the other camp, and asked if we could get together. She said she'd like to. We did, corresponded every day during the year, visited each other three times, and fell deeply in love. We decided to marry the following summer. (TR) Elaine's first visit to my home. (BR) On Twin Thumbs, with Sunlight Peak behind, during a backpack through the Needle Mountains and the Grenadier Mountains in Colorado.

260. We had enjoyed Cheesman Park in Denver on our first date. The classic art, rose gardens and mountain view seemed a perfect combination as we planned our wedding later in the year. Elwyn Arps, an old climbing friend, was my "best man", and his wife, Louisa, who was a member of the Denver Women's Press Club, arranged for our reception in their historic building.

261. The three pictures illustrate some of the favorite things we enjoy sharing: (T) The peerless Pennsylvania autumn colors; (M) Indian archaeological sites (here at Uxmal, Yucatán, Mexico); (B) Mountaineering (here exploring Mt. Lassen's crater, with Mt. Shasta barely visible behind).

262. Ski runs have colorful, intriguing names. Some of our favorites I've cited in quotes. (TL) Winter scene in Glenwood Canyon, CO. (MR) "Last Alamo" at Keystone, CO. (BL) At Steamboat Springs, CO. (BR) A frosty Snowmass, CO.

263. (TL) High on Snowmass. (TR) On lift at Winter Park, CO. (ML) Vail Village, CO. (BL) Elaine at Vail. (BR) Near Wolf Creek Pass, CO.

264. On summit of Purgatory, Durango, CO, with views of Needle Mountains. (ML) On lift at Purgatory. (MR) Lovely cross-country terrain near Molas Pass. (BL) Starting down "See Forever" at Telluride, CO.

265. (TL) Peak Eight, Breckenridge, CO. (TR) Breckenridge base. (ML) Elaine at Telluride. (B) Looking down on what used to be the old mining town of Telluride. (MR) At Copper Mountain, CO.

266. North Peak at Keystone, from "Mozart".

268. (TL) With Dudley Shimmel as Sancho Panza, ready to start a performance during the premier run of <u>Man of La Mancha</u>. (MR) Ready to attack windmills. (BL) With Lynn Carr, who played Dulcinea, ready to explain why Quijote did the things he did by singing "The Impossible Dream".

269. (TR) Gayle Gearhart, director of the play and also a former student, who encouraged me to try out for the part of Don Quijote. (ML) Dulcinea inspires the restoration of Don Quijote's memory, near the end of the play. (BR) The triumphant moment, just before Quijote collapses and dies.

270. (TL) Alonso Quijana is transformed into Don Quijote by his squire. (R) They mount and ride forth adventuring. (BL) Quijote exulting in the Golden Helmet, actually a barber's tray. (BR) Quijote sings his love song when he first discovers Aldonza, a serving maid, and conceives her as a high-born lady worthy of his service. (MR) Quijote attacks the mule drivers after they have violated Aldonza.

271. (TL) A band of Gypsies tempt Quijote and Sancho. (ML) Quijote sings "The Impossible Dream" to Aldonza. (TR) Quijote is confronted by the Knight of Mirrors (actually his niece's fiancé, using this as a means of attempting to erase Quijote's "delusions"). (B) The entire cast receiving an ovation at the end of the play. (All pictures by Mrs. John Hess).

272. Near Parker Dam State Park, Pennsylvania.

273. All pictures in our yard or near our home.

274. (TM, ML, BL, BR) In snow-filled woods on Rockton Mountain, near Clearfield. (1 and 2L) At home. (4L and MB) Grand Portage, Minnesota.

275. In our pasture.

276. (TR) Large-scale model of the way the mountain will look when finished. (ML) Mount Rushmore memorial has the faces of Washington, Jefferson, Lincoln and Teddy Roosevelt carved on the cliff. But they are more bas-relief, not in the round. (BL) The heroic bust of Jan Paderewski, one of the greatest pianists who ever played, and who became Prime Minister of Poland. Ziolkowski's statue won a World's Fair first prize. The sculptor had this piece, along with other marble statues he had created, mounted on large pine tree stumps behind his home-museum at the Crazy Horse site. Jealous, unprincipled vandals clandestinely defaced these beautiful works of art while the family was away. PARNASSUS: A mountain in Central Greece. The name has come to stand for, collectively; "those who believe in art for art's sake", or "the world of poetry or poets", or "any center for great artistic endeavor". Following the death of their father, Ziolkowski's children are now carrying on the work of sculpting the mountain.

277. (TL) A carving Ziolkowski made in a pine log of how he envisioned the countenance of Crazy Horse. (TR) The base of a statue in City Park in Denver, memorializing the Scotch poet, Robert Burns. (ML) The resurrected summer "tourist train" of the Denver and Rio Grande Railway about to depart Durango for its daily trip up the canyon to Silverton. (MR) Camping beneath the Wham Ridge of Vestal Peak, one of the Grenadiers.

278. (TL) Camp in Chicago Basin. (TR) Meadows in the Grenadier Mountains. (ML) Descending toward No Name Creek's origin from Twin Thumbs Pass. (BL) Camp with view of Knifepoint, 21 years after first climbing it.

279. (TR) Elaine on summit of Knifepoint, 1981. (MR) The peerless flowery meadow "close to the base of Knifepoint's buttresses" (as I described it in 1960). (BL) The remote camp by the "tarn of the friendly marmots", while traversing from the Needles Mountains to the Grenadiers. (BR) View from camp at outlet end of Balsam Lake.

280 - 281. (T) Summer view of East Brady Narrows. (The Narrows Inn, long-since closed). (B) Same scene in autumn, taken in 1963.

282. (BL) St. John's Lutheran Church, Highland, PA. (BR) With fellow workers at the Clark Candy Co.

283. (TL) At our Highland home. (TM) Grandmother and grandson. (TR) With Marjorie and our children at a birthday celebration in our Clearfield yard. (MR) With Elaine in mother's Perrytown Place apartment. (B) With great-grandchildren at New Smyrna Beach, FL. (BR) St. John's cemetery, where she now lies beside my father.

284. (TL) Faded colored sketch, which Joe Breth made of our home from the opposite pasture and gave us. (BR) The hillside from which he made the sketch. (MR) On a rock formation he called "Sudden Presence" near Ridgeway, PA. NOTE: Joe was in his late twenties, working in the environmental field, based in Ridgeway. He was in the process of establishing a windmill industry in Clearfield, but had not yet transferred his residence. On the way home one evening, he was tragically killed in a head-on collision. He and I had been in the midst of a joint literary-artistic endeavor to be published in <u>Summit</u> magazine. He was illustrating my series of poems entitled "Summer Shangri-Las" with his exquisite colored ink sketches. The premature death of one so uniquely talented was especially wrenching.

285. (TR) In the Bald Eagle Valley, PA. (ML) Along the ten-mile bicycle path in Oil Creek State Park, Titusville, PA. (BL) Along the Tow Path of the old Chesapeake and Ohio Canal, bordering the Potomac River. 190 miles of it between Cumberland, WV and Washington, DC are open and maintained by the National Park Service. (BR) Near Ole Bull State Park, PA.

286. (TL and BR) Sinnemahoning State Park. (TR) Along the Blue Ridge Parkway, VA. (ML) Along the Youghiogheny River,

Ohiopyle State Park, PA. (BL) Ferns and laurel on Penfield Mountain, near home. (TL, R and MR) Farmlands in spring and fall near Home Camp, PA. (BL) Along Dubois Water Reservoir.

288. I first met Elwyn and Louisa Arps in 1952 at a Colorado Mountain Club climbing camp. We grew to be close friends. As the years unfolded, their home in Denver became like a second home for me. We went on various mountain excursions together and they always insisted that I stay with them on my way to and from climbing camps where I was guiding. Louisa authored some popular historical books, including Denver in Slices and High Country Names. (See also note on page 260). COLLAGE: (T) At Ute Indian Museum, Montrose, CO. (M) Near Robert Burns Memorial in Denver's City Park. (B) In front of the Denver Museum of Natural History, where their Front Range Panorama is located.

289. COLLAGE: (T) Our families on the summit of Mt. Evans, CO, 1966. (M) View across Grand Lake from cabin toward Rocky Mountain National Park. (B) Rocking by the fireplace in the unique cabin. (BR) Louisa and friend beside Grand Lake cabin.

290. (T) Sunset at lake in northern Kansas where we camped in 1984. (BL) The Great White Throne in Zion National Park. (BR) On summit of Angels Landing in Zion, on our honeymoon, 1980.

291. (ML) Looking down on Virgin River from Angels Landing (M) The cliffs we verged on Angels Landing. (MR) Elaine beneath the Weeping Wall. HYNER VIEW is a few miles downriver from Renova, PA.

292. (T) A sailing vessel passes near Bass Harbor, ME.

293. (T, L and R) Elaine climbing Precipice, and view out to islands in Acadia National Park. (B) Summit of Champlain Mountain.

294. (TR) Cathedral of Learning, University of Pittsburgh (Garroway). (ML) In Phipps Flower Conservatory. (BL) Outside Heinz Chapel. (BR) Cathedral of Learning from Carnegie-Mellon campus.

297. (TL) Elaine on a huge rock outcropping near the top of a narrow ridge which we climbed, across from Stevenson Lake's boat launch and beach areas. We spotted this ridge while biking along the far side of the reservoir. The ridge was unusually narrow, and had at least a dozen rock towers and cliffs, mostly hidden in summer by the foliage of tall trees, but somewhat more detectable in early spring when the hardwoods are devoid of leaves. (TR, BL and R) Autumn scenes along the Sinnemahoning Park road.

298. (TL and R) American Falls, Niagara Falls, NY. (BL and R) Horseshoe Falls from Maid of the Mist, and at the top edge.

299. (TL) Bridal Veil Falls. (TR) American Falls from Maid of the Mist.

300. (T) At base and near the brink of Yosemite Falls, one of the loftiest cataracts in the world, at 2,425'. MIDDLE COLLAGE: Base and top of Vernal Falls, and giant cedar forest. (BL) Approaching Half Dome's steep granite. (BR) On Half Dome's summit, during our honeymoon.

301. The Mediterranean Sea at our elbows, Torremolinos, Spain.

302. The friend who organized the project is Richard Humphries, who has turned his property in southern Lancaster County, Pennsylvania, into an intriguing place to teach children respect for nature and stimulate their imaginations. It is called Gnome Country, and currently hundreds of school children are benefitting from his programs in spring, autumn and at Christmas.

308. (BL) Leaving for Summer School. (T) Just after receiving her Master of Science in Library Science degree.

309. (TR) Elaine in the library which she organized and built from scratch at the Clearfield Campus of Lock Haven University. (B) Giving a review of five medical and health books to "Books-Sandwiched-In" at the Shaw Public Library, Clearfield.

310 - 311. I've listed favorite programs, performers, composers, selections, and a bit of music from two pieces which I've performed publicly quite a few times. "To a Wild Rose" is from Highlights of Familiar Music (Presser), and "Intermezzo sinfonico" is from Amsco's Cello Solos Series No. 40.

312 - 313. These pictures of our grandchildren, Jennifer and Ryan, were taken during visits to their three Florida homes in Seminole, Plantation and New Smyrna Beach, between 1978 and 1988. The last one (313 BMR) was taken near the top of Copper Mountain, during a joint visit to Colorado in 1988. The blue water scene on page 313 was taken at Blue Spring, Florida.

314. (TR) Over spruce row from home, 1991. (TL) Toward valley in front of home, 1962. (ML) Pine Ridge Indian Reservation, SD, 1959. (BL) Over Indian River from Kristan's home in Bethune Beach, 1988. (BR) On Oroville Lake, CA, 1979. NOTE: I used some of my outstanding foreign sunset photos in A Lifelong Love Affair with Mountains.

315. (TL) From summit of Squaw Peak, AZ, 1982. (TR) From the Parthenon, Athens, Greece, 1969. (MR) 19,795' Nevado Tocllaraju with alpenglow, from our already dark base camp in the Quebrada Ishinka, Cordillera Blanca, Peru, 1965. (BR) From south shore of Lake Ontario, 1992. (BL) On Florida's Panhandle Coast, 1982.

318 - 319. Our yard and home in winter, 1993.

320 - 321. Sunset gleaming across Snowmass Lake, Elk Range, CO, 1990. NOTE: The two poems quoted here are at the top of my lifelong favorites.